Inside the Olympic Industry

SUNY series on
Sport, Culture, and Social Relations

CHERYL L. COLE AND MICHAEL A. MESSNER, *editors*

INSIDE
the Olympic Industry
power, politics, and activism

HELEN JEFFERSON LENSKYJ

Foreword by
Varda Burstyn

STATE UNIVERSITY OF NEW YORK PRESS

Published by
State University of New York Press, Albany

© 2000 State University of New York

For information, address State University of New York Press,
State University Plaza, Albany, NY 12246

Cover photo of Olympic stadium in Sydney used with permission. Copyright © 1999
    by Toby Hillier
Cover photo of protest march in Tokyo, 1990. From the collection of Jan Borowy.

Production by Kristin Milavec
Marketing by Patrick Durocher
Composition by Doric Lay Publishers

Library of Congress Cataloging-in-Publication Data
Lenskyj, Helen Jefferson, 1943–
        Inside the Olympic industry : power, politics, and activism / Helen Jefferson
    Lenskyj ; foreword by Varda Burstyn.
            p.   cm. — (SUNY series on sport, culture, and social relations)
        Includes bibliographical references (p.) and index.
        ISBN 0-7914-4755-3 (cloth : alk. paper) — ISBN 0-7914-4756-1 (pbk. :
    alk. paper)
        1. Olympics—Planning.   2. Olympics—Economic aspects.   3. International
    Olympic Committee—Corrupt practices.   I. Title.   II. Series.

    GV721.5 .L42 2000
    796.48—dc21   00-020164

In loving memory of my mother,

MARGARET IRENE JEFFERSON,
1898–1997

CONTENTS

FOREWORD

The Olympic Games are the great Circus Maximus of planet Earth. They are now mounted every two years, involve roughly ten thousand athletes from over two hundred nations, and, in the 1990s, the price tag per Summer Games topped $2 billion per city. Thanks to television, radio, newspapers, magazines, and, more recently, the Internet, during the weeks of the Olympics billions of people venerate the athletes who become Olympic champions, and the host city gets to strut its stuff. The entire enterprise is swathed in tinselled layers of marketing and hype—by the International Olympic Committee (IOC), by the National Olympic Committees (NOCs), by the transnational corporations who pay tens of millions of dollars to sponsor the Games, by the television networks that pay hundreds of millions of dollars to broadcast them, and by host cities and national governments who have invested hundreds of millions of taxpayers' dollars. All this marketing draws on the myth of the redemptive power of "pure sport" for athletes, for their spectators, and for local and national communities; and on the unquestioned assumption that the Games will bring economic and social benefits to those who host them.

The myth of the redemptive power of pure sport received a body blow in 1988, when Canadian sprinter Ben Johnson tested positive for steroids at the Seoul Games. In the wake of Johnson's fall from grace the world learned what had been an open secret in Olympic circles: that banned performance-enhancing practices were normative, not aberrant, in the lives of many aspiring athletes. With those revelations came a temporary tarnishing of the Olympic rings. But the myth that the Games are an unalloyed good for host communities, a plum to be had for the most worthy and deserving, remained firmly in place in the public imagination and mass media. *Inside*

the Olympic Industry changes all that. At last, in this powerful and com-
pelling book, we have a resource that permits the citizens and political representatives of communities who contemplate bidding for, and mounting, a
set of Games to understand the key issues that will face them if they enter
the Olympic fray. Here, without hype, we have the reality, not the myth.

The winning of a bid for the Olympic Games is the result of a long
process that typically costs aspiring hosts tens of millions of dollars. These
funds are provided by both private and public sources, in the hope that a city
will win the Olympic prize. As Helen Jefferson Lenskyj shows, that process
has been largely funded by public monies but dominated by local elites—
industrialists, media moguls, owners of hotels and tourist attractions, advertising companies—for whom the bid process itself provides marketing
opportunities to associate themselves with the Olympic rings. The city that
wins then enters a long process of preparation, invariably involving major
facilities and infrastructure projects that radically change the face of the host
city and cost the public hundreds of millions of dollars.

Like the use of banned performance-enhancing drugs, the corruption of
the bidding process at the heart of the IOC has been an open secret in
Olympic circles for a very long time. In 1986, after the IOC met in Lausanne to award Barcelona and Albertville the 1992 Summer and Winter
Games respectively, William Oscar Johnson and Anita Verschoth wrote in
Sports Illustrated (October 27, 1986) that more than $100 million were spent
by the thirteen cities competing for the bids, even though the awarding of
the Summer Games to Barcelona and the Winter Games to Albertville were
foregone conclusions. Their article chronicled in detail the astounding
extravagances lavished upon the IOC members by the contenders. They
described the bid week in Lausanne as "surreal," marked by "a peculiarly
pushy brand of civic boosterism with the high-tech cool of professional
trade-fair barkers and filmmakers, plus some hard-headed techniques of
public relations and personal persuasion that never *ever* ruled out raw
bribery" (emphasis in original). Indeed, so consistent have been the types of
corruption employed in the bid process, that it has been possible to identify
a classic "bribery package" of perks, privileges, services, and funds handed
out to "Olympic family" members by eager committees in bid cities.

Despite the long-standing knowledge of corrupt bid processes, flagrant
violations of lofty Olympic rhetoric, and dishonest business practices, these
issues were never honestly described or critiqued in the mass media, and certainly never fundamentally challenged. Johnson and Verschoth concluded
their catalogue of excesses by saying that "it was all probably necessary—and
inevitable." With one sentence they normalized and condoned what they had

indignantly described, and implicitly dismissed the outcry that would surely have followed otherwise. Then in 1992, British journalists Vyv Simson and Andrew Jennings wrote their Olympic exposé, *Lords of the Rings* (Vyv Simson and Andrew Jennings, *The Lords of the Rings: Power, Money, and Drugs in the Modern Olympics*. Toronto: Stoddart, 1992), in which they traced the growth of the IOC and international Olympic organization into a powerful and corrupt global industry under the leadership of Juan Antonio Samaranch. This book so angered Samaranch that he provoked a Swiss prosecution of Jennings (for "lampooning"), and Jennings was convicted and fined in a Swiss court. The court decision notwithstanding, Samaranch was understandably disturbed. Many serious scholars and journalists accepted the substance of the claims of *The Lords of the Rings* as sound. Hence, the publication of that book constituted the first major hit on the credibility and integrity of the IOC itself. But despite some accomplished subsequent whistle blowing from other quarters as well, the flagrant conflict-of-interest violations that pass for business-as-usual practice in the IOC, the Olympic family, and Olympic Solidarity programs, and in the sports federations and bid committees, continued to flourish within the Olympic system largely unprotested.

Then, late in 1998, the lid finally blew off the Olympic pot. Allegations of wrongdoing and investigations in one city provoked investigations in others; different levels of the Olympic industry judged each other publicly and harshly. The massive corporate sponsoring component of the industry demonstrated its absolute commitment to maintaining the optics—if not the reality—of purity in the Olympic Games, and threatened to walk if the Olympic rings continued to be tarnished. Thanks to all this Olympic drama, it has finally been possible to see much more clearly who comprises this Olympic industry and how this industry functions. It has also been possible to judge the industry against its own rhetorical ideals. It is an understatement of Olympian proportions to say that its practices have been found wanting.

From late 1998 to the summer of 1999, the revelations that emerged in the IOC, NOC, and city-based investigations—described at length and in detail by Lenskyj—threatened to shred into tatters the veil of mystification that has long surrounded the games. Yet, one year after the revelations came to light, there is still little promise that either honesty or accountability have been established. Despite the loud cries of "foul" and the long lists of scandalous misdemeanors and crimes that appeared in the press, the basic structures and norms of the Olympic industry, which combine the worst features of corporate and club organizations, were not fundamentally questioned or changed. Lenskyj provides a comprehensive catalogue and analysis of Olympic corruption, and in the process makes clear the impossibility of meaningful reform within existing Olympic structures. This in itself is invaluable truth telling.

But arguably the most important contribution this work makes is to document and analyze issues that were hidden even more deeply under layers of media boosterism—that is to say, the harmful impacts on cities of hosting the Games themselves. This book provides, for the first time, close and fascinating readings of numerous case studies of anti-Olympic and Olympic watchdog organizations around the world. In case after case, Professor Lenskyj shows that the enrichment of Olympic and local elites, which has taken place through the preparation and hosting processes of Olympiads, has almost always been accompanied by the disenfranchisement and exploitation of the many, and the outright oppression of the least powerful of a city's residents. These problems are the local expression and result of the corrupt processes and the totally unaccountable Olympic industry structures that have recently come to public light.

Because of what has amounted to a de facto mainstream media blackout of organized anti-Olympic struggles, most people know little about the efforts and concerns of hundreds of citizens groups that have coalesced to combat the Olympics in cities around the world for more than twenty years. The anti-Olympic coalition that came together in Nagano, Japan, and whose composition and positions Lenskyj discusses, prepared a list of many of the problems identified by these groups, and presented these to Samaranch. The list included:

- environmental destruction;
- huge and expensive facilities financed with taxpayers' money but not serving the needs of local communities;
- restrictions of citizens' freedom of movement and civil liberties during Olympics;
- Olympic venues and infrastructure given priority over more important public services;
- distortions in the local economy and hindrance to sustainable economic development;
- students and children mobilized as "volunteers" and deprived of their rights under the Convention on the Rights of Children;
- corruption in the host city selection process;
- impossibility of democratizing sport under Samaranch;
- and commercialism of athletes, sport, and sport venues, resulting in damage to individuals and the environment.

Helen Lenskyj's studies unequivocally confirm these problems. Thanks to the patterns in the impact of Olympic Games preparation identified in her overview and case studies, we can add to this list the criminalization of poverty—a process that permits poor citizens to be driven from their homes and neighborhoods so that Olympic development can occur; and the institutional censorship of protest by mass media thoroughly implicated in Olympic boosterism. Clearly, it is important to identify the systemic flaws in Olympic business practice. But it is perhaps even more important to realize the extent to which the Olympic system's lack of accountability to democratic community involvement has resulted in a series of very serious negative consequences for host cities.

As the case studies included in this book clearly show, the main culprit in maintaining public ignorance about both Olympic corruption and the Games' negative impacts are the mass media. It is impossible to escape the conclusion that the structural integration of the media into the Olympic industry has turned them into promoters—not journalists or critics—of all things Olympic. In all the cases explored in this book, an integration of media, politicians', IOC, NOC, and local Olympic committees' interests was strongly in evidence during both bid and preparation processes. This elite integration resulted in systemic media censorship of opposition to the Games and of analyses of their problems and negative consequences. This has taken place largely through the powerful act of pure omission, with a strong dose of distortion, ridicule, and minimization thrown in for good measure. The Olympic industry is a large component of what Sut Jhally has termed the "sport-media complex" (Sut Jhally, "The spectacle of accumulation: Material and cultural factors in the evolution of the sports/media complex." *The Insurgent Sociologist*, 12:3 [1984], pp. 41–45). One of the great lessons of the past decades is that when the media's economic interests in a sporting event or institution are significant, journalists turn, in their majority, from reporters to impresarios. It was only when revelations of wrongdoing and corruption emerged on a scale impossible to ignore that the vast majority of media made space for some critical coverage. However, the increasing economic integration of the mass media with sport will mean that even this remarkable period of revelations will not result in any significant change without large-scale citizen mobilization, stringent, new conflict-of-interest rules, and structural reform in the Olympic industry itself.

Helen Jefferson Lenskyj is a professor of sociology at the Ontario Institute for Studies in Education in Toronto. She has been an indefatigable campaigner for equality rights in sport, and her works on women and sport (*Out of Bounds: Women, Sport, and Sexuality*, 1986; *Women, Sport, and Physi-*

cal Activity: Research and Bibliography, 1991; countless articles) are known around the world. An enthusiastic recreational athlete, her goal in writing this book has been to clearly demonstrate the towering hypocrisies and self-serving strategies of local and international elites at the expense of ordinary mortals and their communities. She has abundantly demonstrated that the disadvantages of the less affluent and less powerful have been exacerbated, not ameliorated or uplifted, by the Olympic industry. The crimes committed against such populations, via forced dislocations and the criminalization of poverty and dissent, have been serious by any democratic standard. This alone should be cause for grave concern. At the same time, these case studies show that it is more than the economically disadvantaged who stand to lose out when their communities are involved in Olympic megaprojects. The environmental harms and the long-term economic problems Olympic Games bring in their wake—from higher taxes and rents to a legacy of expensive buildings that are of little use to a community—are a very high price that all citizens pay for mounting these huge hallmark events.

What we may hope, along with Professor Lenskyj, is that the information that boiled over the Olympic pot in 1999 will reach and influence athletes and communities, and begin a process of serious reevaluation of the worth of the Games and the Olympic industry. We may hope that the studies presented here will promote a growing disengagement from a structure that is systemically elitist and unaccountable and, therefore, damaging to the very communities it purports to help. As the growing scholarship on professional sport has shown, the gaps between the glowing rhetoric of sport and its true impact on individuals and communities is wide indeed. This book helps us to see the reality for what it is, and gives us the information we need to begin to meaningfully narrow that gap.

VARDA BURSTYN

ACKNOWLEDGMENTS

When I began conducting research on Toronto's Olympic bid more than ten years ago, I had no idea that a book of this kind would be the outcome. I owe the greatest debt to the tireless community activists in Toronto, Sydney, and Atlanta, whose work has been the inspiration for *Inside the Olympic Industry*, especially to friends and colleagues in the Bread Not Circuses Coalition in Toronto, the Atlanta Task Force for the Homeless, Greenpeace, Green Games Watch 2000, Rentwatchers, and Shelter New South Wales. Their individual contributions have been acknowledged in the introduction and throughout the book. They have all been extremely generous with their time and support, even while they were swamped with the everyday demands of their advocacy and frontline-service work.

I would like to acknowledge the invaluable help and support provided by colleagues and friends from universities in Canada, Australia, and New Zealand, and to Judi New for sparking my interest in Sydney 2000's environmental issues. Thanks are also due to the helpful staff at the Sydney Organizing Committee library. I am most grateful to colleagues, students, and support staff in my home department, Sociology and Equity Studies in Education, Ontario Institute for Studies in Education, at the University of Toronto, for ongoing help and support, to Liz Green, Jane Ku, and Grace Puja for their hard work as research and editing assistants, Jeanie Stewart for her computer expertise, and the copy editor, Alan Hewat.

Dale Cotton, Kristin Milavec, and the staff at SUNY Press worked diligently toward very tight deadlines, reviewers Varda Burstyn, Jim McKay, Michael A. Messner, and an anonymous reader provided just the right balance of support and critique needed at the revision stage, and Varda wrote the Foreword in her usual lively and incisive style—thanks to all for your most valuable contributions. I also want to acknowledge the strangers, as well as the friends, who encouraged me in this work by telling me, "It's time people spoke up about the Olympics!"

Lastly, but most importantly, I would like to thank my partner and my children for their love and support. Without them, none of this would have been possible.

ABBREVIATIONS

ABC	Australian Broadcasting Commission
ACLU	American Civil Liberties Union
ACOG	Atlanta Committee for the Olympic Games
AHC	Aboriginal Housing Company
AOC	Australian Olympic Committee
ATSIC	Aboriginal and Torres Strait Islander Commission
BNC	Bread Not Circuses Coalition
CBC	Canadian Broadcasting Corporation
COA	Canadian Olympic Association
CODA	Corporation for Olympic Development in Atlanta
ESD	ecologically sustainable development
FBI	Federal Bureau of Investigation
FCPA	Foreign Corrupt Practices Act
FOI	Freedom of Information
GGW2000	Green Games Watch 2000
ICAC	Independent Commission Against Corruption
IOC	International Olympic Committee
LOOC	Lillehammer Olympic Organizing Committee
MPP	Member of Provincial Parliament (Ontario)
NBA	National Basketball Association
NBC	National Broadcasting Company
NCOSS	New South Wales Council of Social Service
NIAC	National Indigenous Advisory Committee
NOC	National Olympic Committee
NSW	New South Wales

OATH	Olympic Advocates Together Honorably
OCA	Olympic Coordination Authority
OECD	Organization for Economic Cooperation and Development
OPIRG	Ontario Public Interest Research Group
RCMP	Royal Canadian Mounted Police
SIA	social impact assessment
SIAC	Social Impact Advisory Committee
SLBE	Salt Lake Board of Ethics
SLOBC	Salt Lake Olympic Bid Committee
SLOC	Salt Lake Organizing Committee
SOBC	Sydney Olympic Bid Committee
SOCOG	Sydney Organizing Committee for the Olympic Games
TOBid	Toronto 2008 Olympic Bid Corporation
TOOC	Toronto Ontario Olympic Committee
UN	United Nations
UNSW	University of New South Wales
U of T	University of Toronto
URPS	Utahns for Responsible Public Spending
USOC	United States Olympic Committee

KEY PLAYERS

Anita Beaty, director, Atlanta Task Force for the Homeless

John Bitove, CEO, Toronto 2008 bid committee

Jan Borowy, founding member, Bread Not Circuses Coalition (BNC), Toronto

Ken Bullock, member, Salt Lake Organizing Committee (SLOC)

François Carrard, director-general, International Olympic Committee (IOC)

John Coates, president, Australian Olympic Committee (AOC)

Phil Coles, member, International Olympic Committee (IOC), Australia

David Crombie, chair, Toronto 2008 bid committee

John D'Alessandro, president, John Hancock Financial Services

Anita DeFrantz, member, International Olympic Commitee (IOC), United States

Arthur Eggleton, executive, Toronto 1996 bid committee

Mahmoud El Farnawani, Olympic agent

Rene Essomba (deceased), member, International Olympic Committee (IOC), Cameroon

Sergio Santander Fantini, member, International Olympic Committee (IOC), Chile

Jean-Claude Ganga, member, International Olympic Commitee (IOC), Congo

Mike Gorrell, journalist, *Salt Lake Tribune*

Kevan Gosper, vice president, International Olympic Committee (IOC), Australia

Pirjo Haeggman, member, International Olympic Committee (IOC),
  Finland
Joe Halstead, commissioner of economic development, Toronto
John Harrington, journalist, Salt Lake City
Paul Henderson, president, Toronto 1996 bid committee
Marc Hodler, member, International Olympic Committee (IOC),
  Switzerland
Murray Hogarth, environment editor, *Sydney Morning Herald*
Sandy Hollway, CEO, Sydney organizing committee
Andrew Jennings, coauthor, *The Lords of the Rings* and author, *The New
  Lords of the Rings*
Dave Johnson, vice president, Salt Lake Organizing Committee (SLOC)
Frank Joklik, former president, Salt Lake Organizing Committee (SLOC)
Un Yong Kim, member, International Olympic Committee (IOC), Korea
Michael Knight, New South Wales Minister for the Olympics and Sport
Glenda Korporaal, Olympic business journalist, *Sydney Morning Herald*
Alfredo La Mont, director of international relations and protocol,
  United States Olympic Committee (USOC)
Mel Lastman, mayor, Toronto
Mike Leavitt, governor, Utah
Carol Ann Letheren, member, International Olympic Committee (IOC),
  Canada
Darryl Luscombe, toxics campaigner, Greenpeace Australia
Jacqueline Magnay, Olympic journalist, *Sydney Morning Herald*
Shagdarjav Magvan, member, International Olympic Committee (IOC),
  Mongolia
Keva Mbaye, vice president, International Olympic Committee (IOC),
  Senegal
Rod McGeoch, head, Sydney 2000 bid committee
David Miller, councilor, Toronto
Mike Moran, assistant executive director, United States Olympic
  Committee (USOC)
Charles Mukora, member, International Olympic Committee (IOC),
  Kenya
John Niland, vice chancellor, University of New South Wales (UNSW)
Francis Nyangweso, member, International Olympic Committee (IOC),
  Uganda

Lowitja O'Donoghue, former head, Aboriginal and Torres Strait Islander Commission

Steve Pace, head, Utahns for Responsible Public Spending (URPS)

Charles Perkins, Aboriginal activist

Richard Pound, vice president, International Olympic Committee (IOC), Canada

Jacques Rogge, member, International Olympic Committee (IOC), Belgium; Sydney 2000 coordination commissioner

Bert Roughton, journalist, *Atlanta Journal Constitution*

Charles Rutheiser, author, *Imagineering Atlanta*

Juan Antonio Samaranch, president, International Olympic Committee (IOC)

Norman Seagram, executive, Toronto 1996 bid committee

Michael Shapcott, founding member, Bread Not Circuses Coalition (BNC), Toronto

Tom Sheridan, head of independent examination, Sydney organizing committee

Vyv Simson, coauthor, *The Lords of the Rings*

Randy Starkman, sport journalist, *Toronto Star*

Peter Tallberg, member, International Olympic Committee (IOC), Finland

Mark Tewksbury, founding member, Olympic Advocates Together Honorably (OATH)

Michael Walker, councilor, Toronto

Paul Wallwork, member, International Olympic Committee (IOC), Samoa

Tom Welch, former president, Salt Lake Organizing Committee (SLOC)

Introduction

INSIDE THE OLYMPIC INDUSTRY presents a critical analysis of the politics of Olympic bids and preparations from the perspective of all those adversely affected by the social, economic, political, and environmental impacts of hosting the Olympics. The resistance efforts of international anti-Olympic and watchdog organizations, whose activities have long been underreported and underresearched, are the center of the analysis. Events in 1998–1999, when allegations of bribery in the Olympic industry were finally investigated, marked the beginning of the end of a long era in Olympic history characterized by secrecy and corruption. At the end of the twentieth century, the voices of Olympic whistle blowers and critics are finally being heard.

OLYMPIC INDUSTRY: THE KEY PLAYERS

The ultimate authority on all things Olympic lies within a group of businessmen, bureaucrats, politicians, diplomats, sport officials, retired military men, and others who form the International Olympic Committee (IOC). Its membership prior to the 1998 controversy comprised seven women and 109 men. Members elected before 1966 had life membership, and those elected after that date retired the year they reached the age of eighty. A member's responsibility was to represent the IOC to his or her country of origin, rather than to be accountable to that country's national Olympic committee (NOC). This arrangement helped to secure the IOC's key role in the global integration of competitive sport.

Juan Antonio Samaranch assumed the presidency in 1966 and subsequently played a key role in appointing more than eighty new IOC members. In the late 1990s, the powerful IOC executives included: Marc Hodler (Switzerland), president of the international skiing federation and Salt Lake City 2004 coordination commissioner; vice presidents Richard Pound (Canada) and Kevan Gosper (Australia); and Sydney 2000 coordination commissioner Jacques Rogge (Belgium), all of whom emerged as key players in the events of 1998–1999.

In the years following the overwhelming commercial success of the 1984 Summer Olympics in Los Angeles, one of the IOC membership's main responsibilities was to select future host cities from the growing list of bidders spurred on by hopes of reproducing the Los Angeles experience. The technical merits of a bid were assessed by an IOC evaluation committee whose members had expertise in relevant areas. During visits to each bid city, the evaluation committee examined plans for security, transportation, accommodations, finance, government support, competition sites, Olympic villages, etc. At the same time, dozens of IOC members—sixty in the case of Sydney, Australia—were in the habit of visiting bid cities with their spouses prior to the selection of future host cities. These trips, taken at bid committee expense, purportedly enabled IOC members to see the proposed sites and facilities for themselves in order to cast an informed vote. It was this practice that generated most of the abuses disclosed in November 1998, when evidence of improper exchanges of gifts and services between bid committees and IOC members came to light.

Over the last three decades of the twentieth century, dozens of cities around the world spent millions of dollars developing bids to host the Summer and Winter Olympics; eighteen had the dubious honor of doing so. Despite boosters' promises, most host cities experienced more negative than positive social, political, economic, and environmental impacts. As was the pattern with other hallmark events and other subsidized public sport arenas, the Olympics left behind limited benefits—the "bourgeois playground" legacy—to be enjoyed, for the most part, by the more privileged sectors of society, while the powerless disproportionately bore the burden.

The following discussion will draw upon the experiences of several bid and host cities since 1968, with a particular focus on Salt Lake City, Atlanta, Toronto, and Sydney—four cities that were directly involved in the Olympic bribery controversy. It was through these cities' bid and organizing committees that networks developed between Olympic industry personnel and local politicians, corporate leaders, entrepreneurs, university administrations, and the mass media. Events in these four cities are revisited as I develop the key themes of the book: bribery investigations and outcomes; "Olympic family" ideology; grassroots resistance; negative social, political, economic, and environmental impacts; and the role of the mass media. In the analysis of anti-Olympic and watchdog groups presented in chapters 6 to 8, I examine developments in other bid and host cities, including Berlin, Amsterdam, Barcelona, Melbourne, Seoul, and Lillehammer.

It is customary to use terms such as *Olympic movement* and *Olympic family* in reference to the IOC and its extensive international network, which is expected to reach 42,000 members in the case of the Sydney 2000 Olympics. The Olympic family includes: one hundred and ninety-eight national Olympic organizations from member countries; up to twenty-eight international sport and multisport federations governing Summer and Winter Olympic sports; all ongoing bid and organizing committees; the mass media numbering about four thousand in Sydney; and, on occasion, the athletes. Rather than contributing to the mystique and elitism that terms such as *movement* and *family* connote, I prefer to use the term *Olympic industry*. In doing so, I am following the example of progressive physical education and sport scholars in the 1980s who correctly recognized that to call the initiatives aimed at increasing North Americans' physical activity the "fitness movement" rather than the "fitness industry" was to obscure the fact that the majority were prompted by the profit motive. I demonstrate that, despite the persuasive rhetoric, most aspects of the Olympics are organized to maximize power and profit rather than to promote the welfare of individuals and groups engaged in sport as a healthy and fulfilling human activity.

APPROACH AND METHODOLOGY

It is difficult for a sport sociologist to develop a critique of the Olympic industry without appearing to be uninterested in, unmoved by, or opposed to any kind of sporting competition—a position that Olympic boosters routinely attempt to discredit with the label *naysayer*. At the same time, I do not plan to adopt the common defense of listing my own recreational sporting credentials by way of proving that I am simply a sport lover in critic's clothing. I will state, however, that I would not have devoted twenty years of my academic career to the study of sport if I thought that it had no individual or social value. More importantly, I would not have spent more than twenty-five years as an activist in social justice movements working toward equity for women, lesbians, gays, bisexuals, and other disadvantaged minorities if I thought that community organizing was a futile enterprise. My single goal in writing this book is to promote social justice for oppressed groups whose disadvantages are exacerbated by the Olympic industry.

Olympic scholar John MacAloon (1992) was critical of Olympic research-ers for their general failure to employ ethnographic methods in their work. Conversely, I would claim that Olympic scholars rarely, if ever, apply these methods to groups engaged in Olympic resistance. The research and analyses in this study take "the view from below": That is, the critiques, concerns, actions and interventions of Olympic watchdog groups representing disad-vantaged minorities whose voices have generally been silenced by the power of the Olympic machine.

My own participation in events surrounding the current Toronto Olym-pic bid includes: active membership in the Toronto Bread Not Circuses Coalition (BNC) since May 1998; consultations with two of the founding members (Jan Borowy and Michael Shapcott); involvement in the commu-nity consultation process of the Toronto 2008 bid committee, attendance at almost all of the bid committee's public events; deputations to Toronto Council on behalf of BNC; and meetings with representatives of Greenpeace and Toronto Environmental Alliance.

During the earlier Toronto bid process for the 1996 Olympics, I was con-tracted to prepare a report on women in the Olympics for the Toronto Olympic Task Force. In this capacity, I accessed all the relevant reports and documents from Toronto City Council and the Toronto Olympic Task Force, and participated in a consultation investigating the social impact of the Games. Toronto newspaper reports during the period of high media cov-erage (November 1989–April 1990) were also collected. At that time, I con-sulted BNC member Jan Borowy, who gave me copies of the coalition's 1989–1990 publications. In 1999, she provided me with materials that she had collected while researching European anti-Olympic organizations, as discussed in chapter 6.

In April and May 1999, I had meetings in Sydney, Australia, with mem-bers of Greenpeace, Green Games Watch 2000 (GGW2000), Rentwatchers, Shelter New South Wales (NSW), and the Non-government Task Force on the Homeless, and attended the Bondi Olympic Watch protest meeting. I had individual consultations with Darryl Luscombe (Greenpeace), Brett Hoare (GGW2000), Will Roden and Rob Plant (Shelter NSW), Beth Jewell (Rentwatchers), Darren Godwell (University of the Northern Territory, Aboriginal activist), and Murray Hogarth (*Sydney Morning Herald* environ-ment editor). Additionally, I examined published and unpublished docu-ments produced by these individuals and organizations, either in hard copy or on their web sites. In the cases of Salt Lake City and Atlanta, I accessed reports by Olympic watchdog groups such as Utahns for Responsible Public

Spending (URPS) and the Atlanta Task Force for the Homeless, which were provided on their web sites, and consulted with the executive director of the task force, Anita Beaty.

In terms of official sources within the Olympic industry, I relied primarily on the documents, reports, and communications provided by national and international Olympic organizations: the IOC, the United States Olympic Committee (USOC), Salt Lake City bid and organizing committees, Sydney bid and organizing committees, and Toronto's two bid committees (1996 and 2008). IOC, USOC, and Salt Lake City resources were accessed through their respective web sites. In the case of Sydney, I collected relevant materials on every annual visit since 1990. In July–August 1993 and April–May 1994, I monitored newspaper reports, obtained materials from the Sydney bid committee office, and witnessed the public advertising campaign. On trips to Sydney in 1997, 1998, and 1999, I visited the Homebush Bay Olympic site and Visitor Center, as well as completing a guided tour of environmental initiatives organized by the Royal Australian Institute of Parks and Recreation. I accessed the Sydney organizing committee (SOCOG) library in 1998 and 1999, and the University of New South Wales (UNSW) Center for Olympic Studies library in 1999. Where necessary, I supplemented print materials collected on these visits with information provided on government, university, Olympic, and community organization web sites.

Additionally, I accessed international newspapers, wire services, and radio and television transcripts through their web sites. In this task, BNC Webmaster Joey Schwartz provided valuable assistance in circulating information electronically to members. Terry Walker, of Canadian Broadcasting Corporation's (CBC) *Sports Journal*, provided transcripts of interviews with Salt Lake City journalists conducted for the 1999 CBC television program on the Olympic scandal and the media.

In light of my own and others' critiques of the Olympic industry's powerful influence over media coverage, it would be foolish of me to treat the mass media as a complete and reliable source. However, given the fact that the Olympic industry dedicates millions of dollars to public relations campaigns, it is fair to assume that any erroneous media reports would be quickly challenged or corrected—even to the point of suing the source for libel, as was the case with the *Toronto Star* in 1999. Hence, although I have clearly differentiated between mass media and Olympic industry reports, I am proceeding on the assumption that any glaring errors of fact or interpretation in the former were soon corrected by the latter.

INSIDE THE OLYMPIC INDUSTRY: AN OVERVIEW

The discussion begins with the allegations of bribery involving the Salt Lake Olympic Bid Committee (SLOBC) and IOC members, which became public in November 1998. A review of subsequent events, up to the point where formal investigations were launched by the IOC and other organizations inside and outside of the Olympic industry, is presented in chapter 1. Chapter 2 provides the historical background for these events, examines early allegations and responses, and concludes with an analysis of four major investigations conducted by the IOC, USOC, Salt Lake Board of Ethics (SLBE), and SOCOG in 1998–1999.

As the investigations proceeded, it became clear that bid organizers in most cities continued to judge the various arrangements to influence IOC members' votes by Olympic family standards rather than by criteria based on ethical business practices or international antibribery agreements. Their persistent denials of wrongdoing and their framing of such acts as being either aid to sport in developing countries or acceptable and commonplace behavior within the Olympic industry are analyzed in chapter 3, where I deconstruct the ways in which two key structures—the Olympic family and the Olympic Solidarity Program—contributed to shaping relationships and value systems. In this chapter, I examine how racist and colonialist discourses defined IOC members from developing countries as "other," specifically in terms of their (alleged) flawed ethics and business practices. In doing so, I challenge IOC assertions that issues of geography, culture, and race played no part in the investigations and their outcomes.

I completed most of the research related to the Toronto 1996 bid in 1992, and the Sydney 2000 bid in 1994, and integrated two conference papers to produce a 1996 journal article (Lenskyj, 1996). This article, revised but not updated, constitutes the first section of chapter 4 and demonstrates the state of the art in terms of accessible information and critique of the Sydney bid at that time. Whereas Sydney's successful bid for 2000 reflected minimal community consultation, Toronto's failed bid for 1996 included public accountability procedures and intervenor funding for community groups to prepare their own social impact reports. The efforts of the BNC Coalition in 1989–1990 to raise public awareness about the 1996 bid and its impact on citizens—especially on disadvantaged populations—were largely responsible for the first bid's more democratic procedures, whereas in the case of Toronto's bid for 2008, the process was significantly less open. The second section of this chapter, titled "Toronto Tries Again," focuses on the 2008 bid process and its shortcomings, including its failure to engage in authentic community consultation and its dominant corporate agenda. When a city where homelessness had been declared a national disaster mounted two Olympic bids in ten years, there was little doubt about politicians' and Olympic boosters' priorities.

Chapter 5 provides a broad discussion of the social, political, and economic impact of the Olympics. Although the "politics of place" and hallmark event literature provides useful insights into the problems of the Olympics' impact, I argue that it is necessary to deconstruct the "Olympic spirit" rhetoric and the myths of the "pure athlete" and "pure sport" in order to understand the specific allure of the Olympics that differentiates it from other hallmark events. It is the intersection of world-class-city and Olympic-spirit rhetoric that boosters exploit in order to sell Olympic bids to taxpayers who ultimately shoulder the burden of Olympic deficits. In this context, any critique of Olympic bids and preparations is recast as unpatriotic and disrespectful to the dedicated young athletes who, according to this pseudo-religious discourse, epitomize the Olympic spirit and deserve to fulfil their Olympic dreams. The aspirations and dreams of homeless people, whose very survival is often threatened by hallmark events, are explicitly and shamelessly ignored.

Chapters 6 and 7 document the activities of anti-Olympic and watchdog organizations in Olympic host cities since 1968, specifically in relation to the social, political, and economic impact. Human rights and democratic decision-making issues are the central focus of these chapters. Of particular relevance to academic readers, chapter 6 includes a critical analysis of "The University Connection" where I examine university administrations' complicity in the Olympic industry, and student, staff, and faculty resistance to the creeping corporatization of campuses, with Olympic industry connections constituting only one example of this growing trend in North America and Australia. An analysis of the social and political issues in Atlanta and Sydney is presented in chapter 7, with a focus on resistance mounted by watchdog groups such as the Atlanta Task Force for the Homeless and Sydney Rentwatchers. As this chapter shows, a key tool employed by those in power during preparations for Olympics and other hallmark events is the "criminalization of poverty," whereby local ordinances render the survival strategies of low-income and homeless people criminal offences in order to remove them from the streets, thus creating an unflawed image of a world-class city in the eyes of Olympic visitors.

Environmental issues are the subject of chapter 8, with the remediation of the contaminated Homebush Bay site of the Sydney 2000 Olympics serving as a case study to illustrate the limited successes of community-based environmental groups in the face of the Olympic machine. I identify the shortcomings of the Olympic industry's corporate environmentalism as applied to environmental challenges in Sydney, with particular attention to the low priority placed on authentic community consultation.

The vital role of the mass media in shaping public opinion, usually in the interests of the Olympic industry, is analyzed in detail in chapter 9. In recent years, bid committees in Berlin, Atlanta, and Sydney exerted considerable influence over media coverage of the bid, in many cases for the purpose of hiding the huge budgets devoted to entertaining IOC members and their families during bid city visits. Following disclosures of bribery and corruption, however, some investigative journalists abandoned their uncritical stance and published articles exposing the key players in Olympic scandals. In doing so, they joined a small number of critics in the mainstream and alternative press who challenged Olympic industry rhetoric.

Although there is no doubt that the mass media played a major role in these debates, I have chosen to position the critical analysis of the media near the end rather than the beginning of the book in order to avoid detracting from the resistance efforts of individuals and organizations through grassroots activism and counterhegemonic journalism. In the earlier chapters, as already noted, I have relied, where possible, on official statements and reports originating within the Olympic industry rather than on media reports of these documents in order to provide a clear starting point for subsequent discussion of ways in which the mass media took up the controversies.

In conclusion, I argue that the reforms proposed in mid-1999 failed to address the root causes of bribery and corruption within the Olympic industry. Advocating "evolutionary" rather than radical change, the reforms attempted to limit opportunities for IOC members and bid committees to abuse their privileges, and proposed increased athlete representation and greater financial transparency. As long as the Olympics remain a source of enormous profit for the major sponsors and television networks, and as long as Olympic-spirit and world-class-city discourse continues to disguise the real costs to taxpayers and the real impact on already disadvantaged populations, the proposed reforms pose no threat to the status quo and hold no promise of significant change.

1

Salt Lake City
the beginning

O N NOVEMBER 24, 1998, the Salt Lake City television station KTVX reported that a 1996 letter in its possession indicated that the Salt Lake Olympic Bid Committee (SLOBC) had awarded a "scholarship" to the daughter of the late IOC member from Cameroon, Rene Essomba (Gorrell, 1998a). The central role of the mass media in releasing this evidence foreshadowed the events of the next several months when new examples of Olympic scandals became top international news stories, often on a daily basis.

According to IOC accounts, this was the first actual documentation of corruption in the bid process and marked the beginning of a new era of Olympic politics, as the issue of the buying and selling of Olympic votes, dating back to the 1980s and earlier, suddenly became the major preoccupation within the IOC and the international Olympic industry. Subsequent statements by former SLOBC leaders confirmed that six relatives of IOC members and seven other individuals had received approximately $400,000 in financial aid or "scholarships" in a program that began in 1991 after Salt Lake's unsuccessful bid for the 1998 Winter Olympics. At this time, IOC rules permitted bid cities to give IOC members gifts valued at no more than $150. Later evidence of excessive gift giving, hospitality, and services provided to IOC members and their relatives included medical treatment, employment, shopping trips, and holiday travel and accommodations.

In the aftermath of several major national and international investigations targeting the IOC, members of former bid committees, and agents acting on their behalf, several Olympic officials, including members of the IOC, the Salt Lake 2002, and Sydney 2000 bid committees, resigned or were asked to step down, or were issued "warnings" of varying severity, while the future of others remained in question.

More important than the consequences meted out to individual committee members, the underlying principles of the IOC and the Olympic industry were now subjected to an unprecedented level of international scrutiny and investigation by organizations as diverse as sport ministries in Europe, federal intelligence agencies in the United States and Australia, and university student groups in Ontario and New South Wales. The Olympics were irrevocably politicized by these events, and the IOC could no longer resort to the position that the Olympic movement transcended politics.

HISTORY OF SALT LAKE CITY'S OLYMPIC ORGANIZING COMMITTEE

The Salt Lake organizing committee (SLOC) had been the center of several controversies in the late 1990s. Its first president, Tom Welch, had to resign in 1997 after pleading no contest to a domestic violence charge, and the "revolving door" of SLOC resignations and appointments early in 1998 was a further cause for concern. The most serious and longstanding issue, fuelled by the committee's secrecy, resistance to public oversight, and alleged conflict of interest among board members, was the possible public liability for any Olympic debt (Packer, 1997). The Olympic scandal exacerbated these financial concerns; within a matter of weeks, the marketability of the Olympic name was seriously damaged and SLOC faced the threat of cancelled sponsorships and a budget blowout.

A minority of SLOC's forty-person board, including Ken Bullock, Utah League of Cities and Towns representative, and Maria Garciaz, Neighborhood Housing Services, had been working toward a more democratic and open process for some time. Both Garciaz's position on the board and Bullock's place on the executive were achieved only after extensive lobbying and, in Bullock's case, a Utah State Legislature resolution. Bullock earned the reputation as an advocate for smaller communities and a watchdog over the SLOC budget. In 1997, he challenged the $12,000 budget allocated to local youth sport, in contrast to the excessive funding for travel and entertaining Olympic officials, and succeeded in raising the community sport legacy to $350,000. He also proposed that SLOC donate surplus equipment to the state's towns and cities after the Games (Packer, 1997). And in January 1999, when the extent of corruption in the Olympic industry became clear, Bullock was one of the very few voices from inside an Olympic organization calling for the resignation of IOC president Juan Antonio Samaranch.

Bullock received a copy of the Essomba letter anonymously in October 1998 and delivered it to SLOC vice president Dave Johnson at the October 8 board meeting. It appears that no official action was taken until after the November 24 KTVX disclosures. SLOC president Frank Joklik's initial reaction, according to one journalist, was to tell the press, "This is a non-story" (Harrington, 1999). By December 8, 1998, however, Joklik acknowledged that financial aid and "scholarships" valued at approximately $400,000— what the Salt Lake bid committee and the USOC termed its "National Olympic Committee (NOC) Assistance Program"—had been delivered to thirteen individuals, including six relatives of IOC members, during the bidding for the 2002 Winter Olympics.

At this early stage, most Salt Lake City officials implicated in the controversy employed the "humanitarian aid" rationale and, although public disbelief and cynicism quickly surfaced, many Olympic officials clung to this explanation and protested their innocence to the end. Welch and Joklik, along with USOC assistant executive director Mike Moran, took the position that to call the NOC Assistance Program "a shoddy bribe" was "an unfair characterization" and "a sort of defamation" of what they portrayed as the altruistic Olympic family ethos of helping IOC members from poorer nations (Gorrell, 1998b). Only three months later, in a very different context, Moran faced the media again as chair of a press briefing on the USOC Special Oversight Commission Report, which was unequivocal in its condemnation of SLOBC's participation in the IOC's "broader culture of improper gift-giving" (USOC, 1999, p. 27).

According to the explanation that Joklik gave in December, it wasn't surprising that six of the "scholarship" recipients were relatives of IOC members because "these people tend to be leaders of sports programs" and have better education and political experience (Gorrell, 1998c). This was a creative attempt to justify what earlier critics had termed "a preferential exchange between social elites" (Tatz & Booth, 1994, p. 12). In the first of a long series of finger pointing, Welch claimed that "these kind of [scholarship] programs have been around for ever. The USOC was doing it long before we were" (Welch quoted in Gorrell, 1998b). The extent to which such arrangements conformed to IOC Olympic Solidarity Program guidelines will be examined in chapter 3.

On December 9, National Public Radio newscaster Howard Burkess phoned Swiss IOC member Marc Hodler to tell him about the television disclosure of the Essomba letter. Although Hodler did not go on air, Burkess reported his response: that it was not "legitimate" for the Salt Lake bid committee to have made "scholarship" payments to IOC family members (Carter, 1998). Hodler repeated his assertion that such actions constituted bribery at numerous impromptu interviews with the press at the IOC headquarters in Lausanne, Switzerland, throughout the week. He also claimed that buying and selling of votes dated back to the 1996 bids, and that between 5 and 7% of IOC members were open to bribery. A week later, he revised his estimate to twenty-five members. The IOC executive issued a statement disassociating itself from Hodler's claims; it was rumored that Hodler had been instructed to stop talking to the press, an allegation that Samaranch quickly quashed (Gorrell, 1998e).

Hodler further alleged that four agents, including one unnamed IOC member—readily identified as Congo member Jean-Claude Ganga (Gorrell, 1998g)—could have influenced the outcome of the site selection process for the last four Olympics: Atlanta 1996, Nagano 1998, Sydney 2000, and Salt Lake City 2002. These agents, according to Hodler, demanded fees of between $500,000 and $1 million, and one man boasted that no city in fifteen years had won the Games without his help. Hodler initially implicated the Sydney bid in his allegations, but by December 16, having received assurances from the Sydney bid committee, he said he was satisfied that Sydney's bid had been "clean" (Korporaal, 1998a; 1998b).

THE HODLER RULES

Marc Hodler, eighty years old at the time of the controversy and a member since 1963, was known as one of the earliest whistle blowers within the ranks of the IOC. His first attempts to reform the bid process in the early 1990s had been prompted by widespread rumors of excessive gifts, services, and hospitality. Whether these were demanded by IOC members or forced upon them by bid committees was a moot point at that time.

Hodler subsequently developed guidelines known as the Hodler Rules, which were adopted by the IOC in February 1994. The stated IOC rationale for the guidelines was to reduce costs to candidate cities (IOC ad hoc Commission, 1999a), not to address abuses of the bid process. The rules included a $150 limit on the value of gifts or benefits to IOC members or their relatives and a prohibition on any arrangements, transactions, or contracts between bid cities and IOC members/relatives. A two-phase bid process was introduced, with four finalists determined by the IOC six months before the final vote. IOC members, with one accompanying person, could only visit these four cities, with a maximum stay of three days, or five days in the case of long-haul travel.

Although bid cities found to have breached the rules could be excluded from the Games, there was no mention of sanctions for IOC members who did so (except for the standing provisions for expulsion in the Olympic Charter). Despite rumors to the contrary, it did not appear that the IOC was empowered to take away a host city's right on the grounds that the bid process was fraudulent; war, civil unrest, or other dangerous situations, as well as breaches of the host city guarantees and obligations, constituted the only grounds for rescinding the contract.

During the bidding for 2002, Salt Lake City and the other bid cities operated under the 1994 rules, whereas the Sydney bid committee was subject to slightly different rules that had been in force since February 1992. In both instances, restrictions covered the same areas, most notably relationships between candidate cities and IOC members (number of visits, gifts, travel costs, entertainment, etc.); the maximum value of gifts at that time was $200.

Now characterized as the "free-speaking IOC member" in the press, Hodler continued with a series of media interviews on the gift-demanding practices of IOC members from Africa, Europe, and the Americas. Although he stressed that his overriding interest was to show that Salt Lake City was "the victim of blackmail and villains" (Gorrell, 1998f), many SLOC officials took issue with his unequivocal labelling of their NOC Program as bribery, in part because Hodler was the IOC member designated to oversee Salt Lake City's preparations, and had been perceived as their friend and supporter.

Salt Lake Tribune Olympic reporter Mike Gorrell initially described Hodler as "pouring fuel on the incident and turning it into an international controversy that taints the reputations of SLOC and the IOC," while Utah's governor Leavitt agreed that efforts should be made to avoid "negative reflections . . . on the dignity of the Olympic Games" (Gorrell, 1998d). But as new and unequivocal evidence of corruption came to light, Hodler reiterated his interest in rooting out systemic corruption for the good of the Olympics. For Hodler, at least, the dignity of the Olympics rested on more than a public relations image, and there is no doubt that he was instrumental in the IOC executive committee's decision to launch a formal commission of inquiry. Although the commission later revealed that Hodler's allegations were based on hearsay, in hindsight it can be seen that the weight of evidence collected during various formal investigations eventually turned the tide on the Olympic industry.

THE INVESTIGATIONS BEGIN

On December 11, 1998, the landmark date when the IOC finally acknowl-edged that it had sufficient factual evidence to proceed, president Samaranch announced the formation of an ad hoc commission led by vice president and Canadian IOC member Richard Pound, a lawyer, to investigate the bribery allegations and to make recommendations by January 23, 1999. For the interim, no IOC members were permitted to visit cities bidding for the 2006 Winter Games. By mid-January, the names of twelve IOC members under suspicion were circulating through international wire services: Agustin Arroyo (Ecuador), Bashir Attarabulsi (Libya), Jean-Claude Ganga (Congo), Zein el Abdin Gadir (Sudan), Anton Geesink (Netherlands), Pirjo Haegg-man (Finland), Un Yong Kim (Korea), Charles Mukora (Kenya), Louis N'Diaye (Ivory Coast), Sergio Santander Fantini (Chile), David Sibandze (Swaziland), and Vitaly Smirnov (Russia).

The IOC ad hoc commission marked the first move in an avalanche of international investigations conducted in the United States, Canada, Eur-ope, Australia, and Japan. One week later, SLOC instructed its own internal board of ethics (SLBE), established in 1996 and led by retired Chief Justice Gordon Hall, to review the bid process, a move that prompted criticism that this was a toothless panel relying only on information provided by SLOC itself (Gorrell & Walsh, 1998).

The next development, on December 22, was the formation of the USOC's Special Bid Oversight Commission, led by former senator George Mitchell. The following day, the U.S. Justice Department, the Federal Bureau of Investigation (FBI), and U.S. Customs announced formal inves-tigations into the Salt Lake bid. Unlike the other nonjudicial panels, the fed-eral probes covered criminal activities and had the power to subpoena wit-nesses and records and to empanel grand juries. In late January, Utah State Attorney General Jan Graham announced a state investigation, and in February, the General Accounting Office (Congress) and the House Com-merce Committee established investigative subcommittees led by Represen-tatives John Dingell and Fred Upton respectively.

In early January, another dimension of IOC "gift giving" made interna-tional news with the first of a number of reports of expensive gifts that bid committees had sent to Samaranch, including Salt Lake City's gift of guns valued at $1,600 and a $28,000 samurai sword from the Nagano bid com-mittee. The IOC quickly responded with the rationale that since the presi-dent did not vote, and since such gifts were housed in the IOC Museum, these could not be construed as bribery. However, as many media critics pointed out, Samaranch's practice of personally selecting IOC members provided ample evidence of his powerful influence over the host city selection process. Asserting that he was not accountable to the press, Samaranch subsequently announced that he would put his presidency to the vote at the next IOC session.

On February 6, somewhat belatedly in view of the evidence of Sydney bid committee's involvement in "scholarship" programs, the Sydney Organizing Committee for the Olympic Games (SOCOG) announced its first independent review of the records of the Sydney Olympic Bid Committee (SOBC), to be led by former auditor-general Tom Sheridan and completed before the March 16 IOC meeting in Lausanne. Up to that time, Sydney bid committee members had assured the public, the media, and IOC whistle blower Marc Hodler that all their actions had been clean and above reproach. In an attempt to fend off calls for an investigation, SOCOG president Michael Knight, also the NSW Labor government's Minister for the Olympics and Sport, claimed that in the leadup to a state election, such an inquiry would be perceived as political opportunism (since the bid had been organized when a Liberal government had been in power).

THE RESIGNATIONS FOLLOW

By early January, documents compiled for the various American investigations showed that SLOBC had provided IOC members and families with benefits and cash payments in contravention of the IOC rules. As a result, Joklik and Johnson resigned on January 8, SLOC terminated Welch's consulting contract and pension, and other SLOC members who had served on the bid committee were given administrative leave. Alfredo La Mont, USOC Director of International Relations and Protocol, resigned on January 14, citing a "previously undisclosed business relationship" with SLOC (U.S. Olympic official, 1999). The SLBE Report subsequently revealed that La Mont and his business associates had contracts with SLOBC from 1990 to 1992 to arrange meetings, collect information, and provide other lobbying services with IOC members—in other words, he worked as an agent while holding a senior USOC position.

As the evidence of corruption mounted, the first IOC resignation occurred when Finnish IOC member Pirjo Haeggman—one of the first two female members appointed in 1981—stepped down on January 19, 1999. Two other IOC members under investigation—Attarabulsi and Sibandze—resigned shortly before the January 24 release of the IOC Commission of Inquiry report, and Mukora left a few days later.

In 1993, SLOBC had tried unsuccessfully to obtain paid employment for Haeggman's husband, and in 1994 had arranged an eighteen-month consulting contract with an engineering company. However, the $33,750 payment that Haegmann had received was documented in SLOBC's financial records, even though his environmental study was unrelated to the committee's activities, and it appeared that the company did not reimburse SLOBC (SLBE, 1999, p. 25).

Allegations of the benefits that the Haeggmans had received in North America implicated not only SLOBC but also the Toronto Ontario Olympic Committee (TOOC), led by former Olympic yachtsman Paul Henderson, during its bid for the 1996 Olympics. In 1989, TOOC had arranged for Haeggman's husband to work for the Ontario Ministry of Natural Resources for twenty months as a forestry inventory specialist. Trevor Isherwood, a Ministry official, claimed that Henderson had initiated the hiring process and later pressured the Ministry to continue employing Haeggman, whose performance was allegedly adequate. When Haeggman resigned from the job four days before the IOC vote for the 1996 Games, Henderson blamed Isherwood for jeopardizing Toronto's chances of gaining Pirjo Haeggman's vote (Buffery, 1999c; Ontario government job . . . , 1999).

Repeating his earlier assertions that the Toronto bid had been clean, Henderson subsequently claimed that there had been no impropriety in the arrangements with the Haeggmans and no conflict of interest when the Ontario government, a financial partner in the Toronto bid, had hired an IOC member's husband. Henderson initially made vague reference to an "exchange program" between Canada and Scandinavian countries (Buffery, 1999b), but soon began to cite the "friendship and hospitality" argument that was a mainstay among most of those implicated in the IOC controversy (Buffery, 1999c).

It was also revealed that TOOC had paid the Haeggmans' rent of $1,000 (CAN) per month, an amount later described by Henderson as a loan and not a gift or bribe. He claimed that these arrangements were known to the IOC and the bid committees in Atlanta and Salt Lake, and had been "cleared" through Samaranch (Christie, 1999b)—although, according to an Australian newspaper report, Samaranch claimed to have no recollection of this (Lusetich, 1999). In a later allegation, it was claimed that Henderson himself had provided employment and accommodation for the son of another Finnish IOC member, Peter Tallberg.

In light of events surrounding the Salt Lake City investigation, it could be argued that TOOC's activities not only demanded a formal investigation but that a systematic inquiry would have been more efficient than the gradual leaking to the media of various pieces of information, most of which were neither complete nor accurate. However, TOOC had a clear advantage over the Salt Lake and Sydney bid committees in that it took early control of the debate, particularly in the mass media.

Although Haeggman resigned from the IOC, she stated that she did not know about the dealings between her former husband and the bid committees, and correspondence cited in the SLBE report generally confirmed her claim. One isolated report dated March 13, 1999, noted that Haeggman had requested the IOC to reinstate her (Vincent, 1999d), perhaps when it became clear that some fellow IOC members—Un Yong Kim (Korea) and Phil Coles (Australia), for example—appeared, at least at that stage, to have successfully avoided expulsion even in the face of evidence of serious misconduct. And, as several African sport officials observed, charges were more likely to stick to a Black* or minority IOC member than to a White one, and more likely to target a Black or minority recipient than a White donor of a bribe (Selsky, 1999; Vincent, 1999c).

TORONTO ONTARIO OLYMPIC COMMITTEE: NO INVESTIGATION

In Toronto, Henderson's arrangements with the Finnish IOC members prompted Olympic watchdog groups and some city councilors to call for an audit of TOOC's files, which at that time were in Henderson's possession. The *Globe and Mail* reported on the contents of one public document related to the TOOC bid: a videotaped interview between Henderson and a university film student in 1990 which the community-based Bread Not Circuses Coalition (BNC) made available on its web site on January 28, 1999. In the video, originally released at a BNC news conference in 1990, Henderson described how TOOC kept some of its cash-generating schemes concealed from the IOC, the Canadian Olympic Association (COA), and the Toronto City Council. The corporate boxes in the SkyDome, for example, would not be mentioned in the bid in order to maximize profits for Toronto (Christie, 1999c).

Although Henderson was in Australia for yacht racing, he was in frequent e-mail and phone communication with selected Toronto journalists who reported not only his defense of the Haeggman arrangements, but also his attack on IOC members and their travel scams (Buffery, 1999a)—prob-

---

*The words Black and White have been capitalized throughout in order to draw attention to the significance of skin color in the social construction of ethnic identities.

lems that TOOC had documented and presented to the IOC executive in January 1991. This new topic deflected some of the media attention from Henderson's relationship with the Haeggmans and the Tallbergs. On his return later in January, he blamed the media for the scandal (Buffery, 1999d). However, the same media were called to a press conference conducted by Henderson and two former TOOC executive members, Norman Seagram and Arthur Eggleton, a few days later. At this event, the IOC executive meeting to which TOOC and other unsuccessful bid committees had been summoned in January 1991 was recast as a brave initiative by Henderson et al. to blow the whistle on IOC members' misconduct. The fact that in 1998–1999, Toronto Council and a group of business and sport leaders were engaged in a new bid for the 2008 Olympics soon deflected attention from the shortcomings of the 1996 bid process. Moreover, TOOC had the advantage of avoiding a federal criminal investigation that, in the SLOBC case, found that a Salt Lake City businessman was guilty of a misdemeanor tax violation when he offered a fraudulent job to the son of IOC member Un Yong Kim.

In the next development involving TOOC, Toronto's former auditor claimed that he had identified irregular cash payments, including improper cash payments, in TOOC's budget but that Eggleton had told him not to pursue the matter. Eggleton denied receiving this information (De Mara, 1999a; Walker, 1999). TOOC's financial records, finally made public in March 1999, provided further evidence of irregularities and possible conflicts of interest. The mayor and several councilors, as well as BNC, called for a forensic audit of TOOC's records, but, after several delays, Toronto Council finally decided that a full audit would be too costly and settled for an internal investigation.

By this time, some councilors were arguing that attention should be on the current bid for the 2008 Olympics rather than on events of ten years earlier (Christie, 1999d). For their part, however, critics were interested not only in uncovering irregularities in the last bid but also in establishing accountability and openness in the current bid, particularly since many of the same players were involved. The new TOBid committee had promised a clean bid, but with international scandals casting doubt on what constituted "clean" in Olympic parlance, it was clear that the situation called for more decisive action. To that end, TOBid attempted to preempt critics with its February announcement of the formation of an ethics committee. However, the USOC had established such a committee in 1991 and SLOC had done so in 1997; the Toronto group had been incorporated for six months and had been meeting for two years before external events prompted it to follow suit. In another late start, the COA only began working on its code of ethics in 1997.

CONCLUSION

Well before the results of formal investigations were made public, evidence of the tangled webs surrounding Olympic bids was appearing in the global media on a daily basis. SLOBC leaders initially defended the practice of providing gifts and services to IOC members and their families on the grounds that this constituted either aid to sport in developing countries, or assistance to poor relatives in the Olympic family. It was not necessary for bid committees to develop particularly creative strategies to circumvent the poorly policed Hodler Rules on gift giving, although it was later revealed that they did, in fact, put considerable money and effort into identifying the needs and interests of particular IOC members and their families. It soon became clear that the Salt Lake case was not an isolated example of impropriety, but part of a complex system of relationships among bid committees in the United States, Canada, and Australia, and links between members of bid committees and the IOC. The system began to crumble in the face of allegations and disclosures of conduct unbecoming the lofty Olympic ideal.

The ways in which both the mass media and the Olympic industry attempted to shape public debate following the November 1998 television disclosure of improper arrangements between SLOBC and IOC members have been described in detail in order to set the stage for an analysis of the four major investigations that took place in the next few months: the IOC ad hoc Commission of Inquiry, the investigation of the independent examiner for SOCOG, the SLBE, and the USOC inquiry. It is beyond the scope of this discussion to provide details of similar inquiries conducted in Nagano, Lillehammer, Stockholm, and elsewhere. The next chapter will provide the historical context for the allegations and investigations, and will analyze the findings of the four inquiries.

What is the Olympic Ideal?

2

The Scandals Unfold

a long history

IN THE PERIOD 1989–1990, six cities were bidding for the 1996 Summer Games: Athens, Atlanta, Belgrade, Manchester, Melbourne, and Toronto. In late 1990, after the IOC selected Atlanta, the German news magazine *Der Spiegel* alleged that Atlanta officials had used corrupt methods, including cash bribes, free hospital care, and scholarships, to win votes (Jennings, 1996). In 1991, Marc Hodler, the IOC member responsible for monitoring the bid process, supported the allegations about Atlanta and also made reference to Salt Lake City's under the table transactions during its unsuccessful bid for the 1998 Winter Olympics, according to one account (Henetz, 1998).

Soon after the *Der Spiegel* story appeared, the committee from Athens, a city that had been considered a favorite, announced its intention to consult with other bid committees about corruption. The head of the Melbourne bid committee, John Ralph, later told a local newspaper that he had contacted Samaranch to propose a meeting to deal with the situation (Williams, 1999). The unsuccessful bid committees were called to Lausanne and all except Athens complied. Ralph was personally unable to attend but sent Ron Casey and John Coates. The Toronto Ontario Olympic Committee (TOOC) was represented by its chair, Paul Henderson, and executive members Norman Seagram and Arthur Eggleton. It is ironic that two of those called upon in 1991 to expose abuses of the bid process—Coates and Henderson—were themselves central figures in the subsequent controversies.

On January 9, 1991, Henderson presented a twenty-six-page report to President Samaranch and the IOC executive—François Carrard (director-general), Françoise Zweifel (secretary-general), and IOC members Raymond Gafner, Marc Hodler, Keba Mbaye, and Richard Pound—on Toronto's experiences with dishonest IOC members (Henderson, Seagram, & Eggleton, 1991). Although the report documented the abuses in considerable detail, no IOC member was identified by name, an omission that was used by the IOC executive to justify its subsequent inaction. Henderson spoke to the media at the time about some of these incidents, but it is significant that he did not make the whole report public until eight years later, during USOC investigations of IOC corruption—that is, at a time when there was much less to lose by joining the chorus of new whistle blowers. Even in 1999, however, members of many bid committees, including Melbourne's, would speak to the media only off the record (Williams, 1999).

An earlier account of IOC corruption, which included a report of a male IOC member demanding "sex for votes," had been included in a book published in 1987 by Lars Eggertz, the chair of the bid committee for Falun, Sweden. Falun had been an unsuccessful bidder for the Winter Olympics since the late 1970s and hence had a long history with the IOC subculture (Eggertz & Hedlund, 1987, cited in Jennings, 1996). In 1988, IOC executive members Pound and Gafner dismissed the Falun committee's reports of impropriety as the action of a "bad loser" (Jennings, 1996, pp. 131–132). As recently as 1999, in a variation on the "bad loser" rationale, Pound impugned the motives of "outside" critics who complained about the IOC: "Most of the so-called accountability complaints [about the IOC], if you examine their sources, tend to come from those who are outside the tent and wish to be inside, not because the IOC is doing a bad job" (Pound, 1999a, p. 4).

Later in the same speech to the Sport Summit in New York, Pound claimed:

> We have tried for years to get something "hard" so that we could act on all the rumors, innuendo and unsupported allegations that float around out there. . . . We have tried to debrief candidate cities, winners and losers, not just to find general ways to improve our overall process, but also to determine whether there has been inappropriate conduct on the part of any IOC member. None of the bid cities have ever come forward with any evidence. (Pound, 1999a, p. 6)

It is difficult to reconcile Pound's statements with the fact that there were documented complaints by bid committees dating back to 1988. The 1991 TOOC report, for example, described how twenty-six of the sixty-nine IOC members who visited Toronto "broke established rules either by coming with more than one guest, arriving more than once, or staying longer than the allotted time" (Henderson, Seagram, & Eggleton, 1991, p. 9). At least eighteen members engaged in various kinds of "misappropriation of travel expenses and airline tickets," which the report described in detail; these abuses cost TOOC up to $800,000 (CAN). The IOC took some action in response to TOOC's complaints of IOC members' travel frauds. For example, included in Hodler's 1994 rules were detailed guidelines on prepaid airline tickets and nonrefundable travel entitlements that attempted to prevent fraudulent practices.

On the general problem of bribery, Pound was personally aware of the identity of one guilty party outside the IOC. On January 19, 1999, just a few days before the IOC commission's report was released, Pound told an Ontario university audience that, as chief negotiator of television rights for the Seoul Games, he had been offered a $1 million bribe for a television deal (Starkman, 1999a). Like other bid officials in Sydney, Toronto, Manchester, and elsewhere, Pound walked away from bribery attempts, and took no further action.

THE FIRST REPORT OF THE IOC AD HOC COMMISSION OF INQUIRY

The commission released its first report on January 24, 1999, at a press conference broadcast live to North America and Europe. A few days earlier, the IOC had hired the services of a major international public relations company, Hill and Knowlton, to manage, among other tasks, more than one hundred international journalists expected to attend the commission's presentation and press conference. It did not escape the attention of those same journalists that Hill and Knowlton had a checkered history of clients and causes, the most notorious being a $10 million contract with the Kuwaiti government in 1990 to shape American public opinion on the Gulf war (Roche, 1999b; Starkman, 1999f).

By the time the commission released its first report, three IOC members—Pirjo Haeggman (Finland), Bashir Attarabulsi (Libya), and David Sibandze (Swaziland)—had resigned, and one, Rene Essomba (Cameroon), had died the year before. The commission recommended expulsion of six other members on the grounds that "their actions have brought the IOC into disrepute": Agustin Arroyo (Ecuador), Zein el Abdin Gadir (Sudan), Jean-Claude Ganga (Congo), Lamine Keita (Mali), Charles Mukora (Kenya), and Sergio Santander Fantini (Chile). Continuing investigations were in process regarding Un Yong Kim (Korea), Louis N'Diaye (Ivory

Coast), and Vitaly Smirnov (Russia), while Anton Geesink (Netherlands) was issued "a strongly worded warning" (IOC ad hoc Commission, 1999a).

The commission's report stressed that this was not a criminal or disciplinary inquiry, but simply an investigation to determine whether, as IOC members, these individuals had acted in an unacceptable or inappropriate manner and thus violated the Olympic oath. It explained that both the Swiss Civil Code and the Olympic Charter provided only for expulsion—the latter requiring a two-thirds majority vote. In defense of IOC policy, it claimed that the rules were in fact harsh rather than lax since they made no provision for lesser sanctions in the case of simple "negligence" or "carelessness."

Although the IOC commission report cited the Olympic Charter's wording on acting "in a way which is *unworthy* of the IOC," it then stated a few pages later that those who had been expelled should not be treated as "unworthy human beings," rather as individuals who had made "mistakes" (IOC ad hoc Commission, 1999, pp. 12, 14). IOC Director General François Carrard, cited in a *Wall Street Journal* account, elaborated on this topic: "The paradox of the Olympics is that it was founded as a private club. What's happening now is not an impeachment or a judicial process. We are just expelling members for conduct unworthy of the club" (Copetas & Thurow, 1999a). Apparently, given the extraordinarily high standards of conduct in this "private club," an occasional lapse should be viewed merely as a human failing.

On the question of gifts, the first ad hoc commission's report asserted that "IOC members do not request that they receive gifts," but Pound modified that statement in a February address to the Canadian Club, where he acknowledged that "in some of these cases, members of the IOC have been the initiators and in some merely the recipients of improper payments or receipts" (Pound, 1999c). In the second IOC report, however, Pound reverted to his former position: "Where gifts were involved, the Commission was satisfied that they were not sought by the members involved" (IOC ad hoc Commission, 1999b, p. 6).

It is difficult to accept that it was simply "careless" or "negligent" for an IOC member to create "an appearance of conflict of interest" or to commit a "technical" breach of IOC guidelines or that it was less culpable to act as the passive recipient of gifts or benefits with full knowledge that they exceeded IOC limits. Resorting to the common rationale of "friendship within the Olympic Family," the report noted that the "scholarships" grew out of "a structure . . . developed in a context of genuine, often lasting and sometimes very close friendships, which were formed and grew over many years, between certain IOC members and certain senior members of the bid committee" (IOC ad hoc Commission, 1999a, p. 14; see chapter 3). Overall, even though it recommended a number of expulsions, the ad hoc commission under Pound's leadership made a concerted effort to minimize the offences and excuse the offenders.

It was clear from the ad hoc commission's January report and carefully orchestrated press conference that one of the key tasks was to establish a framework for future civil investigations based on the Olympic Charter's standard of review. To that end, the commission had a clear advantage in being the first of several panels to release its findings. Each case in the report included a statement of allegations, the IOC member's response, and the commission's conclusions and recommendations; arguments were based solely on factual evidence at hand. Whereas civil proceedings normally rely on "reasonable probability," Pound claimed that the IOC policy on expulsions (and its absence of policy on lesser sanctions) enabled it to take action (i.e., to expel a member) "only on the grounds of known facts and not on the basis of hearsay"—a higher burden of proof than was usual in civil proceedings.

In fact, in his interviews with the international press, Pound often stated that it was virtually impossible to prove that a gift or benefit to an IOC member constituted a quid pro quo because the vote for host cities was conducted by secret ballot; in Pound's more colorful language, "Would you pay me a million bucks to vote your way if the deal was a secret election? You'd have to have rocks in your head" (Starkman, 1999b). Fully understanding the difficulty of proving a quid pro quo, and accustomed to operating from a position of power in Olympic circles, most IOC members strenuously resisted their expulsions.

Although Pound often lamented that the IOC commission lacked the authority to subpoena witnesses and documents (e.g., Pound, 1999a), he appeared to be displeased with the U.S. Justice Department probe, which issued grand jury subpoenas soon after it began its investigations. As a result, several subpoenaed SLOC members had been advised by counsel that it was not in their best interests to speak to other investigators. In a draft report "obtained by" (media language for "leaked to") the *Wall Street Journal* on January 20, Pound was critical of the U.S. legal process. In his reported words, "We will have to consider what the position of the IOC will be if we are served with a subpoena to appear in front of a grand jury. This is a particularly odious procedural part of criminal law in which the accused virtually have no rights. It was a grand jury which dealt with Clinton matters" (Pound quoted in Copetas & Thurow, 1999a). This criticism of another country's legal system appears to have been dropped from the final IOC commission report, which only referred to the problem of lengthy Justice Department proceedings prolonging the "uncertainty" surrounding the Games.

By this stage, it was clear that such uncertainty was jeopardizing sponsorships and that financial rather than ethical issues were taking precedence in the Olympic industry. A January 1999 *Wall Street Journal* article nicely summed up the key concerns for the Olympic industry: "Tarnished rings? For the Olympics, worrisome clouds over lofty image could undermine 'label' worth billions" (Copetas, Thurow, & Fatsis, 1999). Reports of sponsors' concerns had been circulating since December, when one of Salt Lake City's major contributors delayed its $5 million payment for about a month, and sent SLOC a letter seeking an explanation and assurance that there would be no further scandals (Gorrell, 1999a). According to one anonymous sponsor who spoke to a Salt Lake City journalist, some sponsors were using the scandal as leverage to force SLOC to renegotiate their contracts (Roche, 1999a). In mid-December, the USOC sent letters to hundreds of sponsors and would-be sponsors to acknowledge "impropriety" in the bid process and assure them that reform measures would be taken (Roche, 1999a). IOC's director of marketing Michael Payne and public relations firm Hill and Knowlton embarked on an American damage control campaign in January and February, with some success; Coca Cola, for example, confirmed its commitment to Salt Lake City.

In Sydney, SOCOG CEO Sandy Hollway took the initiative in January by writing to all sponsors to reassure them that IOC expulsions and reforms would address the current problems. In February, however, the *Sydney Morning Herald* carried several reports on Sydney 2000 sponsors' concerns, including Samsung with a $77.5 million (AUS) sponsorship and Holden with about $30 million (AUS) (Evans, 1999c; Larkin & Evans, 1999). A few days later, SOCOG board member Graham Richardson also claimed that some sponsors were using the bribery allegations as an "excuse" to rewrite their contracts, while at the same time asserting, with undue optimism, that Olympic problems were "pretty minor" (Sponsors playing games, 1999).

In other recommendations, the IOC commission extended the investigations to include the last five bids, thus reversing its earlier decision that the Sydney bid was clean. It proposed the formation of a permanent ethics commission composed primarily of non-IOC members to continue the inquiry into IOC members Kim, Smirnov, and N'Diaye, to prepare a formal code of ethics for future bids, and to make recommendations to the IOC executive on all these issues. Its most radical proposal concerned changes to the selection process, beginning with the 2006 Winter Games; all visits to bid cities would be banned immediately and the host city would be chosen by a fifteen-member panel rather than the full membership.

By February, the IOC executive was faced with the threat of revolt by so-called rank and file members who opposed being stripped of their voting rights. It was reported that forty-two members opposed this plan, which required support of two-thirds of the membership in order to be adopted (IOC members revolt, 1999). Although there were strong commercial forces, most notably some of the major corporations, pushing the executive toward more radical reform, the IOC rank and file members held their ground on the city selection proposal, which was eventually modified to allow them to visit the two finalist cities and to vote for the winner.

The president of John Hancock Financial Services, John D'Alessandro, was uncompromising in his critique of the IOC, published in the Sunday *New York Times* on February 14 (D'Alessandro, 1999) and subsequently cited in major newspapers internationally. He not only called for a permanent change to the host city selection process but also proposed a new membership selection procedure to make representatives "accountable to the world community" and an immediate search for a new president. His article drew particular attention to the speedy exoneration of the Sydney bid committee. He complained about the actions of Australian Olympic Committee president John Coates, who had promised cash to Kenyan and Ugandan IOC members on the eve of the IOC vote. Sydney coordination commissioner Jacques Rogge had investigated Coates's actions on behalf of the IOC and within about ten days found them to be "perfectly correct"—an outcome that convinced D'Alessandro that the IOC "investigations" were simply a "classic cover-up."

A greater threat to the IOC than D'Alessandro's rhetoric was the company's threat to disassociate itself from the Olympics unless the IOC cleaned up its "mess"; it cancelled negotiations with NBC to purchase $20 million worth of advertising during Sydney 2000 and removed the Olympic rings from its stationery and billboards, replacing them with SOCOG's logo. A similar but more outraged critique of the IOC appeared in the February 23 issue of *Sports Illustrated*, in which regular columnist Rick Reilly wrote an open letter to Don Logan, Chair and CEO of Time Inc., the magazine's publisher and a major corporate sponsor of the Olympics. Reilly called on Time Inc. and all the other major Olympic sponsors to follow the John Hancock example by cutting all ties with such a corrupt organization. Logan replied by expressing the company's deep concerns about recent events and stating that it had "insisted that the IOC undertake a complete and vigorous examination . . ."; he also assured Reilly that journalistic independence on Olympic stories would be encouraged regardless of the company's commercial interests (Reilly & Logan, 1999).

Although it was clear that the Olympic rings were no longer a blue chip stock, the IOC sent out mixed messages to its sponsors. In remarks following the release of the first IOC commission report in January, Richard Pound, speaking in his "other role" as chair of the IOC Marketing Commission, thanked the IOC broadcast and sponsor partners who had "reiterated their full support for the Olympic Games, even though they have understandably been concerned and anxious that the IOC take quick and decisive action" (Pound, 1999b, p. 2). In February, Pound's speech to the Canadian Club included the assertion that the IOC's reform efforts were "its own initiative and not as a result of any external pressures, including our sponsors and broadcast partners" (Pound, 1999c, p. 2). Other IOC members did not appear to understand that a threat to the Games' global commercial success in turn jeopardized the future of the Olympics. On the issue of visiting and voting for host cities, despite unequivocal evidence of abuses, IOC member Indrapana (Thailand) was reported to have stated, "We are running the IOC, not the media or the sponsors" (Lehmann, 1999b). After all, as an Associated Press story observed, "the primary duty of IOC members has always been to choose Olympic host cities" (IOC members revolt, 1999).

By March 1999, when three major investigations had been completed, it became clear that "duty" was only one factor in members' determination to visit bid cities. The first IOC commission report acknowledged that, since the technical merits of a bid city's proposed sport venues were assessed by international federations rather than the IOC, bid committees concentrated more on impressing IOC visitors with their "hospitality and friendship" (IOC ad hoc Commission, 1999a, p. 8). The Sydney investigation, discussed in detail below, showed that, of the sixty IOC members who visited Sydney, fifteen made side trips or stopovers of more than one day at the expense of the bid committee, in contravention of IOC rules; the most popular destinations were Singapore and Port Douglas, a luxury Barrier Reef resort (Sheridan, 1999). "Travel and entertainment" expenses associated with the sixty visitors and their guests, including air fares, ground transport, accommodation, and gifts, cost the Sydney bid committee $6.9 million (AUS) (Sheridan, 1999, p. 26).

During the second stage of the IOC commission's investigations, letters were sent to twenty-two NOCs involved in bids from 1996 to 2004, and to the six committees bidding for the 2006 Winter Games, asking them to report on any action that might have threatened the integrity of the bid process, including requests for assistance or intervention, acceptance of material benefits by IOC members or their relatives, and acceptance of "excessive hospitality" including multiple visits or more than one accompanying person. Critics, including D'Alessandro, were justly scathing of an official investigation that asked the offending parties themselves to confess their misdeeds. (The other major IOC initiative in January–February 1999 focused on the problem of performance-enhancing drugs. The IOC's World Conference on Doping in Sport was held in Lausanne in early February, and plans were announced to have Samaranch as president and IOC medical commissioner de Merode as vice-president of a new international anti-doping agency. With the IOC's and Samaranch's credibility seriously eroded by the scandal, the proposals met with extensive criticism on all fronts. A full discussion of the international doping issue is beyond the scope of this book.)

SALT LAKE BOARD OF ETHICS REPORT

Two weeks after the first IOC ad hoc Commission report, on February 8, the SLBE released its findings on gifts and benefits made by SLOBC or SLOC to IOC members. In explaining its standard of review, the report noted that the Board had not been instructed to evaluate civil or criminal liability. It referred to the Olympic Charter's standard of ethical behavior and the requirement that members avoid "commercial influence," and further explained that it defined "ethical misconduct" based on whether "a person in our community recognizing IOC protocol, would view the conduct in question as being improper or presenting an appearance of impropriety" (SLBE, 1999, p. 4). This implicit invoking of Mormon community standards, together with the fact that most SLOC officials had Mormon affiliations, set the stage for a higher moral standard in the SLBE investigation.

The SLBE examined extensive documentary evidence and interviewed dozens of witnesses, mostly current or former SLOC employees and trustees. Tom Welch, Dave Johnson, and Frank Joklik appeared before the board, but some other former SLOBC employees declined on the advice of counsel. Information was also provided by three of the IOC members under investigation: Un Yong Kim, Charles Mukora, and Sergio Santander Fantini. As well as presenting clear evidence of Welch's and Johnson's central roles in the "scholarship program," the report alleged that additional IOC members had acted improperly. These members, together with others named by NOCs involved in earlier bids, were investigated by the IOC commission in February. During this period, one member, Mukora, resigned.

The SLBE report included one unusual case in which there was clear evidence that an IOC member (Alexandru Siperco, Romania) and his son had resisted Johnson's repeated attempts to persuade the son, Andrei, to accept airline tickets, housing, and living expenses while he studied at Brigham Young University. Letters cited in the SLBE report showed how Johnson had tried to convince Andrei that such "grants" were approved components of the organizing committee's "scholarship program." Andrei was adamant in rejecting these offers on the grounds that it was not appropriate for him to take advantage of his IOC connection in this manner (SLBE, 1999, Conclusion, pp. 2–3).

By disclosing details of the Siperco case that reflected so badly on the bid committee, the SLBE inadvertently provided fuel for the next IOC ad hoc commission report to blame NOCs rather than the IOC for failure to monitor bid selection processes. While Siperco's was the best documented example of SLOBC's overtures, there were other instances in which Johnson and Welch went to considerable lengths to ensure that expensive gifts were accepted, even to the point of soliciting intervention from third parties.

For its part, the SLBE directed the first four of its nine recommendations at the IOC and the USOC, calling for both bodies to promulgate and enforce all the rules relating to bid cities, IOC and NOC members, and to monitor the bid process more rigorously. Its other recommendations focused on SLOC's future activities, including ethical concerns and financial and policy reviews. Finally, in a challenge to existing power relations within the "Olympic Family," it urged the SLOC "to monitor the ongoing efforts of the IOC and the USOC to promulgate rules governing interaction with IOC members and . . . establish supplementary policies as necessary" (SLBE, 1999; Recommendations).

USOC SPECIAL BID OVERSIGHT COMMISSION REPORT

The next step in the process was the February 1 release of the USOC commission findings. It was this report's forthright critique of the IOC's "broader culture of improper gift-giving, . . . made possible by the closed nature of the IOC and by the absence of ethical and transparent financial controls in its operation" (USOC, 1999, p. 27) that prompted the most indignant reaction from the IOC commission and Richard Pound. While not condoning the actions of SLOBC members, the USOC report claimed that "they did not invent this culture; they joined one that was already flourishing" (USOC, 1999, pp. 27–28). The USOC commission took issue with the IOC commission's statement that IOC members did not request gifts, and pointed out that the SLBE report had documented several instances where they had done so. Reflecting its principal mandate to make recommendations to prevent future abuses of the bid process, the report included nine pages of proposals for "timely, aggressive reform" in IOC and USOC rules and policies.

The USOC commission relied largely on the extensive body of factual evidence collected by the SLBE, as well as conducting its own internal investigations, which included interviews with USOC/IOC members Anita DeFrantz and James Easton, and TOOC's vice-chair Norman Seagram. By the time the USOC commission was calling witnesses, SLBC members Welch and Johnson and USOC Director La Mont had been advised by counsel not to participate pending federal investigations. Based on the existing evidence, the USOC commission concluded that both the SLOBC executive committee and its board of trustees "failed to exercise adequate oversight of the bid and organizing committees," particularly in relation to the large undocumented expenditures incurred through the NOC program (USOC, 1999, p. 16).

Furthermore, the USOC report stated that the SLOBC executive and board should have known about the "long and highly public campaign" of gift giving and scholarships, especially in view of the fact that "a large number of IOC members and their relatives were visiting, attending schools in and finding employment around Salt Lake City" (USOC, 1999, pp. 18–19). Furthermore, since there had been no efforts to keep these details secret, it seriously questioned the SLBE finding that, except for Welch and Johnson, all the other SLOBC members were unaware of the improprieties of the arrangements. In fact, the report found that some senior USOC members were aware that the bid committee was operating a NOC Assistance Program but "never questioned the propriety of that Program or audited its activities" (USOC, 1999, p. 23). SLOBC had used both its own NOC program and USOC's International Assistance Fund "to establish and maintain long-term, vote influencing relationships with the IOC" (USOC, 1999, p. 14). While the report stressed that the disbursement of gifts and services was conducted in a "systematic" way for the purpose of influencing votes, it also stated that it found no "direct evidence" of a quid pro quo (presumably because of the IOC's secret vote) (USOC, 1999, p. 12). However, in the specific case of USOC member La Mont, who had resigned in January, written correspondence between SLOBC and USOC led the USOC commission to propose that arrangements he had facilitated regarding Sudanese athletes' "scholarships" did in fact constitute a quid pro quo.

The USOC report was critical of the USOC itself for failing in its responsibility to oversee the activities of its own members as well as those of SLOBC. In 1989, the USOC site inspection team had noted that Salt Lake City's gift-giving practices were "over the line," and there was evidence that members of the USOC Board of Directors themselves had accepted gifts valued over the

$25 limit during the internal competition to become the American candidate city for the 2002 Games. According to the USOC Report, all three organizations—IOC, USOC, and SLOBC—had failed to develop and promulgate "clearly articulated, binding and enforced rules" during the bid process (USOC, 1999, p. 10).

On the question of IOC responsibility, the USOC report stated that IOC's failure to enforce existing rules, such as they were, led candidate cities to question whether the bid competition was conducted on a level playing field. For the previous fifteen years, it claimed, bid committees had been aware that the merits, capacity, and ability of a city to stage the Games were not the deciding factor. On this issue, the report referred to the TOOC's 1991 presentation to the IOC, in which Henderson et al. had claimed that one of a bid city's four objectives was to demonstrate "why it was in each IOC member's *personal interest* to vote for, and award the Games to that City" (cited in USOC Report, 1999, p. 30; emphasis added). TOOC's report, which George Mitchell termed "the Toronto prophecy" at the USOC press conference, warned that IOC members' visits to bid cities presented "the greatest opportunity for the rules of the bidding system to be abused, either by the Member or by the bid committee. It is here, as well, where the IOC runs the greatest risk of its image being tarnished and its integrity eroded . . ." (cited in USOC Report, 1999, p. 30).

Significantly, the USOC report omitted the rest of that sentence, which went on to say "especially should there exist a competitive press in that City or its bidding competitors" (Henderson et al., 1991, p. 9)—in short, a warning that the risk of scandal was greater if the media found out. Had the USOC been aware of Henderson's well-known hostility to the press, as well as events leading up to the TOOC report, it might have interpreted its contents somewhat differently.

In the area of international relations and bribery, the USOC report made two innovative recommendations: firstly, that the U.S. president should name the IOC "a public international organization" in accordance with the U.S. Foreign Corrupt Practices Act (FCPA); and secondly, that the IOC should not select host cities in countries that are not signatories to the Anti-Bribery Convention of the Organization for Economic Cooperation and Development (OECD), an agreement designed to create a level playing field for international business transactions.

The OECD Convention on Combating Bribery of Foreign Public Officials had been adopted in 1997 with twenty-nine member countries and five nonmembers as signatories. As of November 1998, eleven countries including Japan, the United States, United Kingdom, and Canada had officially ratified the convention, and legislation in twenty-three other countries was in process (OECD, 1998). The two key components of the OECD convention were the criminalization of bribery of foreign officials and the elimination of tax deductibility of bribes. Two years earlier, the United Nations had adopted a Declaration Against Corruption and Bribery in International Commercial Transactions, which committed UN members to criminalize such bribery but had no standing under international law.

Since 1977, the FCPA had prohibited American companies from bribing foreign officials, a rule that was often viewed as disadvantaging Americans bidding on foreign contracts against competitors from countries lacking anti-bribery legislation. In the industrialized world, FCPA is the widely accepted model for addressing the problems of corruption in international business, an area of current concern to the United Nations, the World Bank, and other institutions (Cragg, 1998). In light of subsequent allegations involving Olympic officials, it is interesting to note that proposed amendments to the FCPA legislation in 1998 required language prohibiting bribery not only to obtain business but also to gain any improper advantage, such as to influence judges or others with the authority to hand down a favorable ruling. According to the co-founder of Transparency International, a coalition against corruption in international business, the OECD convention "illuminates the fact that bribery, usually perceived as an ethical issue, is now understood to have political, societal and significant financial implications" (Hershman, 1998). By 1999, those engaged in the Olympic industry had no doubt discovered the truth of this statement.

Americans, according to Hershman, had in the past been accused of trying to export their own brand of morality to other countries, a charge that was echoed by some IOC members in 1999 when USOC, the U.S. Congress, and the U.S. Justice Department were investigating areas in need of reform. Senator John McCain, chair of the Senate's standing commerce committee, together with Senator Ted Stevens, recommended removing IOC's tax-exempt status in the United States and limiting its NBC revenue unless the IOC was serious about reform (Korporaal, 1999j). By March, McCain had arranged Senate hearings to which Samaranch, Hodler, Easton, DeFrantz, and others were summoned, as well as UK investigative journalist Andrew Jennings (see chapter 9).

One of the USOC report's recommendations called for "a substantial majority of IOC members" to be elected by each country's NOC, by international federations and other relevant organizations, in order to promote accountability. USOC president Bill Hybl reinforced this concept later in March when he recommended specifically that the USOC should elect future representatives to the IOC (US chiefs, 1999). A Hamburg journalist subsequently described an "internal USOC strategy paper" that had been delivered to the IOC as an attempt at a "hostile takeover" by Americans using as leverage the fact that $1.5 billion of the IOC's $4 billion revenues (1996–2000) were generated in the United States. Furthermore, USOC would receive $420 million from NBC television rights, giving it almost as much television income as the IOC (Deister, 1999). Financially, at least, USOC posed a serious threat to IOC supremacy.

IOC AD HOC COMMISSION REPORT II

The second IOC ad hoc Commission report was released on March 2, this time with considerably less fanfare. It confirmed the expulsion of Arroyo, Gadir, Keita, and Santander Fantini and recommended that Paul Wallwork (Samoa) be expelled. Warnings of varying severity were issued to the following IOC members: Phil Coles (Australia), Louis N'Diaye (Ivory Coast), Willi Kaltschmitt (Gautemala), Un Yong Kim (Korea), Shagdarjav Magvan (Mongolia), Anani Matthia (Togo), Austin Sealy (Barbados), Vitaly Smirnov (Russia), and Mohamed Zerguini (Algeria). Coles, who was issued "the most serious of warnings" was the first White Anglo-Saxon member to appear on such a list. The commission found that he had merely failed to exercise "his best judgement" in accepting excessive gifts, accommodation, and services for himself and family members, and noted in passing that he had "spontaneously" offered to repay expenses not related to his official visit (IOC ad hoc Commission, 1999b, p. 23).

Wallwork's case arose from SLBE allegations that in 1991 his wife had requested and received a $30,000 loan from SLOBC chair Tom Welch. There was evidence that the loan had eventually been repaid without interest. While Wallwork denied knowledge of the loan, the IOC commission report asserted that "facts" indicated that he "would have—or at least should have—known . . . as early as April 1992" and moralized that he "must bear the consequences of his wife's gross misconduct." This harsh language stood in marked contrast to the mildly worded warnings issued to several other IOC members, whose alleged offenses, in the view of most commentators, were equally egregious (Olympic cleanup, 1999).

Three other members under investigation—Henry Adefope (Nigeria), Ashwini Kumar (India), and Ram Ruhee (Mauritius)—were exonerated. Kumar had been identified erroneously in the SLBE report as having accepted travel expenses for an unknown relative ("A. Kumar") who was in fact himself. The commission report noted Kumar's and Ruhee's concern that the SLBE had not asked them for explanations before publicizing allegations that were later proven inaccurate. On this issue, Pound was critical of the SLBE for failing to contact members to explain their actions before making their names public (Pound, 1999c). Kumar and Ruhee, however, received significantly less media attention than Australian IOC member Phil Coles, whose first response to being named in the SLBE report had been to threaten the committee and the media with a lawsuit (Gorrell, 1999d). It was not until June 1999, on the eve of the IOC Regular Session, that the Coles investigation was finally concluded.

Pound used the occasion of the second IOC ad hoc Commission report to refute the USOC claim that the IOC promoted a "culture of improper gift-giving." Citing evidence presented in the USOC report, he argued that the lion's share of the blame lay with aggressive bid committee members forcing benefits on "vulnerable" IOC members, who then accepted the gifts, according to this rationale, to avoid embarrassment on both sides. NOCs, rather than the IOC, were responsible for ensuring that bidding processes were conducted ethically, according to this report (IOC ad hoc Commission, 1999b, p. 4).

The IOC held an extraordinary session on March 17–18, followed by a press conference to announce that the membership had endorsed the Commission's recommended reforms. A fourth member, Francis Nyangweso (Kenya), who, with Charles Mukora, had been the recipient of John Coates's checks, was exonerated. President Samaranch announced the formation of the permanent Ethics Commission and the IOC 2000 Commission, which he planned to lead, to reform IOC structure and procedures and to develop the new IOC 2000 Olympic Charter by the end of 1999. In the interim, an "election college" made up of the president, IOC members, international federation and NOC representatives, and athletes would select two finalists for the 2006 Winter Games, to be decided by the full IOC membership in June 1999. Given the unpopularity of the earlier selection proposal, and the fact that Samaranch's leadership was to be put to the vote at the March session, the executive's decision to reinstate the process by which the full membership voted for the host city was strategically sound. As it turned out, Samaranch received an overwhelming vote of confidence (eighty-six in favor, two opposed, one absent) to continue as president, an outcome that gave new meaning to the concept of Olympic Solidarity.

REPORT OF THE INDEPENDENT EXAMINER FOR SOCOG (SYDNEY)

The next official investigation to release its report, on March 12, 1999, was the independent examination of Sydney's bid conducted for SOCOG by retired auditor-general Tom Sheridan. This panel's terms of reference were to report breaches of IOC guidelines, misconduct by IOC or bid committee members, conduct to be further reviewed by the NSW Police or Independent Commission Against Corruption (ICAC), and inadequacies in the SOBC's internal audits or control mechanisms. Many of the findings in this report provided the missing pieces in the international puzzle of Olympic family relationships.

The Sheridan report found that, like other bid committees, SOBC's strategy was to engage in "aggressive marketing" of Sydney as host city, and to gain "the respect, confidence and friendship and ultimately the vote of each IOC member" (Sheridan, 1999, p. 1). In the wake of three other reports on bid committees' inventive methods of influencing IOC members' votes through "marketing" and "friendship," SOBC's approach was by now fairly predictable:

- lavish accommodations, entertainment, and gifts for IOC members and guests during visits;
- employment of "professional lobbyists" to facilitate "friendships" and to ascertain individual members' interests for gift-giving purposes;
- "scholarships" for athletes from selected African countries;
- SOBC lobbying during visits to IOC members' countries;
- financial assistance, education, and/or employment in Australia for relatives of IOC members.

The Sydney bid's Olympic Solidarity program took the form of Olympic Training Centre scholarships, at a cost of approximately $2 million (AUS), awarded to selected African athletes. In July 1993, Australian Olympic Committee (AOC) president John Coates and secretary-general Perry Crosswhite, together with former Australian prime minister Gough Whitlam and his wife, Margaret Whitlam, travelled to Africa "for the purpose of building/strengthening relationships" (Sheridan, 1999, p. 42). Letters dated August 25, 1993, termed "Cooperation Agreements" between the AOC and eleven African NOCs, committed the AOC to two forms of assistance in training athletes: one-year grants to be provided unconditionally, and seven-year grants conditional on the success of Sydney's bid (Sheridan, 1999, pp. 42–43). The terminology is significant: "cooperation agreement" suggests that both parties had something to give—in other words, a quid pro quo—whereas if the word *scholarship* had been used, it would have implied an award granted by the benefactor to the deserving recipient.

A less publicized contribution to an Olympic Solidarity program was put in place as a result of successful lobbying by Aboriginal groups, who had noted in 1994 that only two of the 524 scholarships granted by the Australian Institute of Sport were offered to indigenous athletes. By 1999, a scholarship program for twenty-four athletes was established, with $100,000 from the Indigenous Sport Program and $50,000 each from SOCOG and the AOC—the latter qualifying as an Olympic Solidarity program (Godwell, 1999a). The AOC's $50,000 amount for indigenous sport stands in marked contrast to the $2 million promised to African NOCs in the "cooperation agreement" negotiated during the bid process.

On the matter of IOC members' stops en route to Australia, Sheridan reported that the SOBC had encouraged them to stop in Bangkok or Singapore because of perceptions of Australia's remoteness and concerns about travel fatigue (the flight from Europe, the Americas, or Africa to Sydney took 14–24 hours). It was noted that all IOC members and guests received "red carpet" treatment: top hotels, quality restaurants, banquets and catering, guided tours, chartered cruises, sporting events, and finally, a professional photographer's souvenir record of visits at a cost of $1,000 each (Sheridan, 1999, p. 30). Although Sheridan found that the value of gifts exceeded IOC guidelines, he stated, in a manner reminiscent of the IOC ad hoc Commission report: "I hesitate to suggest that the gift giving involved any misconduct on the part of IOC members . . . the gifts . . . were generic and not of a type designed, or likely, to influence the vote of an IOC member" (Sheridan, 1999, p. 28).

Evidence in the Sheridan report showed that SOBC had encouraged IOC members and guests to take "side trips" within the country, both to "showcase" Australia and to promote relationships between members and the bid committee. Pointing out that side trips and stopovers were offered, not requested, Sheridan found that they could not be interpreted as abuse of power. He noted, however, that IOC members' acceptance of "excessive hospitality" fell under the IOC Commission's definition of misconduct. The SOBC representative who most often accompanied members on these side trips was Phil Coles. Combined with his Paris-based lobbying on behalf of SOBC, these trips no doubt provided Coles with the data for his now well-known dossiers on IOC members' personalities and preferences.

In addition to the usual approaches to hospitality, SOBC took innovative steps to impress IOC members, most notably the elaborate arrangements to transport seven Mongolian wild horses from the Western Plains Zoo in Dubbo, NSW, where a successful breeding program had produced twenty-four horses, to Mongolia, where such horses were now extinct. When Mongolian IOC member Shagdarjav Magvan expressed interest in the horses during a side trip to the zoo in 1993, the bid committee embarked on a two-year project to transport seven horses to Mongolia. These arrangements involved, among others, the Zoological Parks Board, the Monarto Zoo in Adelaide, the Department of Foreign Affairs and Trade, the prime minister's office, and the Mongolian minister of foreign affairs, at a total cost of $240,000, with $20,000 provided by SOBC and $115,000 in "AusAid" from Foreign Affairs. Sheridan concluded that, while the program fitted the zoo's mandate and Magvan derived no personal benefit, there was "little doubt that the Bid Company contributed to it in an effort to secure Mr. Magvan's votes" (Sheridan, 1999, p. 48). The report did not explain the circumstances of this particular side trip but it is possible that SOBC planned the 200-mile excursion from Sydney to Dubbo for the express purpose of showing Magvan Mongolia's national symbol, the wild horse, which he reportedly was "astounded" to discover at the Australian zoo (Lehmann & Zubrzycki, 1999a).

It seems likely that all the bid committee's attempts to portray Sydney as a world-class city and to counter the stereotype of Australians as unsophisticated and uncultured were related to what is known in Australia as the "cultural cringe"—an apologetic and defensive position vis-à-vis the rest of the (Western) world. At the same time, however, Australians take pride in an independent national spirit that rejects obsequiousness outright (Booth & Tatz, 1994). As a *Herald* commentary noted in reference to protocol required in Samaranch's presence—standing when he leaves the room, for example: "In an egalitarian country like Australia, such pomp and pretence is alien" (Masters, 1999). SOCOG, too, rejected obsequiousness; an in-house contest to name its new cafeteria produced, among other suggestions, "John and Tony's Sandwich Ranch"; needless to say, this send-up of the president's name was not the winning entry.

Sheridan's conclusions provided further evidence of the "cultural cringe" dilemma:

> On one view the hospitality provided to IOC members when they visited Sydney could be seen as lavish—the best hotels, good restaurants and expensive tours. Whether the degree of lavishness means that the hospitality accepted by IOC members was incompatible with the status of an IOC member is a difficult question which I do not intend to answer. In terms of the Bid Company's conduct in this regard, it would have been difficult—and counter-productive given its aim—to provide less than first-rate hospitality. (Sheridan, 1999, p. 31)

In other words, Sheridan wasn't going to risk appearing "the ignorant Australian" by criticizing IOC protocol. After all, a senior member of Nagano's organizing committee had defined the expenditure of more than $27,000 (CAN) on each of sixty-two IOC members as normal. "What was offered was definitely not excessive. It was normal. In business, entertainment is far more extravagant" (Nagano's gifts normal, 1999). In Canada, the mayor of Quebec City had affirmed that the bid committee never exceeded "the usual rule of hospitality," which apparently included intervening on immigration issues on behalf of IOC members or their families (Hospitality the rule, 1999). Finally, remarks by Dr. Jacques Rogge, Sydney's IOC Coordination Commissioner, asserted that "lavish" treatment alone was not a problem: "You have to differentiate between what is a breach of the line and what is so-called lavish treatment" (Rogge quoted in Korporaal, 1999i).

In conclusion, Sheridan found three major deficiencies in IOC guidelines: no monitoring of adherence, lack of clarity, and "the potential for significant support (benefits) to be made available outside the guidelines" through government-to-government support or NOC support (Sheridan, 1999, p. 1).

CONCLUSION

These four major investigations into the conduct of IOC and bid committee members confirmed rumors, suspicions, and allegations that had been circulating since at least the 1980s. There was unequivocal evidence that rules guiding gifts, hospitality, and services had been ignored by all parties. Clear patterns on the part of bid committees emerged from the reports: lavish accommodations, entertainment, gifts, and services for IOC members and their families; contracts with professional lobbyists to brief bid committees on individual IOC members; scholarships for athletes from developing countries; and financial assistance, higher education, and/or employment in the bid city or region for relatives of IOC members. From the other side, it was also apparent that some IOC members and their relatives were the recipients of extensive benefits from bid committees around the world. In this climate, it was highly unlikely that a bid committee would jeopardize its chances of success by failing to entertain IOC visitors in the manner to which they had become accustomed, or by refusing requests for other favors—as the *Sydney Morning Herald* quipped, "Job for the boy." However, the results of several major inquiries amply demonstrated that many of the bid committees' actions were unwise, unethical, and, in some cases, illegal.

3

Olympic Family Solidarity

creative connotations

IN THIS CHAPTER, the analysis will focus primarily on the sociocultural context of Olympic bids and preparations, and the ways in which social structures within the Olympic industry influenced individual behavior. Within the international Olympic industry, two institutional structures—the Olympic family and the Olympic Solidarity program—contributed in different ways to shaping relationships among the various Olympic players. Transcending internal Olympic structures were the racist and colonialist discourses that defined people from developing countries as "other." In relation to charges of corruption in the Olympic bid process, this "otherness" was manifested in paternalistic and/or racist assumptions about the ethical values and business practices of African and other nonwhite Olympic officials. It is not the purpose of this analysis to produce a list of villains and victims, a task better suited to the mass media and the legal system. Instead, I propose to demonstrate that, contrary to IOC assertions, there is no doubt that issues of geography, culture, and race permeated all these events.

OLYMPIC FAMILY SYSTEMS

Olympic family is the metaphor used to described the extensive network of individuals and organizations involved in the international Olympic industry. Links between members of this family are forged not only on the playing field, but also in the boardroom. Although former Olympic athletes are well represented on the IOC and NOCs, politicians and businessmen with no elite sport experience are now joining the family as bid and organizing committee members; the composition of Toronto's 2008 bid committee provides one example (see chapter 4). The shared bond assumed to unite diverse family members is Olympism, which the Olympic Charter defines as follows:

> Olympism is a philosophy of life, exalting and combining in a balanced whole the qualities of body, will and mind. Blending sport with culture and education, Olympism seeks to create a way of life based on the joy found in effort, the educational value of good example and respect for *fundamental ethical principles*. (IOC Charter, 1997, p. 8; emphasis added)

The definition of Olympism assumes a common international understanding of "fundamental ethical principles," some of which are identified for IOC members in the Olympic Oath: "I undertake . . . to keep myself free from any political or commercial influence and from any racial or religious consideration . . ." (IOC Charter, 1997, p. 26). In light of these lofty principles, as well as Western liberal "tolerance" for racial diversity, it is not surprising that the IOC felt the need to claim that "race" was not a factor in the expulsions and warnings issued to culpable members, the vast majority of whom were not White.

According to Richard Pound and others, the IOC is "one of the most successful international organizations of the twentieth century" (Pound, 1999a). Unlike other international organizations, however, its members represent the IOC in their respective countries, rather than acting as delegates of their countries to the IOC, an arrangement that at best frees them from national government interests or pressures, and at worst reinforces the concept of the IOC as a private club. In either case, it is not entirely valid to compare an association with this kind of structure to an international organization composed of national delegates. Moreover, while supporters cite IOC's longevity and stability as markers of success, critics view the same features as evidence of its self-perpetuating, undemocratic ways of functioning. Equally important, the unique IOC structure exempted it from one of the most significant global efforts to create a level playing field for international business transactions, namely the 1997 OECD Convention on Combating Bribery of Foreign Public Officials.

Until the 1950s, Africa and Asia were seriously underrepresented in the Olympic family; in 1954, only two Africans and ten Asians were included in the IOC. By 1998, African and Asian members each represented about 20% of the IOC membership. With the first women members invited to join in

1981, the public face of the IOC was no longer exclusively White and male. Yet Europe remained the most powerful bloc, and, given the requirement of a two-thirds majority vote, even an African/Asian alliance could not out-number the Europeans and North Americans. Among those whom Sama-ranch recruited from developing nations and the communist bloc were men who had political or corporate power, rather than sport administration expe-rience, in their own countries: for example, Charles Mukora (Kenya), a director of Coca Cola Africa; Alex Gilady (Israel), an NBC-TV executive; Kun Hee Lee (Korea), the president of Samsung; and Francis Nyangweso (Uganda), a retired major general in Idi Amin's army.

Within the IOC, power tended to accrue to members from the North, to those from recent host countries (which were entitled to one additional IOC member), and to individuals who wielded international influence in sport or political circles. The unofficial list of potential successors to Samaranch cir-culating in 1999 comprised individuals from one or more of these categories: Anita DeFrantz (United States), Kevan Gosper (Australia), Richard Pound (Canada), Un Yong Kim (Korea), and Jacques Rogge (Belgium).

THE OLYMPIC FAMILY: AN EXPENSIVE GUEST

The term *Olympic family*, when used in reference to protocol requirements during the staging of the Games, encompasses IOC members, their staff and guests, presidents and secretaries-general of 198 NOCs, and up to twenty-eight international federations, members of current organizing and bid com-mittees, major corporate sponsors and accredited media personnel—esti-mated at approximately four thousand for the 2000 Summer Olympics in Sydney and thirty-five hundred for the 2002 Winter Games in Salt Lake City (Warchol, 1999; Performance Audit Review, 1998). Athletes numbering approximately ten thousand comprise the biggest but arguably the least pow-erful and prestigious branch of the family. Australian Immigration authorities estimate a total of 42,000 Olympic family visitors to Sydney in 2000.

Although IOC guidelines since 1992 have limited bid committees' lav-ish spending on gifts, receptions and hospitality during members' visits, pro-tocol requirements for the Olympic family during the Games are somewhat less restrained. Previously classified details of the SOCOG and Salt Lake City contracts that appeared in the media in 1999 confirmed that the job of hosting members of the extended Olympic family—not including the ath-letes—would cost the organizing committees millions of dollars. Informa-tion about these practices had been published before (e.g., Jennings, 1996; Hill, 1992) but had much greater impact in the wake of allegations about some IOC members' "unworthy" behavior, particularly their expectations and/or demands during bid city visits.

Equally important, the budget figures for protocol expenses appeared in the *Salt Lake Tribune* and *Sydney Morning Herald* at a time when taxpayers in those future host cities were justifiably concerned that the major Olympic legacy for them would be a debt, not a profit. For example, the Salt Lake and Sydney bid city contracts required a high level of security for key Olympic family members, especially those who qualified as "visiting dignitaries"; about four hundred personal security officers were to be employed for that purpose in Sydney (Macey, 1999; Ryle, 1999). A hospitality zone for the Olympic family was to be provided adjacent to each venue, and Salt Lake's budget for their breakfasts alone was $750,000 (Warchol, 1999).

Cities that had hosted IOC or NOC meetings were already familiar with their hospitality and security demands. As UK Olympic scholar Christopher Hill aptly noted in relation to security requirements during IOC meetings— the takeover of the best hotel, the sniffer dogs, the traffic diversions—"it is important to remember that there is a difference between an IOC Session and a G7 summit meeting" (Hill, 1992, p. 263). Furthermore, the costs of city, state, and national police force involvement, as well as the extra demands on customs and immigration officials, are usually excluded from official Olympic budget figures and, like other infrastructure bills, are borne by the taxpayers.

Some of SOCOG's hitherto unknown expenses had been made public in late 1998 following the November release of the Auditor-General's independent examination of SOCOG's budget. At that time, "Games Services" (accommodation, ticketing, accreditation, transport, and security) were estimated at $177.4 million (AUS), of which $139.4 million would be provided by the NSW Government. $72.5 million was allocated for 1,800 limousines needed for four thousand members of the Olympic family and $41.2 million for security. An additional budget item lists "Olympic Family Services" at $14.5 million (Performance Audit Report, 1998; Appendix 11.11). A February report noted that Olympic family transport was required for the twelve-day period before and after the Games as well as for their duration (Ryle, 1999). It is interesting to compare these figures with SOCOG's medical budget of only $8.1 million.

In March 1999, in accordance with the board of ethics recommendations, SLOC opened its records and meetings to the public. While its budget, as approved by the board of trustees in October 1998, was organized in categories different than Sydney's, security was projected at approximately $15 million, "risk management" $17 million, "protocol" $10.1 million, and transportation $28.6 million. By comparison, SLOC's medical budget was $4.7 million (SLOC, 1999).

SOCOG's long-standing budget problems were brought to the public's attention with the November 1998 Performance Audit's prediction that the government would have to cover a shortfall $660 million higher than the figure projected in the 1997 budget. By January 1999, concerns about expensive habits of Olympic officials and the chilling effects of the "tarnished rings" on sponsorships prompted SOCOG to take some cost-cutting steps, including the proposal that limousines be replaced with buses to pick up Olympic family members at their hotels (Sydney runs a bus, 1999). This apparently audacious request to the IOC attracted considerable international media attention. In response, the IOC offered to provide officials with cars, courtesy of an Australia Mercedes dealership that was also an Olympic sponsor, a move that further entrenched the image of pampered IOC members exploiting their privilege. The *Herald* noted, without comment, that SOCOG also had a sponsoring dealership, namely, Holden; in other words, SOCOG could offer the equivalent of a Ford while the IOC sported Mercs (Korporaal, 1999h).

The next week, another *Herald* story on the limousine issue noted, again without comment, that the relevant SOCOG committee had changed its name from IOC Family Services to IOC Relations and Protocol Committee (Ryle, 1999)—perhaps in an attempt to disassociate itself from the growing negative connotations attached to the Olympic family name. A January 23 *Herald* commentary, for example, observed that "only one other global organization uses the word 'family' as frequently and obsequiously as the IOC, and that's the Mafia" (Masters, 1999), while a *Toronto Star* article a few weeks later called the finger pointing and intrigue within the IOC a "dysfunctional family feud" (Starkman, 1999d; see also Walkom, 1999a).

By June 1999, during the IOC session in Seoul, SOCOG and IOC reached an agreement negotiated by NSW Olympic Minister Michael Knight that eliminated some of the entertainment costs, including the traditional cultural celebration preceding the pre-Games Olympic Congress ($350,000 [AUS]), sight-seeing and shopping tours for IOC spouses, and flowers in hotel lobbies and lounges, but limousines for IOC members were still included (Magnay, 1999b).

The compromise was not reached without conflict. Conveying the message that the IOC was still a private club—despite the fact that SOCOG was a member of the Olympic family, at least for the duration—Swiss member Denis Oswald was reported to have stated: "It is not appropriate for SOCOG and Michael Knight to take the tone of a schoolteacher and give us a lesson in what has to be done" (Magnay, 1999c). IOC executive members complained that SOCOG had concentrated on cutting perks that were not even required in the host city contract, while failing to note that the IOC paid for tickets and hotel accommodations; it was acknowledged, however, that the contract did require the social program and the special airport reception area to speed up IOC processing through customs and immigration, as well as free hotel rooms for about thirty senior IOC members and their administrative assistants. But, as Sydney's Coordination Commissioner Jacques Rogge emphasized, SOCOG would receive $1.5 billion as its share of television revenue (Magnay, 1999c).

OLYMPIC SOLIDARITY PROGRAM

As explained earlier, the notion of "Olympic assistance" was used as a rationale for SLOBC's and SOBC's arrangements with African and South American IOC members, and the various investigatory committees subsequently either expelled or warned some of the IOC members involved. The tenuous connection between these committees' scholarships and the IOC's Olympic Solidarity Program is worth examining.

The Commission for International Olympic Aid was established in 1961 to support sport development in newly independent countries in Africa and Asia. In the early 1970s, renamed the Olympic Solidarity Program and allocated a share of IOC television revenues, it became more effective in redistributing some of the IOC wealth to needy countries. According to Olympic scholar Barrie Houlihan, self-interest as well as altruism prompted these initiatives, which served in part to lock sports organizations from the developing world into the Olympic family at a time when the Games of the New Emerging Forces posed a threat to the IOC monopoly on world sport (Houlihan, 1994).

Olympic Solidarity programs were organized jointly by the IOC and NOCs with technical assistance provided by international sport federations. Objectives included the training of athletes, coaches, and administrators, the creation of "simple, functional and economical" sport facilities, and the organization of national, regional, and continental competition (IOC Charter, 1997). Throughout the 1990s, there was growing emphasis on scholarship programs, such as those offered by elite sport training centers in the former USSR, Germany, United States, and Australia, for coaches and athletes, including youth athletes (under twenty) considered to have Olympic potential. Transportation costs for some athletes participating in the

Olympics in Seoul and Nagano were covered by the Olympic Solidarity Program, while SOCOG agreed to pay $30 million (AUS) for airfares for athletes and their equipment to be transported to Sydney in 2000.

Evidence cited in the IOC Commission and SLBE report showed that SLOBC, possibly in collaboration with USOC (there were conflicting accounts of USOC involvement) undertook scholarship programs without channeling them through the IOC. For their part, bid officials quoted in media reports alleged that some IOC members made direct requests for cash or sporting equipment for domestic sport programs or facilities. Others took the less direct method of showing Western bid committee members the destitute living conditions and impoverished state of youth sport in their home countries. It was the sight of boys playing soccer in the dirt, according to SLOBC chair Tom Welch, that prompted him to donate $50,000 to IOC member Ganga for youth sport in the Congo (Gorrell, 1999b).

When AOC president and Sydney bid committee member John Coates saw living conditions in eleven African countries during a 1993 tour, he was not only moved to provide financial assistance ("scholarships") to a needy country, but was also struck with a practical solution to the problem of strengthening the Sydney bid. Discovering that one of the major highways in Mali had been funded by the Chinese government, he realized, according to Australian news reports, that Sydney's sport facilities alone would not win votes of IOC members from developing countries, whose athletes had little chance of medal success (Salvado, 1999). In other words, Coates implied that, while Western IOC members were motivated by lofty ideals of sporting success or bid cities' relative technical merits, African IOC members needed more material incentives. Hence, under the rubric of the AOC's "co-operation agreements," Coates offered additional funds to African IOC members on the eve of the vote for the 2000 Olympics.

Coates was not alone in making these kinds of allegations about African IOC members. Even whistle blower Marc Hodler was reported to have said, "[A]bout 50 IOC members are not interested in winter Games and are not familiar with winter sports. They ask their wives where they want to spend their holidays in the winter" (Gillis, 1999). He thus implied that members from tropical or semitropical countries relied on material incentives to vote for a particular candidate city for the Winter Games. It is hard to imagine that similar allegations directed at members from Western countries would have escaped censure: would an Australian member be accused of ignorance of winter ice sports such as ice hockey? And would a Western member be characterized as more "vulnerable" to bribes for these reasons?

HOW TO WIN FRIENDS IN THE OLYMPIC FAMILY

In their presentation to the IOC executive in 1991, TOOC members asserted that in order to be awarded an Olympic Games, one of the bid city's objectives must be to "demonstrate why it it is in each IOC member's personal interest to vote for, and award the Games to that City" (Henderson et al., 1991, p. 3). There is no evidence that IOC executive members challenged this particular interpretation of the bid process. In fact, according to the SLBE report, Samaranch himself had provided the same kind of advice to Salt Lake bid officials Tom Welch and Dave Johnson in 1989: "Mr. Samaranch advised them to become personally acquainted with as many IOC members as possible and to become part of the 'Olympic Family.' Several witnesses . . . including Mr. Welch and Mr. Johnson, described the Olympic Family as a relationship of trust, mutual support and commitment among individuals involved in the international Olympic movement" (SLBE, 1999, p. 5).

Despite these efforts to cultivate "friendships," Salt Lake lost the 1998 Winter Olympics to Nagano, a host city whose bid committee's campaign to influence IOC visitors was later revealed to have cost thousands of dollars per member. Salt Lake bid supporters then met to develop a more effective strategy: to focus on winning the "hearts" of IOC members. A document cited in the board of ethics report listed the bid committee's goals: "Establish and maintain long-term, vote influencing relationships with IOC members, . . . with other key people of the Olympic Family (International Winter Sports Federations, National Olympic Committees, US Television, Press/Media, Marketing, Consultants, etc.) . . . [and] with USOC" (SLBE, 1999, p. 7). The methods of achieving these goals, as described in the report, ranged from sending greeting cards to IOC members and their families to providing unlimited credit for their shopping excursions; one major department store made a $250,000 value-in-kind donation to the bid committee through this arrangement (SLBE, 1999, p. 32).

In another strategy to become part of the Olympic family, SLOBC leaders visited IOC members overseas: "[W]e were invited to their dinners and their homes and their sporting events and we became a part of them," Welch was quoted as saying. He claimed that free medical services for Congo member Ganga's mother and $10,000 for the Chilean member Santander Fantini's mayoral campaign were simply examples of "the way people in this city do business . . . you support your friends and their causes" (Gorrell, 1999b). Sydney bid chief Rod McGeoch had also worked on becoming "good friends" with all the IOC members; as well as travelling to every possible sports meeting to meet IOC members, he played host to about eighty IOC visitors to Sydney (McGeoch & Korporaal, 1994). Not all of those involved with bid committees managed to keep up the facade that they were building genuine friendships with IOC members; several claimed that they would not choose to spend time with some IOC members or their families, and admitted feeling relief when the visits came to an end.

In the late 1980s when Toronto was bidding for the 1996 Olympics, TOOC chair Paul Henderson claimed in a public meeting that all of his friends were Olympians (see chapter 4). Ten years later when TOOC's employment of Finnish IOC family members came under scrutiny, Henderson repeated the claim—"All my friends are Olympic people" (Henderson, quoted in Vincent, 1999a)—while COA president Bill Warren agreed that all those involved were friends (Vincent & Ruimy, 1999). Henderson had been vice-president of the international yachting federation at the time when a Finnish man was president, while Canadian IOC member James Worrall had been honorary consul-general to Finland, and all these arrangements had promoted good relationships with the Finns (Christie, 1999a). One lone voice—Toronto 2008 bid committee chair David Crombie—called for a "crystal clear" distinction between "'my friends' and those who are going to judge the vote" (Crombie, quoted in Vincent, 1999b).

Henderson's claims of exclusive friendships with Olympians in no way diminished the allegations against TOOC. Under his leadership, according to TOOC's report and press conference, as much as $900,000 (CAN) was spent ($800,000 to satisfy IOC members' demands for cash travel allowances and other services, more than $20,000 on the Haeggmans' accommodations, and a further unspecified amount to cover other expenses) in an attempt to influence, or, at the very least, not to alienate IOC members.

TOOC members' reliance on the friendship rationale was typical of bid committees as well as Olympic officials. IOC member Peter Tallberg, whose sons had been employed in three bid cities, was quoted as saying: "The IOC has no rules against normal friendly and family connections" (Saunders & Partridge, 1999). And Richard Pound claimed that, because he and Phil Coles had been friends since 1960, it was appropriate for them to have dinner together the same week that Pound was investigating allegations of Coles's misconduct in accepting improper gifts from the Salt Lake bid committee (Starkman, 1999c).

Such statements reinforced the concept of the Olympic family as a private club whose specially privileged members were exempt from the rules of other commercial international organizations, or indeed from the most basic rules of honest business dealings. In fact, it is tempting to suggest that the sense of entitlement manifested by many male college and professional athletes (see, for example, Benedict, 1998; Burstyn, 1999) has found its way into the Olympic industry, where many former Olympic athletes now hold positions of power and can redefine right and wrong on their own terms. During the IOC, SLBE, and Sheridan investigations of 1998–1999, several uniquely Olympic definitions of "ethical" came to light. For example, on the numerous occasions when the Salt Lake bid committee gave, and IOC members received, cash, scholarships, gifts, and services, these were considered ethical if they took place in the open. This was reportedly the reasoning behind the exoneration of John Coates. Australian IOC member Kevan Gosper was reported to have been satisfied that Coates's actions were proper because, "It's not unusual for encouragements, incentives, to be part of the bid as long as they are out in the open," while Coordination Commissioner Jacques Rogge, who investigated the payments on behalf of the IOC, concluded "It was legal, legitimate . . . no under the table payment. Everything was straightforward" (Magnay & Riley, 1999a; Korporaal, 1999d).

Not surprisingly, the "moral relativism" argument also emerged early in the process. With Salt Lake City bribery allegations setting the standard, Atlanta bid committee member Charlie Battle appeared to believe that his committee had been justified in exceeding the IOC gift limit, because "everybody was doing it." A *Washington Post* report quoted Battle's reasoning as follows: "We didn't do anything illegal, immoral, unethical or what I felt was improper given the context of lavish hospitality and entertainment that was the accepted route. . . . We felt like we conducted our bid in the spirit of what we felt were the guidelines that were given to us" (Battle quoted in Brubaker, 1999).

President Samaranch himself took the moral relativism argument to new depths when, according to a *Toronto Star* report, he claimed that since only about $1 million was involved in the Salt Lake bribery scandal, it was less serious than the European Union scandal, which involved about one billion dollars (Vincent, 1999e).

Formal and informal relationships between individuals and groups comprising the Olympic family have generated connotations of "friendship" that differ from the usual understanding of that concept. It is possible to identify four key dimensions to the kinds of "friendship" that Salt Lake City, Sydney, and Toronto bid committees and their agents developed with IOC members before and during the bid process:

- friendship as the opportunistic cultivation of personal relationships with IOC members and their families in order to influence their votes;

- friendship as the rationale for giving IOC members and their families money, gifts, and services in excess of IOC guidelines;
- friendship as the "natural" outcome of one's personal identity as a one-time Olympic competitor with a circle of exclusively "Olympian" friends;
- friendship as the mutually profitable relationship typically promoted during international business transactions, with gifts or services provided where necessary to satisfy local customs and to oil the wheels of commerce.

Several factors rendered these kinds of friendships problematic. Friendships in the Olympic family developed between parties with unequal power—that is, bid committee members seeking votes, and IOC members holding the power to select host cities. The secret ballot system made it impossible to prove that a quid pro quo had ever occurred, thus potentially allowing "friendships" to be exploited by both parties.

IOC and NOC members were permitted, sometimes encouraged, to serve as members of a city's bid committee, on the grounds that they had extensive experience and expertise on these matters; this arrangement actively promoted conflict of interest situations. Ostensibly in order to host a nonpartisan Olympic Games, bid cities were also permitted and encouraged to have politicians serving on bid and organizing committees. This arrangement disenfranchised citizens when elected representatives were pressured to put Olympic interests ahead of public interests, as was the case in Sydney where Olympic Minister Michael Knight was also the head of SOCOG. In all these situations, the already blurred distinctions between various roles and responsibilities were further complicated by the avowed bonds of "friendship" that linked members of the Olympic family.

THE AGENTS: MODERN OLYMPIC MATCHMAKERS

In the early stages of the Olympic controversy, it became clear that several recent bid committees had developed links with IOC members using the services of agents, consultants, and lobbyists. It could be argued that, if the much-touted bonds of friendship within the Olympic family united bid committees and IOC members, it would not be necessary to employ the services of an agent to act as a kind of Olympic matchmaker. Despite Olympic family rhetoric, it appears that agents were necessary in part to bridge "cultural" differences; they were "cultural navigators" according to one account (Infantry, 1999b). For example, an agent associated with a number of bids, Mahmoud El Farnawani, was valued for his skills in interacting with African and Mediterranean IOC members; he was originally from Egypt, had experience as an athlete, coach and administrator in those regions, and reportedly understood African culture. A more important role of agents was, of course, to facilitate "friendships" between bid officials and the IOC in the hope of influencing members' votes.

The notion of "cultural" differences was exploited in a number of official accounts not only to justify excessive gift giving but also to imply that any criticism of international diplomacy and cultural practices outside North America merely displayed the critics' lack of "cultural" awareness. The first report of the IOC ad hoc Commission provided more than a half-page of explanation about these practices: "To some degree, there is an international practice and custom of giving gifts within the Olympic Movement and it has become almost a matter of protocol to do so . . . in relation to candidate cities . . . it is simply a matter of courtesy and generalized promotion of the city" (IOC ad hoc Commission, 1999a, p. 11).

The second report of the IOC commission acknowledged that gift-giving practices needed to be "strictly regulated," but it expanded again on the "cultural difference" rationale:

> [G]ifts viewed as improper in some parts of the world are looked upon with a totally different perception in many other areas. Thus, for some highly respected, totally honest and incorruptible [IOC] members, any ongoing relationship, including with members of all bid committees, is by definition based on very personal friendship. This naturally and openly implies exchanges of gifts, visits and personal attentions. For such members, receiving gifts from bid committee members was perfectly normal and natural. . . . In many societies, these exchanges are viewed as an honourable tradition and are not corruption. (IOC ad hoc Commission, 1999b, pp. 10–11)

After the two IOC commission reports had established the "cultural difference" discourse, it became more difficult to criticize "gift exchanges" without appearing ignorant and/or racist. The concept of "exchanges," however, did not match evidence provided in the IOC commission report, which failed to mention any instance of reciprocity. Samaranch appeared to be the only IOC member to state that he gave as well as received protocol gifts (Gross, 1999). It seems reasonable to assume that other IOC members accused of accepting improper gifts would have drawn attention to the fact that they were givers as well as recipients of gifts, if indeed they were.

To the limited extent that claims of culturally specific practices may have some validity, they did nothing to explain the actions of some IOC members, such as Australian Phil Coles, whose own White, Western, Anglo-Saxon cultural traditions closely approximated those of the Salt Lake and

Atlanta bid committee members implicated in his case. A cynic might argue, of course, that it was precisely the shared Western preoccupation with money and material benefits that permitted the arrangements between Coles and SLOBC as documented in the SLBE report (SLBE, 1999).

When IOC whistle blower Marc Hodler made his allegations of corruption in the IOC, he stated that agents were the "real culprits" and would be included in the investigation (Infantry, 1999a). One of four agents to whom Hodler referred, Mahmoud El Farnawani, lived in the Toronto region and had a long history of voluntary and paid work on behalf of various bid committees, with media reports listing Atlanta, Athens, Istanbul, Nagano, Salt Lake City, Sydney, and Toronto. The IOC ad hoc Commission report as well as reports from Sydney and Salt Lake City confirmed that he had been employed by a number of bid committees.

In 1989, when Toronto was bidding for the 1996 Games, TOOC president Paul Henderson used El Farnawani's voluntary services to assist in "marketing" Toronto to IOC members. For his part, El Farnawani was disappointed with this experience, claiming: "Definitely I *delivered the votes* I promised; others did not" (El Farnawani quoted in Infantry, 1998; emphasis added) Commenting favorably on El Farnawani's usefulness in June 1998, Henderson was quoted as saying: "He has a small group of IOC members—six or seven—that he knows very well" (Infantry, 1998). However, according to a December newspaper account, Henderson, responding to TOBid member Jim Ginou's queries about El Farnawani in March 1998, had offered this advice: "Keep a long way away from him . . . you've got to be squeaky clean . . . powerbrokers . . . can't deliver [votes]" (Infantry & Starkman, 1998).

Also in December 1998, in an interview with the *Sydney Morning Herald* shortly after the Salt Lake City allegations became international news, Henderson was unequivocally critical of agents. He told how, during NSW Olympic minister Bruce Baird's visit to Toronto in 1991, he had warned him: "There are three or four of these guys, and when you start to bid, these pariahs [*sic*] come along . . . you get addicted by the bidding deal, and these consultants feed on your desire for information" (Moore & Korporaal, 1998). At the same time, Henderson shared his own inside knowledge of the personal preferences and idiosyncrasies of IOC members with Baird.

None of this was news to Baird, who disclosed in January 1999 that he had been approached by an agent seeking bribes in 1992, and had also been contacted by an IOC member (later identified as Jean-Claude Ganga) seeking an inducement to vote for Sydney prior to the 1993 IOC session (Minister says, 1998; Korporaal, 1999e). Equally relevant was Baird's statement that the Sydney bid committee had hired El Farnawani as part of its costly campaign to influence IOC votes.

Baird complained that, although El Farnawani had as many as forty dinners with IOC members from Africa and Middle Eastern countries and "their friends and relatives," votes from these delegates apparently went to Istanbul and not Sydney (Lehmann, 1999a). It was El Farnawani, according to several reports, who acted on behalf of Coates in offering "assistance" to African sport programs through IOC members Mukora (Kenya) and Nyangweso (Uganda) the night before the IOC vote for the 2000 Games (Byers, 1999). The Sheridan report later showed that in 1993 the Sydney bid committee had a $180,000 (AUS) contract (including travel expenses) with El Farnawani to focus on Africa, as well as a $100,000 contract with another agent, Gabor Komyathy, whose contacts were in eastern Europe (Sheridan, 1999, p. 35).

SOBC took a unique approach to the concept of lobbying when one of its own IOC members, Phil Coles, and his partner Patricia Rosenbrock set up a lobby team in Paris for the last four months of the bid in 1993. The rationale was to provide Coles and others with opportunities to "travel amongst the voting members, visit them, socialize with them and provide hospitality to them when they might be travelling through Paris." According to documentation cited in the Sheridan report, Coles had "the legitimacy to call upon his fellow members in accordance with bidding city guidelines" (Sheridan, 1999, p. 36). In other words, this was an opportunistic attempt to influence IOC members from western Europe, an important area not covered in the other consultants' territory. While the guidelines limited IOC members to only one visit per bid city, they did not cover the possibility of offshore lobbying such as this SOBC enterprise.

The subsequent scandal over the character assessments (later called "character assassinations") of IOC members jointly prepared by Coles and Rosenbrock amply demonstrated the cynical exploitation of "friendships" in the Olympic family context, where members of bid committees ingratiated themselves with IOC members, their wives (or husbands), and their families to influence votes. This is not to suggest that there were no authentic friendships between individuals who shared common interests in Olympic sport; no doubt such bonds existed among many of those involved. However, in the context of the Olympic bid process, there is evidence to suggest that many such "friendships" were nurtured solely for utilitarian purposes.

This was not the first time that bid committees had assembled dossiers on IOC members. Jennings claimed in 1996 that all bid cities had done so for many years, citing, for example, an investigative television program, *Monitor*, that had obtained Berlin's notes on IOC members in 1992 (Jennings, 1996,

p. 190). Coles and Rosenbrock's four hundred pages of handwritten notes on more than a hundred IOC members and wives ranged from relatively innocuous information on their interests to racist, sexist, and ageist allegations about their personalities. By 1999, although the existence of dossiers appeared to be old news, the specific contents still attracted attention. The *Sydney Morning Herald* helpfully provided the complete set of notes on its web site for several months, thus permitting any interested person to find out, as Jennings might have put it, "the shoe size of the second daughter" of an IOC member.

It is noteworthy that, after the publication of the first *Lords of the Rings* book, Jennings and Simson were accused of showing "contempt towards the IOC, its president and its members, criticizing their personalities, their behavior and their management" (Jennings, 1996, p. 303) and subsequently convicted by a Swiss judge. In Coles's case, on the other hand, the IOC did not censure the offensive content of the dossiers but rather treated their public release as an unpardonable invasion of members' privacy. Coles's and Rosenbrock's major offenses were to pass the information on to another bid committee, according to some accounts (Lehmann & Zubrzycki, 1999b). The IOC Special Commission did not expel Coles, but merely issued the "severest of warnings," citing his poor judgment in allowing the notes to be circulated outside of SOBC. On the matter of allegations about gifts provided by the Athens bid committee, which *Sydney Morning Herald* investigative journalists had pursued (see chapter 9), the Commission claimed that these were not proven and hence not pertinent (IOC Special Commission, 1999).

SLOBC adopted the same strategy of compiling dossiers during its 1991–1993 bid campaign; in fact, it was revealed in 1999 that Coles and Rosenbrock's notes had been obtained by SLOBC through an unknown route (IOC Special Commission, 1999). One former SLOBC member described vice-chair Dave Johnson's approach with some admiration: "Dave could tell me how many children [an IOC member] has, where he went to school, what his anniversary is, his avocations, his hobbies . . . if they like Godiva's chocolate or a certain kind of wine, Dave would have it available in their rooms" (Egan, 1999). The findings of the Salt Lake board of ethics left no doubt about the exploitation of this knowledge in order to influence votes. The situation can be interpreted in at least two ways. As well as portraying the SLOBC committee as victims of the IOC culture of improper gift giving, it is also possible to view IOC members from developing countries as dupes of the predominantly White SLOBC who, in the guise of friendship, manipulated them to gain votes.

SLOBC spent about $161,000 in consulting fees and expenses for El Far-nawani between 1993 and 1995 to lobby IOC members in Greece, Libya, Morocco, and Tunisia, and to monitor activities in other bid cities. A second agent, Mutaleb Ahmad, Secretary-General of the Olympic Council of Asia, received $62,400 to lobby members from the Middle East and North Africa, and an undisclosed amount was paid to Frank Richards, a Utah businessman with South American experience. Two consulting companies linked to USOC Director of International Relations and Protocol Alfredo La Mont were also contracted by SLOBC to arrange meetings and provide other lob-bying services with IOC members, for a total of more than $45,000 (IOC ad hoc Commission, 1999a; SLBE, 1999). La Mont subsequently resigned from the USOC.

The problem of "addiction" to winning the bid identified by Toronto bid leader Paul Henderson had been mentioned by Salt Lake City and other bid committees, but Henderson's 1991 portrayal of vulnerable bid officials at the mercy of piranha-like agents (presumably this is what he meant by "pariahs") was a new theme. In his January address to the Sport Summit, Richard Pound echoed Henderson's sentiments when he explained that the commis-sion was "looking into the issue of the so-called 'agents' who prey on the vul-nerabilities and naivete of bidding cities. By the time we are through with so-called Olympic 'agents,' I doubt that it will be a profitable business—if it ever was" (Pound, 1999a, p. 6).

It is important to note that all except one of the agents identified during the various official investigations had non-Western origins (Africa, conti-nental Europe, Asia, and South America). On the other hand, the bid com-mittees that had used agents' services were: two American (Salt Lake City and Atlanta), two Canadian (Toronto 1996 and Toronto 2008), and one Australian (Sydney), as well as the committees for Athens, Nagano, and Istanbul. Hence, most of the scenarios to which Pound and Henderson alluded involved predominantly White, Western bid committees allegedly being "preyed" upon by non-Western agents.

The draft report of the IOC ad hoc Commission, "obtained by" (in media language, leaked to) *Wall Street Journal* reporters, made reference to two agents involved in recent bids; one was said to have offered twenty-five votes for $2 million while the other promised nine European votes at $50,000 to $100,000 per vote (Copetas, Thurow, & Fatsis, 1999). This item, like others mentioned in the newspaper article, was omitted from the commission's final report. When asked about the investigation by a *Toronto Star* journalist in January, Pound stated that there was no evidence "to sug-gest the agents acted improperly. . . . Not all agents are bad agents" (Infantry,

1999b). In the same vein, Claire Potvin, identified as a domestic project consultant in a Toronto 2008 bid committee's document (TOBid, 1999), distinguished between "consultants," who "know the Olympic world," and "agents," who believe they can trade on their consulting experience to make a profit by "influence peddling" (Infantry, 1999b). As these individuals came increasingly under suspicion during the 1999 investigations, it became clear that geography, race, and culture also played a role in distinguishing between "good" and "bad" agents.

When the Toronto 2008 bid committee signed a contract with El Farnawani in June 1998, officials boasted to the media that he was their "secret weapon"—an agent with many friends and considerable influence among African IOC members. His role was to "influence" and "secure" votes, according to the *Toronto Star* interview with bid committee members (Infantry, 1998, p. 4). El Farnawani was a member of the Toronto group attending meetings of the Association of National Olympic Committees in Seville, together with bid committee chair David Crombie and two other local consultants. El Farnawani's lobbying strategy exemplified the utilitarian approach to "friendship" that many bid committees valued: "You have to earn the trust and friendship of an individual, study all about the person and not make it seem like you're just after their vote" (Infantry, 1999a). Soon after El Farnawani appeared to be a player in the Salt Lake City controversy, Toronto bid officials reported that he had completed his five-month, $35,000 (CAN) contract but had not proven "a good fit" with the committee; he had only produced a four-page report and verbal advice and his contract had been terminated (Infantry & Starkman, 1998).

The Toronto bid committee had ignored Bread Not Circuses's request for copies of financial statements and contracts for almost twelve months, but the initial contract with El Farnawani was obtained by a *Toronto Star* reporter in December 1998. Signed by bid staff member Jeff Evenson, it stated that El Farnawani's role was to investigate "the general context in which the international Olympic bid strategy should operate" and provide "strategic advice on the development of a strategy for *securing the support* of members of the International Olympic Committee" (Infantry & Starkman, 1998; emphasis added).

In February 1999, when the Toronto bid committee held a public board meeting, its financial statement showed that more than $137,000 had been paid in fees and expenses to El Farnawani and Carlos Garcia, another consultant whose role had not been disclosed publicly before this time. At the press conference following the meeting, Crombie stated that the two agents had been contracted to give advice on Toronto's "winnability"—a very different concept from the earlier stated purpose of "securing" IOC members' support. Although a copy of El Farnawani's contract was circulating among journalists at the press conference, the committee continued to ignore BNC's request.

LIBERAL DISCOURSE OF CULTURAL DIFFERENCE

Despite IOC denials, it was not a coincidence that the vast majority of IOC members alleged to have acted improperly were from Africa, Asia, or South America. Predictably, White Western responses to the bribery allegations fell into two main categories: liberal and racist.

The first response was denial that race played any part in the situation. In Richard Pound's words, "This is not an issue of geography, culture or race and should not be perceived that way. It is a matter of individual conduct in an organization that places the highest importance on its members' personal integrity" (Pound, 1999a, p. 6). This statement was delivered shortly after international wire services disclosed the names of IOC members under investigation, the majority of whom were Black or people of color. In his statement to the press during the IOC special session in January, Pound repeated the same denial.

A related type of response called for an understanding of the situation of IOC members in developing countries; sport programs in their homelands, it was argued, were in desperate need of financial support, and these IOC members were therefore more vulnerable to offers of "scholarships" or "aid" (Vincent, 1999c). IOC vice president Keba Mbaye (Senegal), for example, stated: "Those [members] who are most in need are also those who are the most open to offers which sometimes verge on the provocative" (Mbaye quoted in Selsky, 1999).

In a less convincing version of this rationale, it was claimed that the IOC members from developing countries (and their families) were themselves in need of money, education, or medical services, and hence were more susceptible to gestures of "friendship" from bid committees. For their part, bid committees members from wealthy countries could not reject requests for assistance from needy Olympic family members whom they had come to regard as "friends" (often because one or both sides had instrumentally cultivated such relationships).

Explanations relying on "cultural difference" arguments categorized non-Western IOC members as more susceptible to bribery because it was an essential part of doing business in certain parts of the world. John Coates, for example, offered the following explanation to a *Herald* reporter: "The difficulty is its [IOC] membership comprises men and women from throughout the world, from developed and developing countries, from Western and former Eastern bloc countries, not all of whom have societies which understand and accept the corporate governance values we demand" (Coates quoted in Masters, 1999). Commenting on the first IOC report, Canadian IOC member Carol Ann Letheren, in a *Toronto Star* report, claimed that IOC members, given their mix of cultures, may have been confused about what constituted acceptable behavior, and that the IOC Ethics Commission would provide leadership on "how these things are seen in the business world, and the IOC is a business" (Letheren quoted in Freeman, 1999). Ironically, both Coates and Letheren were members of NOCs whose own corporate governance and attitude regarding conflict of interest came under public scrutiny in the 1990s. In hindsight, it could be argued that the "cultural relativism" concept did not distinguish between Western and developing countries, but rather distinguished between the "business world" and the world of Olympic sport.

More overtly racist interpretations simply portrayed all IOC members from developing nations as exploiting the privileges of membership to obtain maximum benefits for themselves and their families. TOOC vice-chair Norman Seagram, for example, alleged that, while many IOC members were wealthy, those from poorer nations treated the IOC as "a meal ticket" and "their way of making a living . . . any possible benefit they could gain from that association, they would take it" (Seagram quoted in Buffery, 1999a). People associated with the Salt Lake City bid made similar references to IOC members who expected to receive lavish gifts, and those who were more interested in the perks than in Olympic sport (Cates, 1998; Mims, 1998).

Conversely, others invoked the elite nature of the IOC to defend members against such charges, by claiming that members named in bribery allegations were in fact independently wealthy and hence couldn't possibly have accepted bribes. Defending IOC member Un Yong Kim, Australian Kevan Gosper was quoted as saying: "There is no suggestions that he sought money. Kim is a wealthy man in his own right" (Gosper, quoted in Korporaal, 1999c). On the matter of Samaranch's acceptance of valuable guns from the SLOBC, Australian IOC member Phil Coles claimed that these were simply "a gift of hospitality" to the leader of an international organization. "He's not even a hunter," added Coles (Evans, 1999a).

CONCLUSION

The blurred distinctions between business transactions and "friendships" within the Olympic industry permitted improper interactions to be hidden under the twin umbrellas of Olympic family and Olympic Solidarity, as demonstrated in this analysis of abuses of friendships, however defined in Olympic industry contexts: opportunistic cultivation of personal relationships, ties between Olympic family members, bonding among former Olympic athletes, or mutually profitable networks among parties engaged in international business transactions.

Contrary to the rhetoric that puts sport and athletes at the center of the Olympics, it is clear that personal gain and the profit motive animated a significant number of IOC, bid, and organizing committee members. Moreover, the variables of geography, culture, and race were undeniably operating in the Olympic family context. Explanations based on these factors were used to justify bribery by presenting it as "humanitarian aid" to developing countries; conversely, cultural differences were invoked to excuse those who accepted improper gifts on the grounds that their country's poverty made them vulnerable, or their socialization (outside the purportedly higher moral system of the Western world) led them to view bribery as an integral part of doing business. The fact that the "cultural difference" theory failed to explain the behavior of Australians John Coates and Phil Coles was generally ignored; perhaps it was taken for granted that they would be quickly exonerated, as indeed they were.

Geography, culture, and race also shaped the views of whistle blowers, some of whom also resorted to cultural difference explanations. Grassroots critics of the Olympic industry, joining in the general condemnation of IOC corruption, faced the challenge of doing so while at the same time resisting racist and colonialist discourses that named Black and minority IOC members as the most culpable, and thus led the mass media to put these men's images on front pages around the world.

4

Toronto and Sydney
Olympic Bids
when winners are losers

THE 1970S AND 1980S WERE MARKED by increased political awareness and activism among disadvantaged groups in a number of Western countries, as well as in developing nations. Community-based movements involving women, Blacks, ethnic minorities, working-class people, gays, and lesbians enabled members of these groups to develop effective strategies for meaningful citizen participation and resistance. It was in this social–political context that struggles were waged in Toronto, Canada, and Sydney, Australia, over the process of bidding for the right to host the Summer Olympic Games of 1996 and 2000 respectively.

The first section of this chapter presents an analysis of events surrounding the Toronto 1996 and Sydney 2000 bids, while the second section critically examines Toronto's current bid for the 2008 Summer Games. The focus will be on the ways in which politicians, sport leaders, corporations, and the media attempted to manufacture public consent, and the ways in which individuals and groups resisted such attempts. The analysis will

---

The first section of this chapter is a revised version of an article published in the *Journal of Sport and Social Issues* 20:4, 1996, pp. 392–410, titled "When Winners Are Losers: Toronto and Sydney Bids for the Summer Olympics."

assume basic principles of participatory democracy, as pioneered by popular educators Saul Alinsky, Paulo Freire, and others: that citizens have the right to participate in decisions that affect their futures; and that *conscientization* and community activism are effective routes to self-determination (Alinsky, 1971; Freire, 1973; Horton & Freire, 1990). Furthermore, the analysis will employ neo-Marxist concepts of accommodation and resistance in order to explore the difficulties facing individuals and groups who challenged hegemonic assumptions about the Olympic industry.

COMMUNITY ACTIVISM IN TORONTO AND SYDNEY

Toronto has a history of community activism involving working-class people, women, gays and lesbians, Blacks, and ethnic minorities, dating back several decades. Examples include citizen action to preserve neighborhoods and protect the environment; parent involvement in educational decision making; and women's activism to stop violence (Dehli, Restakis, & Sharpe, 1988; Egan, Gardner, & Persad, 1988; Pierson et al., 1993). Sydney, too, has a history of successful community-based movements involving women, labor, Aborigines, and gays and lesbians, and, in a country with a wealth of endangered natural resources, environmentalist groups have had a particularly high profile in both the informal and formal political process (Hutton, 1987; Sawer, 1990; Scutt, 1987). Sydney, however, lacked some of Toronto's formal structures within municipal government that facilitated community involvement on issues such as public education and neighborhood renewal, and this difference may account in part for the different outcomes of their Olympic bids.

Different public opinion also prevailed in Sydney and Toronto concerning sport in general, and the Olympics in particular, at the time of the bids. Many Australians pride themselves on their unqualified love of sport, although this is just as likely to be expressed in terms of allegiance to a particular team as in personal sport involvement. The Olympics have long been viewed as a means of putting talented young Australian athletes, especially runners and swimmers, on the international stage, and thus bringing world attention to a small, geographically isolated country.

Australia had not hosted the Olympics since the Melbourne Games of 1956, whereas Canadians had recent memories of the 1976 Montreal Olympics and its substantial deficit, as well as the $416 million (CAN) in public money required to host the 1988 Winter Olympics in Calgary. Thus, it was relatively easy for Toronto bid critics to document past Olympic budgets and their drain on the public purse. However, Australians might have recalled other megaprojects where the original estimates and the actual costs were millions of dollars apart. The Sydney Opera House and Expo 88 Brisbane are prime examples.

In their analysis of the Sydney bid process, Booth and Tatz (1994) claim that two other factors defused organized criticism: general skepticism that Sydney was a serious contender; and the seductive and deceptive promise of the Sydney Olympic Bid Committee (SOBC) that the Games would lead to Australia's economic recovery through both the influx of tourist dollars at the time of the Games and the expected long-term boost to tourism and trade. Canada was equally in need of a boost to the economy at the time of the first Toronto bid, but critics pointed to the problems of homelessness, unemployment, and poverty in Toronto as reasons for rejecting, rather than supporting the bid. Further, Canada does not suffer from geographic isolation, and the potential boost to tourism was therefore a less salient issue in Toronto.

Since the 1980s, the rhetoric about keeping politics out of sport has been replaced by the explicit politicizing of the bid process by boosters and critics alike (Simson & Jennings, 1992). Critics identify the burden on taxpayers and disadvantaged groups, and the threat to the environment, while supporters point to the positive effects on the economy and the labor market, and the much-touted "legacy" of sporting facilities and housing. These patterns were evident in debates surrounding both the Toronto and Sydney bids, although the outcomes in each case were dramatically different.

INTERNATIONAL OLYMPIC COMMITTEE REQUIREMENTS

The Olympic Charter—the IOC rules and bylaws—states that the IOC has supreme authority and jurisdiction over "every person or organization that plays any part whatsoever in the Olympic movement." All contracts and agreements affecting the Games must be approved by the IOC. The successful bidder, together with that country's NOC, must enter into a contract with the IOC, and, within six months of the announcement, form an organizing committee that subsequently joins as a party to the contract. No other group is party to such a contract; no level of government, for example, is required to sign an agreement with the IOC. Thus, it is possible for the bid process to be completely controlled by corporations, not governments, as was the case in Los Angeles' private enterprise bid for the 1984 Summer Olympics. Councilors were determined that the private bid should not become a public debt, and a measure prohibiting any public spending on the Olympics was overwhelmingly endorsed by municipal voters. This, however, was an exceptional case. With no other city bidding for the Games, the bid group was in a good bargaining position, and was able to negotiate a contract that circumvented the existing IOC Rule 4 requiring financial liability to be assumed by the host city and organizing committee "jointly and indivisibly" (Hill, 1992, pp. 159–160). Currently, Rule 40 of the IOC Charter (1997) states that financial responsibility for the Games must be assumed by the host city and the organizing committee "jointly and severally."

IOC procedures for bidding and hosting the Olympic Games make virtually no provision for authentic community involvement, with the possible exception of the Olympic Cultural Festival, which calls for considerable volunteer participation. However, even the cultural components are ultimately controlled by the IOC, which reserves the right to approve the entire sport and cultural program. Furthermore, mere volunteer participation in staging the sport and cultural programs does not necessarily ensure a meaningful level of community participation in planning and decision making. In fact, the potential exploitation of thousands of volunteer workers and the negative impact on unionized workers has been identified as a serious labor problem in the staging of the Olympics (Bread Not Circuses, 1990).

IOC Bylaw 61 requires each bid committee to guarantee that "no political meeting or demonstration will take place in the stadium or on any other sports ground or in or near the Olympic village(s) during the Games." Although the safety of athletes, spectators, and workers is obviously a key concern, IOC pressure on host cities to suppress public protest may in fact contribute to its escalation, as citizens protest the suspension of their right to public assembly and freedom of speech. By the late 1980s, it had become commonplace for major international events, such as the Economic Summit held in Toronto in 1988, to be accompanied by dramatic and highly visible police and military surveillance, "street sweeps," and the "cleaning up" of inner city areas—all measures that had a serious impact not only on potential protesters, but also on prostitutes and homeless people. International sport has prompted similarly invasive security measures. In Brisbane during the 1982 Commonwealth Games, for example, the Queensland government passed an act to keep the city "clean" of Aboriginal "dissidents," and gave the police unprecedented powers to seize persons and property (Booth & Tatz, 1994). This kind of police and military intervention was one of the concerns raised by critics of both the Toronto and Sydney bids.

TORONTO 1996 BID: DECISION MAKING

In August 1986, Toronto City Council unanimously declared Toronto's interest in hosting the 1996 Games. Under legal agreement with the City, the Toronto Ontario Olympic Committee (TOOC), established in 1985, became the city's official agent in bidding for the Games. Any recommendations made by TOOC had to be approved by the city council before they were implemented. The Toronto Olympic Commitment, a statement of objectives adopted by the city council in September 1989, required that firm financial commitments from the federal and provincial governments be in place by April 1990. The budget for the Toronto bid as of May 1989 was $14.6 million (CAN); corporate sponsorship (either cash or in-kind) accounted for $7.9 million and the balance of $6.7 million came from the three levels of government. This kind of government involvement, especially at the municipal level, opened up avenues for residents to voice their concerns through their elected representatives.

The Toronto Olympic Commitment identified a number of initiatives aimed at facilitating public participation: a series of evening public meetings; descriptive information (multilingual); community meetings in neighborhoods where venues were proposed; a public meeting of the executive committee; a commitment to achieving a representative organizing committee; intervenor funding for community groups; and a full social impact study focusing on ethnocultural groups, people with disabilities, the homeless, young people, the sporting community, the Native community, people on fixed incomes, and the business community (Toronto Olympic Commitment, 1989). Phase One of the social impact study, a $20,000 project, reported that 47% of the community service agency directors interviewed were in favor of the bid, 24% opposed, and 29% undecided. Subsequent events revealed, however, that TOOC and the city council did not always share a common understanding of public participation.

TOOC's composition was by no means representative of the Toronto community. In May 1989, it comprised two women and nineteen men; of these, there were ten corporate, seven government, and four high performance sports representatives. It was not until five months after the Olympic Commitment objectives were adopted that four new women and nine new men were appointed to TOOC, and two other positions for representatives from organizations were named. However, because TOOC's major task, the preparation of the bid, was completed twelve days before these late appointments, and because the subsequent organizing committee would not necessarily include TOOC members, this was a somewhat empty gesture.

Initially, TOOC indicated general support for the goal of public participation. TOOC president Paul Henderson, a businessman and former Olympic yachtsman, stated in a letter to the city council dated October 6, 1989: "Working together with all segments of our diverse society can only enhance the quality of life for all residents of this unique city." Subsequent letters to the council revealed Henderson's limited notions of public participation: he agreed to designate money for a brochure and to cost-share the community relations officer position with the city, but stated that the other items related to public participation were not "necessary" at that time.

Media and Public Relations

There are interesting parallels, and some key differences, in the media and public relations aspects of the Toronto and Sydney bids. In both instances, bid boosters recognized the media's key role in creating a groundswell of popular support and attempted to obstruct a fair debate of issues, with varying degrees of success.

A November 14 *Toronto Star* article reported on TOOC president Paul Henderson's campaign for "fair" media coverage for Olympics. He had asked corporate sponsors to pressure local press in order to create a positive image of the bid among Canadians (Byers, 1989). In the same vein, in January 1990, TOOC sponsored advertisements in Toronto papers and television, promoting the bid through the slogan, "Go For It." The Bread Not Circuses (BNC) coalition then released a statement of "eleven things they don't tell you in that TOOC ad" (BNC, 1990). TOOC dropped the newspaper advertisement but the television spot remained, and Henderson continued to criticize the media for their alleged negative coverage and their lack of business sense in failing to support the bid (Nunes, 1990).

At the same time, TOOC's involvement in the public meetings required by the city council's Toronto Olympic Commitment represented an attempt to manipulate local media. At the November public meeting, chaired by Toronto mayor Art Eggleton, Henderson himself presented the third deputation of the evening—early enough to ensure television coverage on the late-evening news. He began by identifying himself as an Olympian and stating that all Olympians were environmentalists. In addition to the transparent tactic of exploiting this avenue of community involvement to promote a TOOC agenda, Henderson was criticized, in a *Toronto Star* editorial and elsewhere, for trying to stack the speakers' lists at public meetings (Bread Not Circuses, 1990).

It subsequently came to light that two major television networks, CBC and CTV, were producing promotional materials free of charge, as part of the in-kind services they agreed to provide as "partners" of TOOC. A CBC vice-president claimed that their motive in the partnership was the protection of their business interests, although a CBC sports publicist claimed that CBC supported the bid. Many critics raised the question of conflict of interest on the part of print media, evident, for example, in the number of journalists sitting on TOOC's media advisory committee (Nunes, 1990).

In September 1990, the *Globe and Mail* published an eight-page Olympic Bid supplement, almost half of which was taken up with advertisements by corporate sponsors. Regular *Globe* sportswriter James Christie wrote most of the articles, which were largely uncritical descriptions of the process and the facilities. His article on the Games' legacy (Christie, 1990) reads like a brochure from the bid committee: facts and figures on the nine proposed sporting facilities and their state-of-the-art attributes.

Members of the BNC coalition, comprising antipoverty activists, trade unionists, women's groups, community agencies, and others opposed to the bid, experienced considerable harassment and hostility at the hands of some journalists, although their press conferences were generally well attended by the mainstream media. Other critical community groups also encountered opposition. The Metro Tenants' Association intervenor report expressed concern that "those who raise concerns such as ours are labeled as 'naysayers.' This leads to negative feelings all around and further divides the community. The 'hype' surrounding hallmark events is such that it becomes more difficult as time goes on to effectively raise legitimate concerns" (Metro Tenants' Association, 1990, p. 43).

Overall, the Toronto media adopted a pro-Games position, although they made some attempt to present negative as well as positive perspectives. The more critical columnists such as Gerald Caplan (*Toronto Star*) and Michael Valpy (*Globe and Mail*) were openly opposed to the bid process, which they referred to as hucksterism and a con job (Caplan, 1990; Valpy, 1990).

The heavily print-dependent public information campaign mounted by TOOC was a source of concern to many citizen groups: $180,000 (more than double the amount distributed to intervenor groups) was used to develop and distribute thousands of copies of a four-page information flyer, "Olympic Update," available in five languages, which presented the plans for public participation, identified proposed Olympic venues, and provided details of funding and costs. These "tons of paper," in the view of one critic, constituted "an attempt to pawn off conspicuously biased marketing 'hype' as real information" (Askin, 1989). For those whose names were on the public participation mailing list, printed material received during even one short period (January 8 to February 26, 1990) totalled a stack of paper more than three inches high. A particularly blatant example was the TOOC Proposal for the 1996 Summer Olympic Cultural Festival, replete with hyperbole about the merits of the Toronto program: "a sweeping and rewarding choice of artistic possibilities," "a dazzling array of national and international performances," and "one of civilization's most daring experiments" (TOOC Proposal, 1990, pp. 1, 7, 10). Equally offensive was the proposed exploitation of the labor of ethnic minority groups for these "multicultural" events.

Accommodation and Resistance in Toronto

As early as June 1989, the BNC had proposed that the City provide intervenor funding to community groups to prepare research reports on the social impact of the Games. The coalition also held the first public meeting in early September 1989, two months before the first city-sponsored public meeting (Bread Not Circuses, 1990). BNC argued that, unlike Olympic supporters whose cash reserves were in the millions of dollars, critics of the bid had almost no funding.

Nonprofit organizations intending to serve "clearly identified and recognized community needs" were eligible to apply for intervenor funding. The research areas identified were: housing, tenant protection, environment, waterfront, financial issues, labor issues, multiculturalism, and race relations, as they related to the Olympics (Intervenor Funding, 1989). Of the $100,000 intervenor fund, $70,000 was allocated to seven groups. No funded group investigated the two crucial issues of labor and race relations, which had been identified in the original proposal, and only one dealt specifically with women's issues. Of the ten groups whose proposals were rejected, two—the BASIC Poverty Action Group and Parkdale Tenants' Association—had endorsed the BNC Coalition. Parkdale, a waterfront area with a transient, low-income population, was under particular threat because of the proposed Olympic construction in that neighborhood and the displacement of already marginalized residents. Parkdale Tenants and the BASIC Group, together with Artists/ Environment Forum, the Canadian Association for the Advancement of Women and Sport, Toronto Chapter, and BNC itself, were widely known as critics of the bid.

Despite the selective funding procedures, intervenor reports were not uniformly supportive of the bid. No intervenor report expressed its unqualified support, and most expressed concerns about neglected issues and negative social impacts. The Folk Arts Council surveyed 103 cultural organizations and reported an "overwhelmingly positive" response. However, some concerns were expressed regarding housing, the homeless, transport, traffic, day care, social needs, and the environment. The report expressed the conviction "that the Games would personify Toronto's international lifestyle and multi-flavored demographics" (Canadian Folk Arts Council, 1990, p. 1). As might be expected with a group that promoted a multicultural rather than an antiracist approach, there was no discussion of race relations or the impact of the Games on marginalized racial minorities, and no recognition that members of these groups are overrepresented among the homeless, unemployed, and victims of violence. Their use of a term such as *multi-flavored demographics* trivialized the experiences of these marginalized groups.

People United for Self-Help in Ontario focused on the bid's failure to address access issues for people with disabilities. The Supportive Housing Coalition urged that the Olympic Commitment incorporate the resolution of the housing crisis as one of its objectives. Metro Tenants' Association and the Waterfront Coalition developed a number of recommendations for minimizing the negative impact of the Games on housing and the environment. Two funded groups, Women Plan Toronto and Citizens for a Safe Environment, stated that the city should withdraw the bid and use the public funds on urgently needed local projects, such as environment management, social housing, job training, public recreation, and transit. A second option from Citizens for a Safe Environment proposed an environmentalist Olympics plan to maximize the possible beneficial effects. In the absence of any intervenor report that specifically focused on gender equity, the City's Director of Equal Opportunity presented a number of relevant recommendations for sexual and social equity, specifically in the areas of employment, communications, sport and cultural programs, and access to programs and services. Public meetings held in accordance with the objectives of the Olympic Commitment also yielded a mixed community response. Although supporters of the bid attempted to pack the speakers' list at some meetings, these tactics did not silence those who had serious reservations about the process. There was a clear sense from the official records and transcripts that there was significant opposition to the proposed Olympic bid, expressed through written and verbal deputations, questions from the floor and general discussion. Individuals and groups repeatedly expressed their substantive concerns about the social and environmental impact of the Games, as well as their dissatisfaction with the public participation process and the *fait accompli* nature of the process.

In its role as "official opposition" to the Olympic bid, BNC focused on two themes: poverty and the need for democratic participation. It stressed that the needs of the people of Toronto for housing, good jobs, child care, and a safe and clean city should come first; that scarce resources should not be wasted on "mega-projects"; and that all the people of Toronto should have direct involvement in the decision-making process (Bread Not Circuses, 1990).

The coalition held press conferences, distributed flyers, and sold copies of the *Anti-Bid Book*. For a time, it produced weekly information flyers called "Bread Alerts" mailed out to about a thousand supporters. Approximately fifty community groups and a thousand individuals endorsed BNC, and the official support of the Labor Council of Metropolitan Toronto and York Region in September 1989 provided added strength. It is therefore especially disturbing that a group with such strong labor ties was denied intervenor funding, and that labor issues were largely ignored in the funded groups' reports. BNC did much to raise Toronto residents' awareness of the potential problems associated with the hosting of the Olympics. It succeeded in turning public debate to the issue of poverty and the lack of democratic participation, at a time when the official community consultation processes and education campaigns were perceived by many to be inadequate.

The preceding discussion indicates that the actual Olympic sporting program had a low profile during the Toronto community consultation process; it appears that the hegemony of international sporting competition prevailed. Two exceptions to this trend may be found in the reports of BNC and Women Plan Toronto. The BNC's *Anti-Bid Book* included a critical analysis of high-performance sport as a business and the Olympics as a television spectacle with no necessary relationship to community sport and recreation programs or facilities for Toronto residents (Bread Not Circuses, 1990, p. 20). Similarly, Women Plan Toronto's report questioned the potential benefits for women athletes and provided extensive evidence of gender inequality in the Olympics: fewer sports and events for women, few female coaches, ideological constraints on female participation, and the sports media's sexist biases toward female athletes (Women Plan Toronto, 1990, pp. 29–31). In addition, a proposal put forward by the Director of Equal Opportunity (City of Toronto) resulted in a research report on gender equity in Olympic sports and events (Lenskyj, 1990).

For most of the individuals and groups involved—both supporters and critics—attention focused on the social impact and legacy of the Games, and not simply on the Games as high-performance competition or sporting spectacle. The economic impact was a key concern: supporters portrayed Toronto's hosting of the Games in terms of increased job opportunities, a legacy of housing and recreational facilities, and a healthy financial surplus, while critics pointed to the debt incurred by other host cities and the negative economic impact on already disadvantaged groups such as the homeless and those living in poverty.

This highly politicized response to the Toronto bid was in part a consequence of prevailing economic and housing conditions in Toronto, and mistrust and cynicism directed at elected representatives. More importantly, much of the response was generated by the long-standing conviction in

Toronto's marginalized communities that citizens have the right to participate in decisions that affect their lives, and TOOC's proposal to develop Olympic sites literally in these people's backyards met with widespread opposition.

SYDNEY BID: DECISION MAKING

Events surrounding the Sydney bid were markedly different from the Toronto experience from the outset, so much so that it is not always possible to make valid comparisons. Unlike TOOC, which was formally accountable to the Toronto City Council, the Sydney 2000 Olympic Bid Limited was an independent, incorporated company that did not even make a pretext of being representative or accountable to the community. Several elected officials—municipal, state, and federal—were among its members, but, unlike Toronto, the company was not accountable to an elected body. The bid company had the premier of New South Wales as president. Vice presidents were the minister of transport (also with the portfolio of Minister Responsible for the Olympic Games Bid), the president of the Australian Olympic Committee (AOC), the lord mayor of Sydney, and the chairman (*sic*) of the NSW Tourism Commission (all male). The ten male members of the board included four high-performance sport representatives and six businessmen. The Patron was the prime minister, Paul Keating. Of the forty-five professional staff, only one, the Major Event Review Committee chair, was female.

The Sydney bid company showed considerable interest in environmental issues, most notably through the politically astute move of securing Greenpeace endorsement for its proposed "Green Games" and Olympic Village, which is to be designed and constructed on environmentally sound principles. Many of the Sydney 2000 brochures, posters, etc. were printed on coated, and at that time, nonrecyclable, paper—not an auspicious start for a Green Games. The fact that the proposed site has been a toxic waste dump for many years will no doubt continue to be an issue for debate.

While the Sydney bid demonstrated a high level of concern for the natural environment, it largely neglected the human environment. A social impact report produced by the Office on Social Policy (NSW Government) provided a framework and guidelines, but no social impact study was actually conducted, and the report was not published until after the announcement (Darcy & Veal, 1994). Unlike Toronto, Sydney lacked an organized network of grassroots activist groups that could lobby for greater citizen involvement and more attention to the potentially negative impact on disadvantaged minorities.

For both the Sydney and Toronto bids, Peat Marwick conducted an independent economic impact study, free of charge (Peat Marwick, 1989; 1993).

A more favorable economic picture emerged from the Sydney study, although critics voiced their doubts about the accuracy of any such long-range projections. There was also some debate about the predicted surplus of $6 million (AUS)—a figure highly dependent on the value of television rights—but overall, popular wisdom held that the Games would yield a surplus.

The Sydney bid cost $24 million, with the federal government contributing $5 million; the NSW government originally committed $10 million, but because of successful fund raising in the corporate sector of $25 million, this was subsequently reduced to about $2 million. Corporate contributors were categorized as Gold Supporters, Proud Supporters, and Friends of the Bid, according to their level of generosity; Gold Supporters included Coca Cola, beer companies, television networks, associations of hotels and clubs, airlines and shipping lines, and major corporations. Foreshadowing the high profile of commercial sponsorship in the staging of the Games, a photograph of surfing competition in the June 1993 issue of the Sydney 2000 official newsmagazine, *Share the Spirit*, prominently displayed the Coca Cola logo (p. 13), even though the publication appeared free of advertisements.

In the Sydney bid, approximately twenty-nine cents of every dollar came from public funds, in contrast to forty-six cents in the case of the Toronto bid. However, given the much smaller population of Australia, the impact on the average taxpayer would be higher. Because of the ongoing debates about the estimated Olympic budget, and the high likelihood of error, it is not possible to predict what proportion of the final budget will actually be public money. According to the official statement of the organizing committee dated March 1994, the Games will be "primarily funded by the sale of television rights, sponsorship, ticket sales and merchandise." However, taxpayers and residents will not remain unaffected. For example, the NSW government promised $800 million for the construction of sporting facilities and public transport access to the Olympic site, but stated that any cost overrun would be covered by cutting back on other capital works projects and increasing state taxes.

While supporters took comfort in the fact that about 70% of the facilities were already in place, the omission of these infrastructure items from the Olympic budget cast doubt on the accuracy of any official figures. For example, public works projects such as the third runway at the international airport, the Harbor Tunnel, and the Parramatta River ferry service were planned before the Sydney bid was made official. However, in view of the fact that a bid process has its informal beginnings many years before it is formally constituted, and Australian politicians had a high profile from the outset, it would be naive to assume that there was no hidden agenda behind such projects.

Media and Public Relations

The Sydney 2000 Company mounted a costly and high-profile advertising campaign. Throughout 1993, the year of the IOC decision, the colorful Sydney 2000 and Olympic rings logo adorned every available surface, from chocolate bar wrappers to the entire length of Sydney Transit buses (including the windows). The copyright logo was featured on a wide range of souvenir products on sale in major department stores as well as in some retail outlets set up specifically to market "Share the Spirit" sportswear. Advertisements also appeared in newspapers and on radio and television.

The Sydney 2000 bid offices occupied one full floor of an expensive high-rise office tower overlooking Darling Harbor, one of the proposed sites. The office carpeting carried the ubiquitous logo theme, and there were extensive displays of architects' models and artists' impressions of the proposed facilities. A glossy full-color information folder in English was readily available upon request. I visited the offices in July 1993 and asked the receptionist for print information on the bid for my research. I received the information folder and some additional sheets of budget information. The folder contained the following:

- a copy of the monthly color magazine, *Share the Spirit*;
- a color promotional brochure titled "Sharing the Spirit, Seeking the Games";
- a color brochure titled "Share the Spirit: A Decade of Opportunity for Rural Australia," describing the benefits for Australians living in rural areas, and identifying seven medal-winning Olympic athletes who came from rural backgrounds during the period 1928 to 1992;
- two brochures issued by NSW Public Works Olympics 2000 Project, explaining progress in construction of the Sydney International Aquatic Center and Athletic Center, to be completed by 1994 regardless of the outcome of the bid;
- a twenty-seven-page set of fact sheets with information about facilities, accommodations, transport, communications, health care, budget, etc.;
- a color supplement titled "Sydney's Olympic Village plan wins support from Greenpeace," describing the environmental principles of the village plan, which included halting global warming and ozone depletion, maintaining biodiversity and stopping toxic pollution;
- a color supplement titled "First-class communications link Sydney with the world," describing Australia's media infrastructure and international telecommunications networks.

Current and former government officials (and their spouses) had a high media profile in the Sydney bid process. For example, Annita Keating, wife of the prime minister, was among those who formally presented the bid to the IOC, while former prime minister Gough Whitlam and Margaret Whitlam, with the AOC president, toured eleven African countries and met with African IOC members to sign agreements offering aid to African athletes—a "goodwill" gesture obviously aimed at garnering more IOC votes (North, 1993a). Elected representatives had a much lower profile in the Toronto bid process. Indeed, given their image as political leaders immersed in the serious economic problems of their country, it would have been difficult to imagine Ontario premier Bob Rae presiding over TOOC, or Canadian prime minister Brian Mulroney negotiating with African sports people. In contrast, Australian politicians Fahey, Keating and Whitlam, apparently by virtue of being Australian, male, and White, readily assumed the role of international ambassador for sport.

During the Sydney bid process, the relative lack of local critics aroused some suspicion about the independence of the media, and a freelance journalist later claimed that critical articles had been rejected by several newspapers. The inaugural issue of a small alternative publication, *Reportage*, the Newsletter of the Australian Center for Independent Journalism, University of Technology, Sydney, eventually published these and other critical articles in September 1993—the same month that the IOC announcement was made and therefore too late to sway public opinion (Editorial, 1993).

An editorial in Sydney's major daily newspaper, the *Sydney Morning Herald*, voiced strong objection to the state government's alleged attempt to straitjacket media coverage on the grounds that any criticism would undermine the bid. It endorsed a television producer's view that freedom of the press was one of the strengths of the Sydney bid ("The media and the Olympic bid," 1993). The editorial went on to state that the *Herald* had been supportive but not uncritical, and that its insistence on an accurate budget was not an attack. In fact, it concluded, government attempts to control the mass media would diminish Sydney's appeal as a site where journalists, athletes, and visitors might enjoy themselves and express their views freely.

The *Herald* published a number of critical commentaries by reporter Max Walsh, who alleged a cover up of costs in the official version of the budget (Walsh, 1992; 1993a; 1993b; 1993c). However, Walsh's critiques had a relatively low profile in the Financial Section, and the *Herald* more than compensated for these few negative articles with its regular section, *Sydney 2000 Countdown*, in the news section of the paper. Significantly, the Olym-

pics 2000 clippings kit dated March 1994, on sale at the *H*
Sydney, did not include any of Walsh's articles.

Sam North, the *Herald*'s regular contributor to *Sydney 200(* ....,
revelled in unrestrained flag waving and a fondness for military metaphors
to describe the bid process (North, 1993d). A review of a sample of sixteen
Herald articles written by North in 1993 strongly suggests that Sydney 2000
had successfully straitjacketed at least one Sydney newspaper. Not coincidentally, John Fairfax, the *Herald*'s publisher, was one of the corporate sponsors for the bid.

A further indication of the print media's role in drumming up public
interest, by whatever means, was the "Sydney Smiles" competition sponsored
by a smaller tabloid newspaper, the *Telegraph Mirror*. The two winners of the
contest—a man and woman, both White—became "Sydney's Smiling
Ambassadors" to the IOC, with a free trip to Monte Carlo for the presentation of the bid. In a similar vein, teachers organized a contest among Sydney
school children, who were asked to prepare and present speeches about the
Olympics. The winning performance by an eleven-year-old girl earned her a
place on stage as an official presenter to the IOC in September 1993.

Commenting on the alleged constraints on the Australian media, two
Sydney sport sociologists noted that there may have been a government/
media conspiracy, as claimed by some freelance journalists, or that it may
have been "a genuine desire on all sides not to jeopardize the bid by providing competing cities with critical ammunition" (Darcy & Veal, 1994, p. 1).
How the latter differs from a conspiracy is difficult to determine, since the
outcome in terms of freedom of the press is identical. The idea that bid committees from competing cities would keep files on Sydney media coverage of
the bid may indeed be plausible. However, it seems much more likely that
local media campaigns such as those mounted in Sydney and Toronto were
aimed primarily at drumming up support from citizens who would ultimately
carry the financial burden of any Games deficit, not to mention the dubious
privilege of living in a city that is hosting an international sporting event, with
an expected influx of 250,000 visitors. Supporting this hypothesis is a statement by the Sydney bid's communication commissioner, who explained that
it had been their "deliberate intent" not to "overhype" the campaign, but
rather to build public support gradually (Jeffery, 1993). In other words, much
like an athlete's training schedule, carefully paced marketing to the NSW
public would ensure that enthusiasm peaked at the crucial time.

By June 1993, three months before the announcement, it appears that
the marketing was entering its hyperbolic phase. The Sydney 2000 fact sheet
on the cultural program, issued that month, vied with its Toronto equivalent

for gushing prose: "With the dawn of the new millennium, peoples of the earth will look to the Olympic Movement for renewed inspiration." Australia's "multicultural character" is the theme of the proposed cultural program, which seeks, among other goals, to promote "knowledge and appreciation of the unique culture of the Australian Aboriginal Peoples" (Sydney 2000 Fact Sheets, 1993).

The exploitative "zoo" approach to racial minorities is clearly evident in the cover picture of *Share the Spirit* (June 1993), where a beaming IOC president Samaranch is resting his hand on the bare shoulder of a young Aboriginal dancer. The boy was one of a group of Aboriginal school children who "entertained" the president during the IOC visit to the Sydney site with a display of dancing and folklore. A story in the same issue, "Aboriginal sprinter an inspiration to children," is no doubt intended to acknowledge Olympic sprinter Cathy Freeman's successes, but in fact exemplifies the significant underrepresentation of Australian Aborigines in Olympic competition.

Accommodation and Resistance in Sydney

The prominence of government officials in the Sydney bid was reflective of both the extent of government commitment and the general level of confidence in the average Australian taxpayer's totally "irrational" love of sport, in the words of a nonsporting and rather jaded reporter (Gittings, 1993). In 1993, public support for the Games in Sydney and NSW stayed between 82% and 90%, (depending on who conducted the poll), although a gender gap of 5% was reported, with men more likely than women to favor the Games (North, 1993b). There was little need for state intervention in the manufacture of consent; the value of international sporting competition was accepted as "common sense" in most sectors of Australian society.

Along with the taken-for-granted assumption that all Australians love sport, it seems likely that politicians and bid supporters were also relying on the "she'll be right, mate" attitude and the aversion to "whingeing and whining" that have become part of Australian custom and folklore. In other words, the ability to avoid worrying and to suppress any doubts or complaints is considered a virtue in many contexts. For example, after the announcement, a female journalist explicitly called for Australians to stop spoiling the party by worrying about money, which surely would come from the corporate sector. After all, she said, hosting the Olympics will provide an opportunity for the rest of the world to get to know Australia (Price, 1993). Even the former NSW premier was quoted as saying that, aside from the monetary benefits, the real purpose of the Games was the psychological change and the boost to consumer and business confidence (North, 1993c).

Aborigines were one of the few groups to mount organized opposition to the Sydney bid. Throughout 1993, heated debate had been raging in Australia over the Mabo decision, which represented a victory for Aboriginal land rights (Native Title Land Act, 1993). Not surprisingly, the decision was experienced as a threat by mining companies and others who had exploited natural resources on Aboriginal lands throughout the century. A few days after the IOC announcement that the Sydney bid had been successful, Aboriginal leaders threatened to organize a boycott of the Games to force the government to rewrite the land rights legislation. The mainstream media responded with outrage at this so-called "stunt" which threatened "Australia's dream," demonstrating yet again, as Booth and Tatz aptly observe, that "the lack of rights which Australians afford Aborigines are not criteria by which they care to judge themselves as a nation" (Booth & Tatz, 1994, p. 11).

Further evidence of this double standard can be seen in the media hype surrounding the bid competition. Sydney newspapers made much of Beijing's (and China's) poor human rights record, specifically the 1989 Tiananmen Square massacres. Among the members of the Sydney bid team presenting to the IOC in Lausanne in June 1993 was Aboriginal activist and former senator Charles Perkins. According to Sam North, Perkins abandoned Olympic protocol when he stated that, while Australia had race problems, Australian authorities didn't run over people with tanks. Perkins told a press conference that most environmental groups, unions, ethnic groups, and Aboriginal people were onside and that the Games would promote both the economy and race relations (North, 1993e). Clearly, his inclusion on the team was a politically astute, or perhaps a politically opportunistic move. In any event, this apparent lack of solidarity among Aborigines served majority interests very effectively.

ORGANIZING CONSENT: TORONTO AND SYDNEY

In purely pragmatic terms, it could be argued that the Toronto and Sydney campaigns provided graphic examples of winning and losing strategies for organizing consent around the issue of hosting the Olympic Games. Paradoxically, the losers (Toronto) were in fact the winners (Sydney) when judged by the criterion of democratic decision making.

The carefully timed, high-profile public relations campaign in Sydney ensured that the Sydney 2000 logo, and what it signified, was firmly embedded in the consciousness of Sydney residents. At the same time, the mass media were strongly represented in the list of corporate sponsors for the bid, and no doubt some of their in-kind contributions took the form of sympathetic reporting. In the face of this two-pronged publicity campaign, Australians, already avid sports spectators, needed little persuading of the desirability of hosting the Games.

Toronto citizens, on the other hand, were more cynical consumers of TOOC's Olympic package, which lacked much of the public relations gloss that characterized the Sydney bid. Equally important, TOOC was held accountable from the outset to a body of elected representatives—the City of Toronto Council—and thus could not easily bypass the public participation process required by the council's Olympic Commitment statement.

Events surrounding the Toronto and Sydney bids cast doubt on the validity of the bid process long before the 1998 disclosures of corruption. It could be argued that, given the economic disparity between North and South, as well as the political "cold war" between developed countries, bid competitions are not carried out on a level playing field. Moreover, there are dramatic differences between IOC notions of community participation and those of grassroots groups, especially at this historical moment when Australia's and Canada's indigenous populations are fighting for land rights and self-determination, and unemployment and poverty are rampant. Given these conditions in the last decade of the twentieth century, the overriding question might be: should any city/state/nation bear the burden of hosting the Olympic Games?

TORONTO TRIES AGAIN: THE 2008 TORONTO BID

Toronto's bid for the 2008 Summer Olympics had its official beginnings around August 1996, when Olympic supporters under the leadership of David Crombie, chair of the Waterfront Regeneration Trust, formed a group known as the Toronto Olympic Bid Corporation. The committee used the Trust's office space and was assisted by its staff. The activities of this environmental organization, established in 1992 and funded by the provincial government and corporate sponsors, including a major bank, could be classified as corporate or "light green" environmentalism according to the criteria presented in chapter 8.

Crombie was a former mayor of Toronto and a member of the House of Commons with a record of several ministerial portfolios in the Progressive Conservative Party's government. Although this was the most right-wing of Canada's three parties, Crombie himself was usually considered a moderate. In another environment-related role, Crombie chaired the Royal Commission on the Future of the Toronto Waterfront in 1988.

One of the bid committee's first public actions was to send a check for $15,000 (CAN)—provided by the Trust—to the COA in February 1997 in order to put Toronto in the competition as the Canadian candidate to bid for the 2008 Games. The group kept a generally low profile until mid-1998, when news of its activities appeared in the mainstream media. Earlier that year, a commentary by former Toronto councilor and political scientist John Sewell, published in the alternative press, was critical of the secrecy surrounding TOBid's plans: meetings behind closed doors, the absence of a statement of purpose, a firm budget, or even a board of directors. Sewell demonstrated, too, that Crombie's "honor roll" of hundreds of powerful and creative people already volunteering their time to the bid had a negative side: "[T]heir energy and skills aren't available to tackle the big problems the city faces. Crombie is a case in point. His attention on watershed issues has faded in the last few years as he has spent his time on the Olympics" (Sewell, 1998, p. 25).

Early Public Debate

In January 1997, Crombie was one of four panelists invited to a University College (University of Toronto) Olympic Symposium. I was also asked to participate on the panel as a sport scholar, with Herb Pirk, former chair of the Toronto Task Force for the 1996 Olympic Bid (a City of Toronto administrators' committee, not the actual bid committee), and Ed Drakich, president of a Canadian athletes' advocacy organization and a former Olympic athlete. In this "balanced" group, there were individuals representing athletes, sport administrators, the bid committee, and the academy—the latter the only critic of the bid. Because this particular configuration was typical of many subsequent public discussions, I will provide a detailed analysis of the presentations.

Pirk made it clear from the outset that he supported the bid, and after reviewing some of his earlier experiences, concluded by stating that Olympics should not be seen as way of solving "all of society's problems." These, he claimed, should be addressed by other means. This proved a popular defense against critics as the bid gained momentum in 1998—before the bribery allegations dominated the Toronto media. *Toronto Star* sportswriter Mary Ormsby, for example, in a column titled "Games vital to kids' hopes," emphasized the anticipated "grassroots legacy"—improved recreational sport facilities for children—and called on readers to stop being "petulant" about the negative aspects of mounting the Olympics. Like Pirk, she claimed: "They are not about solving social crises" (Ormsby, 1998).

The low priority given to "social problems" by supporters who enjoyed White, middle-class privilege again reflected the view of the Olympics as apolitical—purely a sporting event, not a social and political phenomenon. Apart from the obvious callousness toward those who suffer the most from the inequitable distribution of wealth in Toronto, this approach ignored the well-documented finding that hosting an Olympic event does not merely fail to address, but often exacerbates existing social problems, through the displacement of low-income tenants and homeless people, the gentrification of neighborhoods, and long-term increases in property taxes, as the next chapters will show.

Drakich, as a former Olympic athlete, spoke of the benefits of Olympic sport for individuals and communities, citing his own "goose bumps" at the memory of the community spirit generated by the Games. This approach—"I was an Olympic athlete and it changed my life" (as BNC founding member Michael Shapcott has characterized it)—has long been a popular way of generating community support for the Olympics. Testimonials by former Olympians—usually attractive young men and women emanating courage, commitment, and determination—resonated with many middle-class audiences whose futures, while secure, promised no comparable excitement. Indeed, as the bribery crisis escalated, the public discourse began to focus on two purportedly oppositional groups—"clean athletes" and "corrupt IOC members."

Sport sociologists in the 1970s coined the term *jock sniffing* to describe what popular culture critics might now call the "wannabe" phenomenon. The term referred to the excitement and attraction experienced by many men (and some women) as they rubbed shoulders with high-performance athletes and shared in what journalist Michael Valpy aptly termed the "jock, macho, locker room, towel-snapping camaraderie" of masculinist sport (Valpy cited in Shapcott, 1991). While the jock-sniffing concept is overly psychological, a social analysis of the Olympic industry needs to pay attention to the allure of Olympic sport and the addiction to Olympic bids.

There is extensive research evidence on the role of sport in establishing hegemonic masculinity, one of the most recent and most comprehensive being Burstyn's *The Rites of Men* (Burstyn, 1999; see also Messner & Sabo, 1994). For middle-class, White men past their sporting prime, or for men who were never personally successful as athletes, professional sport provides ready access to a macho version of masculinity. Although Olympic sport is not exclusively male, it shares enough common ground with professional male sport to satisfy most jock-sniffing impulses. For example, the ethos of Olympic sport—faster, higher, stronger—has come to mean that the most widely acclaimed Olympic athletes—the fastest sprinter, the highest jumper, the strongest weightlifter—are all male.

Depending on their financial status, men with these jock-sniffing impulses may buy season tickets, a corporate box, or a professional sport franchise. Alternatively, these privileged (mostly White) men might direct their money and energy toward an Olympic bid. Many of the key players on the Atlanta, Toronto, Salt Lake City, and Sydney bid committees had business or legal backgrounds, while relatively few had recent personal experience as competitive athletes. And, despite the success of Black athletes in North America, White men have held most of the key positions on recent American and Canadian bid committees.

The pro-Olympic position of many Ontario politicians, bureaucrats, and private businessmen was no doubt motivated in part by the desire to experience the male camaraderie and excitement of Olympic sport. In Toronto, the formal presentations of male Members of Provincial Parliament (MPPs) during the final reading of Olympic Bill 77 supporting Toronto's 2008 bid provided ample evidence, as each man apparently felt compelled to describe his own personal link to Olympic sport, however tenuous. One MPP had attended the Atlanta Games with his family, another had witnessed the construction of the rowing course for the Montreal Games, a third had a relative who had competed in the Olympics. Visions of temporary membership in the Olympic family no doubt danced in many politicians' heads during the so-called debate on Bill 77.

It would be difficult to envision parliamentary debate on another social issue—housing, environment, finance, immigration—eliciting as many personal anecdotes from male politicians. Indeed, it is usually female politicians who are criticized for bringing "inappropriate" personal or emotional content into the serious world of politics. Althought the bill passed unanimously, opposition MPPs were not unequivocally supportive of the Olympics and many drew attention to the potential problems. New Democratic Party environment critic Marilyn Churley, the only woman to speak, was also the only member who made no pretentious allusions to personal affiliations with Olympic sport and Olympic athletes.

While introducing the Olympic Bill, MPP Morley Kells, the provincial appointee to the bid committee, used the opportunity to criticize BNC. Complaining about the uneven community support for Toronto's 1996 bid, he stated: "a group known as Bread Not Circuses, funded by the City of Toronto Council, journeyed to Tokyo to speak against Toronto's application. This unfortunate occurrence in effect sealed the doom of Toronto's hopes to sponsor the 1996 Games" (Kells, 1998).

As the earlier discussion in this chapter demonstrated, BNC did not receive any intervenor funding for social impact assessment, let alone money to fly to Tokyo. A private Toronto businessman contributed toward the airfares for the two representatives, who then stayed with members of the

Japanese anti-Olympic group in Tokyo. Furthermore, it is curious that a pro-Olympic politician would credit a grassroots organization with sufficient power to "doom" the bid since it did not serve bid boosters' interest to acknowledge or legitimize the activities of such groups. Indeed, Olympic officials frequently asserted that BNC's protests did nothing to sway IOC votes. Finally, Kells's criticism of BNC carried the implication that, this time, such public opposition should be suppressed.

On February 7, 1999, Kells not only repeated the false allegations about BNC but added more misinformation; he said, according to a *Toronto Sun* report, "The IOC wanted to stay away from political hassles, including environmental concerns" (Blizzard, 1999). The environment was, in fact, introduced as the third pillar of Olympism, together with sport and culture, in 1991, as explained in chapter 8. It soon became clear that this newspaper was embarking on another pro-bid, anti-BNC campaign.

Community Consultation, TOBid Style

When David Crombie became a more visible public presence as TOBid leader in mid-1998, he routinely referred to the "500 volunteers" recruited over the preceding year as a result of his visits to "scores and scores" of community groups and business organizations. According to Crombie's account, the hundreds of Toronto citizens whom he met delivered a clear message concerning their expectations. In his words, the bid should be: inclusive; socially responsible; environmentally progressive; financially sound; and leave a legacy for sport and culture for the twenty-first century (Crombie, 1998; 1999).

While these criteria appeared eminently sound, it soon became apparent that bid committee members' understanding of concepts such as "social responsibility" was light years behind that of grassroots organizations such as BNC, whose own demands, significantly, included democratic as well as financial and social accountability (Bread Not Circuses, 1998). In relation to the "environmentally progressive" goal, too, it is significant that it was not until after community protests that a specific environment subcommittee was formed; the initial optimistic rationale was that all subcommittees would address the environment, even though it was not mentioned in the mandates of most committees. Moreover, all the criteria were generated during closed meetings long before the official community consultation began, and therefore this process did not constitute authentic, inclusive, and open community involvement. At the first *open* meeting of the bid committee on September 1, 1998, Crombie himself made reference to extensive closed meetings held over the preceding summer, chaired by *Toronto Sun* president and former Metropolitan Toronto chair Paul Godfrey.

On March 4, 1998, Toronto Council approved the bid in principle, with the final vote to be taken in July after the bid committee had developed a more detailed proposal. One of the few early opportunities for members of the public to present their concerns was at the June 30 Toronto Council Strategic Planning and Priorities Committee. Although deputations were scheduled to begin at 11 A.M., when the Olympic agenda item was finally discussed at about 1:30 P.M., only two of the five representatives from BNC were still available to speak. Councilors asked very few questions of deputees—indeed, some walked about or talked to each other while community representatives were speaking. Apart from BNC members and forensic accountant Charles Smedmor, who questioned the accuracy of the budget, every deputee spoke in support of the bid.

As anticipated, Toronto Council approved the Olympic report and bid on June 9, with only one negative vote, Michael Walker's. An examination of councilors' voting patterns on a number of motions related to public accountability and democratic process revealed a number of contradictions: councilors with progressive records and reputations did not consistently support these measures, nor did the more conservative members consistently oppose them. Throughout subsequent council discussions of the 2008 Olympic bid, as well as related scandals surrounding the 1996 bid, the SkyDome, and the Air Canada Center (a new stadium for professional basketball and ice hockey), councilors David Miller and Michael Walker were among the most diligent in promoting open and democratic debate.

Miller's motion requiring accountability—public meetings, full disclosure of budgets and financial statements, regular updates and reports—passed 46–6. It was, of course, disturbing to note that *six* councilors would publicly oppose any tenet of a democratic society, let alone something as basic as open meetings and open books. Two other motions on community meetings and consultation passed, while Walker's motion calling for an independent review and analysis of the bid was defeated 8–44, with at least three progressive councilors opposed. Walker's public referendum motion was soundly defeated 2–50, with Miller and Walker its only supporters.

Four of the five equity motions—on public safety, tenant and homeless protection, comprehensive housing strategy, and minority business participation—were successful. On the housing motion, a submission by Professor David Hulchanski, a University of Toronto housing specialist, appeared to have been influential, perhaps because it did not have the disadvantage of being "tainted" by any known association with BNC, although Hulchanski was a strong supporter of the coalition. The motion requiring financial guarantees from federal and provincial governments by November 1999 carried

30–21. On a related issue, a motion was passed requiring Toronto's Commissioner of economic development, Joe Halstead, to develop a City Council task force to provide oversight and independent assessment on matters of social and fiscal responsibility. However, eight months after its creation, the task force had only had one closed meeting, a fact that caused some councilors and critics to express doubts over its effectiveness as a watchdog (DeMara, 1999b).

One of the most antidemocratic votes at the July 9 meeting concerned the motion to incorporate the results of the upcoming community consultation, intended to generate "Olympic Principles," into the final bid proposal. This was defeated 22–31, thus rendering the entire consultation process a meaningless and time-wasting exercise for all participants.

The details of the public consultation process were announced at the inaugural meeting of the Toronto 2008 Olympic Bid Corporation (TOBid) board of directors on September 1, 1998. While this was the first meeting open to the public in the committee's two-year history, it was by no means a "public" meeting. TOBid's Bylaw 4.17, for example, established the protocol for "visitor" behavior: "No person shall display signs or placards, applaud, engage in conversation, use cellular phones, or engage in any other behavior which might disrupt the meeting of the Board, and the Chair shall request persons who engage in such conduct to leave for the remainder of the meeting" (TOBid, 1998).

The goal of the community consultation process was, according to July 7, 1998 memo from Joe Halstead, to "*inform* the general public interested in the bid" and to "involve assistance from those with expertise in six key areas related to the development of the bid"—environment, transport, finance, venues, culture, and social equity (Halstead, 1998, p. 1; emphasis added). This "informing" and "involving"—activities that would occupy deservedly low rungs on the citizen participation ladder—took the form of six all-day (Saturday) workshops, with lunch and transit tickets provided, an open house for feedback on the principles developed at these discussions, and their publication on the Toronto Summer Games web site <www.torontosummergames. com>. The other major component of the consultation process was the hosting of five community council evening meetings in each of the former cities and boroughs of Toronto; as usual, each deputee had five minutes, with no opportunity for discussion unless a councilor raised a question.

BNC representatives participated in all the workshops and community council meetings, but overall found the experience unproductive. The group decided ahead of time that if the workshop agendas appeared to be predetermined, BNC members would not waste a Saturday in this so-called consultation process. Attendance ranged from about twenty-five to fifty, usually including up to ten bid committee and city staff. Facilitators made it clear that they did not want participants to discuss whether they wanted the Games at all, but rather to address the question: "What conditions are necessary for us to support the bid?" In that sense, the agenda was predetermined, but BNC representatives tried to use the opportunity to pose difficult questions of bid staff and to network with other critical participants.

One possible exception to the generally token consultation process was the recommendation that came out of the environment focus group requiring a specific environment subcommittee to be established as part of the bid committee. Largely because progressive city councilor Jack Layton decided to champion the recommendation with the bid executive, the environmental focus group was successful in making this significant change to the committee structure. However, it was clear that a more radical recommendation from a focus group—such as abandoning of the bid or calling for a referendum—would have met with a very different reception from the men in power. And, while those subsequently invited to join TOBid's environment committee included representatives from Greenpeace and Toronto Environment Alliance—two grassroots organizations—no BNC representative was invited, despite the fact that the coalition could have readily provided environment specialists to serve on the committee. Of course, it is likely that BNC would have declined the invitation, had it been offered, on the grounds that it would have jeopardized the coalition's function as a watchdog organization.

In another component of the bid committee's community-related work, its Legacy and Community Enhancement Committee asked the Community Social Planning Council of Toronto to develop a social impact and equity action plan. The action plan, dated January 26, 1999, identified the following objectives: to assess the Olympic impact with particular attention to marginalized groups; to develop plans to avert negative social impact; and to maximize opportunities for social support of youth and ethnic minorities. It proposed the formation of a Social Impact and Equity Committee that included in its eight-person membership two representatives from TOBid, thereby changing the arm's length relationship that one might reasonably expect between a bid committee and those conducting an independent social impact assessment. As further evidence that independence and objectivity might be jeopardized by this arrangement, a short-listed (unsuccessful) candidate for the position of research assistant to this committee told me that the interviewers responded negatively to her approach to social analysis, particularly her statement that it would be difficult to access the views of those most seriously affected by the Olympics—that is, homeless people. The preliminary review of social impact literature produced by the research assistant in August 1999 demonstrated, by both its quality and quantity, that the committee was taking a conservative approach to issues of social impact and had made very limited progress in examining social issues from the perspective of disadvantaged populations.

Belatedly, in light of Toronto Council's July 1998 requirement of full financial disclosure, TOBid finally released a six-month financial statement and a draft Financial Policies and Procedures Manual at its February 8 board meeting. In January, with the bribery controversy escalating, bid committee chair David Crombie had taken every media opportunity to repeat his promise of an "open and "transparent" bid process. The draft manual proposed an independent audit committee to oversee spending, a code of conduct and conflict of interest policy, and the appointment of an ethics commissioner, former associate chief justice of Ontario Charles Dubin. (Dubin had also headed the Royal Commission into the Use of Drugs and Banned Practices Intended to Increase Athletic Performance.)

The view of "visitors" as outsiders and troublemakers was confirmed by BNC's reception at the February meeting. A group of BNC members held a sidewalk press conference beforehand in order to present the BNC report card on TOBid's poor progress on key social, environment, and equity issues. Following this event, BNC members went upstairs to the meeting room. Staff distributing copies of TOBid's Financial Policies and Procedures Manual and financial report at the door told BNC members that they would have to wait their turn, so that all board members could receive their copies first. Some BNC members were then told by hotel security guards that they had to go into the meeting room or leave the building.

Organizers could have avoided this patronizing treatment of visitors and the confrontation with security guards by simply putting aside the one hundred-plus copies required for bid officials and distributing the rest to members of the public. However, the resulting spectacle of casually dressed BNC members being harassed while the more important people brushed past in their expensive suits aptly symbolized the Olympic hierarchy.

Somewhat surprisingly, in view of the strict rules of order, BNC member Jan Borowy was successful in raising a question from the floor during this meeting. It was only after chair David Crombie had answered her inquiry about city staff salaries that a board member interrupted to remind him: "This is a board meeting, not a public debate." Crombie's somewhat more relaxed approach was apparent on another occasion, when he told a meeting of environmentalists in March 1999 that TOBid's environment subcommittee meeting was open to the public. It was not until an assistant passed him a note that Crombie corrected himself, stating that the first meeting was in camera, but that any subcommittee might choose to have open meetings as it deemed necessary.

The timing of the public release of TOBid's ethics initiatives served to preempt the ongoing controversy surrounding Henderson and the 1996 bid, specifically the fact that a majority of city councilors, as well as some MPPs, the Toronto harbor commissioner, and BNC, had called for an independent audit of the failed bid. After the Toronto city auditor's preliminary review in March, mayor Mel Lastman initially supported a forensic audit but then stated that the six-figure cost was too high. The city council's Olympic task force was asked to conduct a review, but had difficulties accessing the bid's financial records eight years later, and in April it recommended that the council abandon the audit and put their attention and energy into ensuring the integrity of the bid for the 2008 Games.

It soon became apparent that the integrity of the current bid needed such attention. Toronto papers reported in April 1999 that TOBid was negotiating a $2.2 million contract with Hill and Knowlton, the same public relations firm that was working for the IOC. Both Hill and Knowlton and TOBid spokespeople provided assurances that this did not constitute a conflict of interest as long as no employee worked on both contracts and efforts were made to ensure no sharing of information that might give the Toronto bid an unfair advantage. Ethics Commissioner Dubin, not too surprisingly, advised TOBid that the "appearance of conflict of interest" must be avoided and hence, the contract should not proceed.

By the time it held its June open meeting, TOBid was putting little effort into the pretext that these were any more than public relations exercises. The event was held at an exclusive private sports club several kilometers from the downtown core and poorly served by public transit. Adjourned after forty-one minutes, the meeting attracted little media attention and very few visitors. The main agenda item was the report from new CEO John Bitove, and no board member raised questions after his presentation. Clearly, the real business of the TOBid continued to be conducted behind closed doors.

In July 1999, when IOC president Samaranch attended the opening ceremonies of the Pan Am Games in Winnipeg, Canada, he was booed by spectators. While there have been earlier examples of organized protesters taking such action, this appears to have been an unprecedented display of censure that may well have negative repercussions for Toronto's 2008 bid.

Another Toronto Issue: Homelessness

On Thursday, January 15, 1999, as the IOC bribery controversy was evolving on three continents, the report of the Toronto Mayor's Homelessness Action Task Force, chaired by Anne Golden, was released to the public. Included in its findings was the fact that, in 1996, 26,000 different people had used Toronto's shelter system, including 5,300 children. The report identified a number of systemic factors contributing to Toronto's problem of homelessness, including the failure of various levels of government to work together, growing poverty, and the shrinking supply of affordable housing, specifically rooming house accommodation and low rental apartments. Another key factor was the lack of political will to adopt preventive measures; the service system focused more effort on emergency and survival help rather than on affordable housing stock (Golden, 1999).

A few months earlier, with the approach of winter and the specter of homeless people dying on the streets, four city councils, including Toronto's, and more than four hundred organizations had identified homelessness as a national disaster across Canada. But, as the Toronto Task Force report noted, a major obstacle persisted as long as municipal, provincial, and federal levels of government were "squabbling" over matters of jurisdiction and responsibility (Golden, 1999, p. 6). It was therefore a disturbing indication of their priorities to witness the Toronto council's and the Ontario provincial government's almost unanimous approval of Toronto's bid for the 2008 Olympics in 1998. The situation was graphically illustrated on Toronto television evening news on February 9, 1999, when the top news stories included the appointment of an ethics commissioner for TOBid and a memorial service for a homeless man whose body had been found on a heating grate outside Queens Park Parliament buildings.

It is relevant to note here that, in another of her official roles, the chair of the Homelessness Task Force, Anne Golden, was a member of TOBid. In its efforts to appear diverse and representative, TOBid included a number of members with backgrounds in charitable organizations and a demonstrated interest in philanthropy, if not social justice. In light of the overwhelming evidence of the negative impact of the Olympic Games on a host city's most vulnerable populations, these contradictions are difficult to explain. While the more progressive supporters of the bid routinely referred to the anticipated economic boost and legacy of affordable housing and improved community recreation facilities, they tended to deny that the Olympics had any negative impact on disadvantaged groups in the host city.

When Toronto last put forward a bid for the Olympic Games in 1989, the cost was $14.6 million (CAN), of which 46% was provided by the three levels of government. Four years later, Sydney's bid cost $25 million (AUS), and the 2008 Toronto bid committee initially estimated costs of $45 million (CAN). During its first year of operation, the Toronto bid committee generated $500,000 from the private sector (Sewell, 1998) but in October 1998, having had limited success in private sector fund-raising efforts, it was forced to borrow $1 million, generously provided by the provincial government in the form of a four-month interest-free loan, in order to pay staff.

The two-page budget in Toronto's interim Bid Book, produced for the purpose of persuading the COA that Toronto should proceed with its bid, was discredited by independent chartered accountant Charles Smedmor in June 1998. The *Toronto Star* carried his analysis and he made several deputations to Toronto Council on these matters. Again in February 1999, the *Star* published a two-part series in which Smedmor dispelled the myths of Olympic profits and legacies (Smedmor, 1999a; 1999b), as well as a scathing critique titled "The Olympic myth of Calgary," by national affairs writer Thomas Walkom (Walkom, 1999b).

Based on the bid committee's 1998 budget figures, Smedmor predicted a $1 billion deficit, which would mean an extra $207 on every Toronto property tax bill for ten years. His reasons for projecting this higher deficit included the bid committee's exclusion of capital costs of Olympic village and media village construction, exclusion of infrastructure costs (e.g., highway construction and public transit expansion), and the inclusion of inflated corporate sponsorship and projected licensing revenues. Moreover, since Atlanta's 1996 Games budget had been used as a model, it ignored factors specific to Toronto, such as the shorter construction season due to severe winter weather (Smedmor, 1998). In terms of Canadian experience, the fact that Montreal taxpayers are still paying off the debt incurred twenty-three years ago hosting the 1976 Olympics, and that Calgary's Winter Olympic left a $416 million debt, must also be taken into account. In short, the budget was both incomplete and distorted.

WARNINGS FROM SYDNEY

Because TOBid, being an arm's length organization of Toronto Council, was exempt from the provincial Freedom of Information (FOI) legislation, citizens' requests for financial accountability during 1998 were unsuccessful. This secrecy was especially alarming in light of the Sydney 2000 situation, where the public and the media had similarly been prevented from accessing financial statements for more than five years because of a 1993 amendment to the NSW FOI Act. During 1998, the *Sydney Morning Herald* filed more than ten requests under FOI laws, most of which were unsuccessful.

In late 1998, the NSW Auditor-General was commissioned to conduct an audit of SOCOG finances, and when his report was released in January 1999—not optimal timing for any organizing committee to come under public scrutiny—it became clear that the charges of excessive secrecy were well founded. SOCOG had failed to include $56.5 million (AUS) in so-called "indirect costs" in its budget. On the other hand, the budget did include "indirect revenues" of $602 million resulting from the predicted boost to the economy. As the auditor-general noted, "limiting costs to direct costs but allowing revenues to reflect indirect receipts mingles incompatible concepts" (p. 3) and produces a distorted budgetary picture. SOCOG's projected $30 million "dividend" to the government was labelled as "largely symbolic" since, by excluding such costs as transport, security, policing, emergency services, garbage collection, traffic diversion—all to be financed by local and state governments—no surplus would be forthcoming (*Performance Audit Review*, 1999).

Another important category of "indirect costs" omitted in the Sydney budget was that of long-term infrastructure planning. It was in SOCOG's interests to omit these costs in order to project a profit from staging the Games. The auditor-general, however, listed several major capital works projects—the Southern Railway from Sydney airport to the city, the Eastern Distributor, and the Homebush Bay and Centenary Drive flyovers—that were not reflected in SOCOG's budget but were in fact essential components of its transportation plan. In my 1992 analysis of these issues (included in the first section of this chapter), I also cited the Sydney Harbor tunnel, the Parramatta River ferry service, and the third airport runway as examples of long-term infrastructure planning that enhanced Sydney's bid but not its budget.

It is not coincidental that in Toronto in the late 1990s, several major public works initiatives were under discussion, including a rail link to the international airport, a bridge to the Toronto Island Airport, expansion of both airports, new sewage pipes and sewage treatment plant, and underground rerouting of the Gardiner Expressway. Of course, politicians and Olympic boosters could well claim that such megaprojects were in the planning stages long before work began on an Olympic bid, and/or that it was advantageous for the city if the Olympic bid served to accelerate projects that might otherwise take years to complete. However, what is sinister about all of these scenarios is that when such infrastructure items are excluded from Olympic budgets, citizens do not have complete and accurate information on the real costs of mounting an Olympic Games.

The NSW auditor's report also noted that since 1993, SOCOG's budget had increased by $760 million to the 1998 figure of $2.7 billion, and he predicted that the deficit would increase from $1.6 billion to $2.3 billion. When he provided his first review of SOCOG's estimates to Parliament in 1993, his recommendations included annual publication and independent audits of consolidated estimates of Olympic operating and capital costs. However, these estimates were not provided until 1998, and no audits were completed until his own 1999 report. It appears that, while a number of community groups were monitoring the social and environmental impacts of Olympic preparations, SOCOG's failure to follow the government's requirements for disclosure and accountability largely escaped criticism until 1998.

CONCLUSION

The fact that no accountability was built into the Toronto 2008 bid process was cause for concern, especially since it was clear from the outset that TOBid planned to solicit financial support from city, provincial, and federal levels of government. The misleading structure of bid and organizing committee budgets, so convincingly documented in the NSW Auditor-General's report, continues to present a serious problem, particularly in the case of publicly funded infrastructure projects that bid and organizing committees conveniently exclude from the balance sheet.

5

The Hidden Costs
olympic impacts and urban politics

T HE DISCUSSION WILL NOW TURN TO the social, political, and economic impact of the Olympics. Environmental impact and its relationship to the other impact areas will be investigated separately in chapter 8, in order to address some gaps in existing approaches. Environmentalists include human health and economic impacts in their work, but there is a dearth of analyses that fully integrate social, political, economic, and environmental concerns. Conversely, the IOC provides environmental guidelines for candidate cities, but makes no similar provision to ensure that bids address the potential negative social, political, or economic impacts on the city, state, or nation.

This is not to suggest that the IOC is uninterested in nonsport issues—the Olympic Charter makes it clear that the IOC has a profound economic interest in protecting its product and its monopoly. Rule 40 confirms that the IOC has no economic liability vis-à-vis a host city's deficit; Rule 61 maintains IOC power over all publicity and advertising; Rule 17 guards against ambush marketing; and Rule 38 gives the IOC veto power over other important meetings or events taking place in the host city, neighboring areas, and Olympic venues for a four-week period (IOC Charter, 1997).

Richard Pound's position on social impact is relevant here. When questioned by two BNC members (Michael Shapcott and Helen Lenskyj) about the IOC's responsibility to set social impact guidelines for host cities, just as it sets environmental guidelines, Pound replied that bid cities would view this as undue IOC interference into their domestic politics. In the same conversation on September 1, 1998, following the TOBid board meeting, Pound stated that our group was "at the bottom of the food chain." His bald assertion captured the Olympic industry's view of community-based resistance.

THE SPORT/POLITICS CONNECTION

Olympic sport, like all major sport enterprises, is constructed by social, political, and economic forces. Since the inception of the modern Olympics in 1896, several macropolitical issues have commanded international attention, the Nazi cooptation of the 1936 Games being one of the earliest examples. There is extensive research on this kind of politicizing of the Olympics (see, for example, Guttmann, 1994; Hill, 1992; Houlihan, 1994; Tomlinson & Whannel, 1984).

The globalization of sport and sport media since the 1960s resulted in extensive coverage of macropolitical Olympic crises. This pattern not only increased public awareness of international politics played out in the Olympic arena, but also created the impression that these were isolated moments, captured in media images of Black Power salutes or police sirens—hence, the simplistic calls to "keep politics out of the Olympics." In reality, Olympic sport has a long and continuous history of overt and covert political activity at both the macro and micro levels.

By the 1980s, several Olympic boycotts had provided the world with unequivocal evidence of the links between politics and international sport. However, while issues such as South African apartheid and Soviet aggression in Asia were continuing political and social realities throughout the 1970s and 1980s, the trajectories of Olympic sport and human rights crossed only every four years, and so politicians' and journalists' calls to keep "politics" out of Olympic sport still resonated with the majority of observers.

As recently as 1998, shortly before the bribery allegations, Toronto and Sydney newspaper editorials were calling for a separation between the Olympics and politics. In the 1970s and 1980s, such calls were usually prompted by boycotts and other macropolitical events, but more recent examples concerned micropolitical issues such as partisan politics and grassroots anti-Olympic activism. In Australia, opposition party politicians were criticized for playing "political games" when they raised valid concerns about the ethics of the Sydney 2000 bid and SOCOG's current budget problems, while grassroots groups were dismissed as un-Australian and opportunistic when they drew public attention to the negative social and environmental impact of the Olympics, or when they threatened to mount mass protests in September 2000 regarding Aboriginal land rights.

It is noteworthy that Australian Labor politicians were not accused of playing "political games" during their 1993 overseas campaigns to promote support for the Sydney bid. Under the rubric of Olympic Solidarity, these efforts, of course, were condoned by the IOC, while Samaranch and others took a dim view of partisan politics or community protest "tainting" the Olympic image. IOC member Jacques Rogge, for example, in his role as Sydney 2000 Coordination Commissioner, warned SOCOG against involvement in partisan politics prior to the 1999 NSW state elections: the IOC position was that the Games "would not be abused or utilized by normal political discussion" (Jeffery, 1998).

On the same topic, a NSW Labor politician claimed that the appointment of Michael Knight to the dual roles of Olympic Minister and SOCOG president was " a masterstroke of political judgment" (McBride, 1998). As well, he implied that this was a major factor in keeping the project on target and on budget—although the latter claim was disputed by the official performance audit later in 1998. When the Sydney water supply became contaminated with cryptosporidium in August 1998, opposition Olympic critic Ian Armstrong and others were justly critical of Knight's "two hats." They claimed that the Olympics were compromised when Knight, as a cabinet minister, was not able to criticize the government's handling of the water crisis and its serious implications for Olympic tourism (Armstrong, 1998).

Either politically astute or genuinely believing President Samaranch's by now predictable words of encouragement to host cities, NSW premier Bob Carr told the legislative assembly that Samaranch considered Sydney's physical facilities "the best he had ever seen" and anticipated that Sydney 2000 would be "the best in the history of the Games." Furthermore, in reference to the organizational structure with its dual role of Olympic Minister and SOCOG president, Carr reported that Samarach "gave 100 per cent approval to the structure. He wishes it had been chosen for Atlanta—he expects it to be in place for future Olympics. He recommends, and the International Olympic Committee wants, this model" (Carr, 1998).

While this arrangement deftly solved the problem of securing state assistance in the event of an Olympic debt, the IOC's support for merging the leadership of organizing committees and sport ministries revealed cracks in the IOC's purported policy of noninterference in domestic politics.

ECONOMICS AND URBAN IMAGE

Since the postwar period, a pattern of urban regeneration facilitated by private/public partnerships has emerged in many cities in North America and Europe (Cochrane, Peck, & Tickell, 1996). Hallmark events such as world fairs and Olympic Games have been credited with mobilizing corporate elites and local politicians in profitable alliances that not only boosted local construction and retail and tourist industries but also generated substantial infrastructure funding from higher levels of government. In such scenarios, private business won on two fronts: an enhanced public image of corporate concern for the welfare of citizens and communities, and a significant profit into the bargain. In the face of this "Olympics as catalyst" rhetoric, however, critics were justly suspicious of politicians and businessmen who promised dramatic improvements in the leadup to an Olympic bid while failing to take adequate action under normal circumstances when urban social problems were equally urgent.

Citing the few cities that have experienced some positive outcomes following hallmark events, Olympic boosters emphasized the unique opportunities to solve the unemployment problem, upgrade public transit, clean up the environment, and construct affordable housing and sport facilities. It is not particularly difficult to produce *some* evidence to support each of these claims. In the well-known Los Angeles example, when the $222 million surplus was revealed, organizations ranging from local bus companies to the IOC applied for a share of the profit; ultimately, 40% of the surplus was allocated to youth sport in Southern California, 40% to the USOC, and 20% to national sports federations (Shaikin, 1988, p. 74). Universities in Calgary and Atlanta benefited from new student housing and sport facilities. In Sydney, former industrial sites were remediated and developed for sport venues, housing and parkland. Since 1972, according to German economist Holger Preuss (1998), the "economic impulse" of the Olympics Games has been responsible for the creation of short- and long-term jobs in most Summer Olympic host cities. On the other hand, a study of the Olympic impact on labor financed by the Barcelona organizing committee (Miguelez & Carrasquer, 1995) concluded that the anticipated economic impulse was limited and only affected some sectors, although it may have helped to delay the negative impact of the international recession. They further reported that small business enterprises saw little benefit, the volume of employment was less than expected, and most jobs were temporary. Both sources acknowledged, however, that employment depended on other economic factors, not only on the Olympic impulse.

According to the hegemonic view, the Olympic impact is positive in every *important* dimension. If this were not the case, Olympic boosters on every continent would hardly put such an extraordinary amount of time and energy, as well as millions of dollars, into bid campaigns. Since those with privilege had the power to define what was important, the criteria for evaluating Olympic impact reflected their social class, race, and gender interests. With recent American, Canadian, and Australian bid and organizing committees, particularly their executive boards, composed primarily of wealthy White businessmen, economic benefits for the private sector within the host city and region usually headed the list of Olympic promises: the boost to urban development, sporting facilities, tourism and hospitality industries, transport and communication, the construction industry, and small business.

Closely linked to the popular economic-boost argument were calls for citizens to support the noneconomic but equally important goal of urban image making. Under normal circumstances, such a nebulous project might take second place to the more pressing social concerns of urban society, but, with a sufficiently sophisticated public relations campaign, an Olympic bid committee can persuade many citizens that image is more important than substance. Consider, for example, the following views attributed to a Toronto councilor:

> [Councilor] Kyle Rae laments the reduction in urban design planners who would attend to the look and feel of the city. He says hoteliers are beginning to get feedback expressing surprise at the number of scuzzy-looking street people and the volume of litter on the streets—both invisible a decade ago. (James, 1999)

This extraordinary callousness—in effect, calling homeless people human litter—became comprehensible, but by no means excusable, when the article went on to compare Toronto (an Olympic bid city) to Vancouver and Barcelona, two cities that had hosted hallmark events in the last decade. The article's unmistakable message was that Toronto should clean up its image if it wanted to be taken seriously as an Olympic contender and a world-class city. Indeed, only a few weeks later, the Metro Toronto Police Department embarked on an eleven-week "Community Action Policing" campaign purportedly to increase police presence in crime hotspots. In practice, this targeted policing was directed at homeless people, panhandlers, and "squeegee kids." One of the official police rationales was to "reassure tourists" (Verma, 1999)—this in a city that was not (yet) an Olympic host.

In the face of this image-making rhetoric, those engaged in grassroots resistance to Olympic hegemony faced the difficult task of moving public discourse away from urban and national chauvinism—"the spotlight of the world will be upon us as we stage the biggest sporting event ever held in the Southern hemisphere," to paraphrase Sydney 2000 promotional material— and into the everyday social world of disadvantaged groups, characterized as it is by racism, unemployment, poverty, and police harassment. In other words, as Jennings would put it, the critics were "pissing on something nice." Not too surprisingly, their efforts often met with hostility.

THE POLITICS OF PLACE AND THE OLYMPIC GAMES

The literature on hallmark events and urban megaprojects serves as a useful starting point for analyzing Olympic impact. Deconstructions of the "politics of place" that operate in these contexts provide insights into the ideological agenda shared by Olympic and megaproject boosters alike—that is, the campaign to persuade citizens that the project will transform their hometown into a "world-class" city, while at the same time enhancing civic identity and community spirit. Hall (1998) identified four prerequisites for a world-class city: a critical mass of visitor attractions and facilities; hallmark events; urban tourism strategies; and leisure and cultural services to support tourism.

In relation to the outside world, the challenge is to transform negative aspects of the city's image (as violent/industrial/undeveloped/unsophisti-cated/etc.) into an attractive tourist product—a "bourgeois playground" (Hall, 1994). At the same time, image makers have to preserve the city's traditional cultural image and authenticity (as friendly/gracious/historic/relaxed/etc.) to satisfy long-time residents and to present a recognizable icon for tourists. Public relations companies play a central role in achieving this balance—for example, the traditional views of Atlanta and its southern hospitality or Calgary and its western (Calgary Stampede) tradition were skillfully blended with the new image of "a world city representing the very cutting-edge of modernity" (Wamsley & Heine, 1996). As Wilson (1996, p. 608) explained in her analysis of Sydney as an Olympic city, world-class has come to mean simply "the standards of facility and kinds of entertainment that affluent international travelers expect anywhere." In the case of an Olympic host city, the construction of state-of-the-art sport venues and facilities, in combination with general urban renewal projects, satisfied the world-class requirement. Equally important, new stadia can be used to attract or keep a professional franchise post-Olympics, a move that further entrenches the city's world-class status, often at considerable cost to the taxpayer (Bale & Moen, 1995; Kidd, 1995). In fact, Eitzen (1996) provided ample evidence of the ways in which "the powerless disproportionately bear the burden" in subsidizing public arenas used primarily for professional sport. It was not a coincidence that several key members of Toronto's 2008 bid committee had close ties with professional sport teams and stadiums, including membership on stadium boards of directors.

The "politics of place" explanations alone, however, provide an incomplete picture of the specific ways in which the Olympic industry and its local boosters exploit noneconomic aspects of the Olympics, most notably their call to citizens to embrace the lofty ideals of Olympics—Hope, Unity, Friendship, and Fair Play—for the good of their country and its young athletes. The pseudo-religious allure of the Olympic spirit rhetoric distinguishes the Olympics from more mundane hallmark events such as world fairs or historical commemorations, and from other urban megaprojects such as downtown revitalization or waterfront regeneration. Hence, any analysis of Olympic impact needs to take into account the relationship between the Olympic industry, masculinity, and power, as well as the symbolic appeal of Olympic sport, captured in the rhetoric of the pure athlete and the Olympic spirit. Indeed, Olympic boosters have a distinct advantage over supporters of a world fair, for example, because they can draw on a hundred years of Olympic ideals that purportedly transcend crass commercialism.

BEHIND THE "OLYMPIC SPIRIT" RHETORIC

Rhetoric about Olympic ideals dates back at least to the late-nineteenth-century origins of the modern Olympic Games—Richard Pound, in fact, claims three thousand years of unbroken history for these "enduring" ideals (Pound, 1999a, p. 2). It is illuminating to compare the rhetoric before and after the bribery controversy, since the minimal changes that did occur were in an unexpected direction. There was, on the one hand, an unprecedented level of criticism and cynicism in the media and on the street concerning all aspects of the Olympic industry. On the other hand, many supporters, rather than abandoning notions of Olympic spirit and ideals, embraced these aspects with greater enthusiasm than ever before.

Atlanta's hosting of the 1996 Summer Olympics prompted an outpouring of Olympic spirit rhetoric in Canada and the United States, as demonstrated, for example, in the reflections of Canadian athlete and TOBid member Sandra Levy:

> The Olympics is truly a paragon of what we, the world, are capable of achieving—international solidarity. It seems like such a utopian concept but once one experiences the utopia in an Olympic village, one really believes that

dreams can come true. . . . The term "Olympic Family" refers to all members
of the village community—a literal attempt to perpetuate a sense of international unity. (Levy, 1996)

There is a striking contrast between her glowing, if idealistic, account and the
disdain shown by some members of the American men's basketball team. As
wealthy, professional athletes, they were apparently uninterested in the camaraderie of Barcelona's Olympic village and preferred to stay in expensive hotels.

The mainstream media played a key role in promoting Olympic spirit
rhetoric. Not only were Olympic stories newsworthy, but many newspaper
and magazine publishers and television networks were major Olympic sponsors. A 1996 *Newsweek* article exemplified media boosterism:

[The Olympics] has bequeathed to the world thrilling examples of courage
. . . heroes to cheer, defeats to shake off, and a little girl who will tumble the
length of a balance beam (biting her lip, ponytail flying, parents blinking
back tears) and in one perfect instant achieve the kind of transcendent
greatness that will live forever in the sports pages of Valhalla. (Adler, 1996)

When the Olympic gymnastics event took place a few weeks later, the predictable image of the courageous young gymnast did in fact appear on millions of television screens, but the knowledge that American gymnast Kerri
Strug was pressured to complete her routine with a twisted ankle was, for
many viewers, not a transcendent sporting moment but an example of
coaches' inappropriate use of power over young athletes.

The *Globe and Mail*, Canada's national newspaper, was no less lyrical in
a 1996 editorial titled "The importance of the Olympics":

The Games are the free trade of sport—they invite athletes everywhere to leap
the walls of parochialism and reach the highest expression of grace and beauty
. . . they invite humanity into a cauldron of competition and hope that its
glow will displace the darkness of the age. For a fortnight, people everywhere
are transfixed. Touched by the spirit of goodwill, inspired by the majesty of
the human form, they refuse to think ill of these Olympic Games. (The
importance of the Olympics, 1996)

In the aftermath of the bribery scandal in 1999, it would have been more
accurate to credit public relations companies with maintaining this (alleged)
uncritical public view of the Olympics. Sports marketing experts, including
IOC director of marketing Michael Payne, advised host cities to take advantage of the "mess" by "using it as a catalyst for reform." Payne went on to say,
tellingly: "It's not just a sports event . . . it's something very special that peo-

ple are passionate about and it must be protected" (Thompson, 1999; see also Cockerill, 1999; Smith, 1999). The validity of his claim was supported in mid-1999, when, after four international investigations had demonstrated the extent of corruption in Olympic circles, journalists, athletes, and fans were still voicing their beliefs in the Olympic spirit.

Toronto Star Olympic journalist Randy Starkman, reporting on Canadian athlete Renn Crichlow's exemplary role as an athlete and advocate, concluded: "Let's face it. The Olympics are unlike any other event in terms of rallying the spirit in our country. Athletes such as Renn Crichlow are the reason why these Games must survive" (Starkman, 1999e). Similarly, a *Sydney Morning Herald* editorial, praising the record-breaking 100m sprint by Maurice Greene, claimed that his run demonstrated "that sport itself has a *redemptive power* that will transcend all the inappropriate activities of the IOC and the Australian Olympic committee when our Games are presented to the world next year" (Our Games, 1999; emphasis added). It should be noted that the pseudo-religious claim that sport has a "redemptive power" is not the same as the liberal position that Olympic sport can be "redeemed" from its present imperfect state.

The *Salt Lake Tribune* made a similar attempt to redirect public attention to the "pure athlete" in the midst of the bribery scandal. A February 1999 story titled "Olympic alumnus tells S.L. it can achieve dream" (Gorrell, 1999e) praised John Naber, motivational speaker and former Olympic swimmer, who, not coincidentally, was visiting Salt Lake City to promote his new book, *Waken the Olympian Within*. Applying the lesson of Olympic athletes overcoming major setbacks to Olympic cities, Naber urged Utahns to view the scandal as "an opportunity to rally forces around the flag . . . to awaken the Olympic spirit in the heart of everyone. This is our chance to do what those Olympians did, to look back and say: 'We overcame.'" In his parting words, Naber predicted that, despite the current impact of the scandal, "people will not be thinking about this" in 2000. Similarly, American Olympic athlete Carl Lewis was reported as saying: "When all is said and done, the athletes got out there and performed and that's what we remember about the Olympics . . . not the organization or other people" (Business as usual, 1999).

This patronizing "people will forget" theme was central to Olympic supporters' attempts to downplay the seriousness of the bribery scandal. It portrayed potential Olympic spectators and television viewers as unreflective dupes with short attention spans and no critical powers, while at the same time exploiting the pure athlete and Olympic spirit rhetoric. In his opening speech to the March 1999 IOC session, president Samaranch provided a perfect example:

The challenge before us is to refocus the world's attention away from the controversy and back to where it belongs: the Olympic Games and the world's athletes. Frankly speaking, the athletes have been lost in this process. . . . These young people should not be kept from pursuing their dreams because of the improper actions of a few. (Samaranch, 1999b, p. 6)

The exhortation to give athletes' Olympic "dreams" top priority had serious consequences for disadvantaged populations and advocates of social justice. To be a critic of Olympic sport was to show disrespect for these young athletes' hard work, dedication, and hopes for the future. The fact that men, women, and children living on the streets of Atlanta, Seoul, Toronto, or Sydney may have had their own dreams—of accommodation, safety, employment, personal fulfillment—had no place in Olympic industry rhetoric, except for the predictable promises that the economic boost would help to solve some (but not all) of these people's problems. The myth of the pure athlete and pure sport ensured that the dreams of the disadvantaged took low priority in the public discourse.

In sport scholarship circles, too, the "Olympic dream" rhetoric was seldom problematized. Debates raged in the 1980s and 1990s over the futile "hoop dreams" of Black youth aspiring to become National Basketball Association (NBA) stars in the face of evidence of the very low statistical probability that they would ever achieve this goal, and the institutional racism that encouraged and rewarded Black youth's athleticism while largely ignoring their intellectual development and futures (e.g., Hoberman, 1997). In contrast, although the probability of becoming an Olympic athlete was equally miniscule, few Olympic scholars made the links between that reality and the exploitation of young athletes' bodies and minds (Donnelly, 1997; Kidd, 1997).

THE MYTH OF THE PURE ATHLETE AND PURE SPORT

There is a longstanding mythology that the athlete/sport component can and should be treated as separate from Olympic administration and infrastructure, a distinction that proved particularly useful for the survival of the Olympic industry in 1999. A statement by Utah state senator Scott Howell exemplified this position: "We can rally together to promote the spirit of the Olympics. We should not forget the athletes who are at the heart of the Games" (Howell quoted in Fantin, 1999a). And in Canada, former Olympic athletes Ken Read and Mark Tewksbury echoed these views:

It is very important at this time of crisis to make a distinction between the Games and the IOC. . . . The heart and soul of the Olympic Games—

summer and winter—are the athletes. They are still out there, most laboring in obscurity, striving for a goal. (Read, 1999)

I believe in it [Olympic ideals] more than ever, we're at a pivotal point. We could reclaim the Olympics for the youth, for the athletes. We could show that it's not just for 114 IOC members. (Tewksbury quoted in Grange, 1999)

Similarly, the athletes' advocacy group OATH (Olympic Advocates Together Honorably) named as one of its objectives "to help create a process that is representative of all stakeholders and that recognizes that the soul of the athletes is the soul of the Olympics" (OATH, 1999).

According to this way of thinking, the pure athlete and pure sport are the true "heart" of the Olympics, while the IOC, NOC, NBC, Coca Cola, doping, etc. are merely peripheral contaminants. These ahistorical and decontextualized notions of the "pure" athlete and "pure" sport are seriously flawed, as any critical sociological or historical analysis of sport and athletes would demonstrate. Indeed, if such arguments were used in the context of professional basketball to defend the pure athlete and the pure game against the evils of the NBA, TSN, or Nike, they would be dismissed as hopelessly naive and anachronistic.

Olympic athletes are not a monolithic group—they are amateurs and professionals, rich and poor, children and adults, ethical and unethical. Athletes participating in the Olympic industry have the capacity, depending on their own social locations, to accommodate or resist Olympic hegemony. In democratic countries, for example, athletes' resistance could take the form of withdrawal from all Olympic competition and the development of alternative kinds of international sport. However, the most popular strategy developed by "pure" athletes in 1999 relied on reform rather than revolution. They invoked a return to a mythic "golden age" when the modern Olympics were simply about sport. OATH took this reform approach, while, predictably, the IOC called for *evolution* rather than *revolution*.

Throughout the scandal, public relations experts constructed a discourse that posited a monolithic group called "the athletes" against the "bad apples" (to use Richard Pound's term) in the IOC. Olympic athletes came to be viewed as expert witnesses—the voices of truth and wisdom. The mandatory interview with the Olympic athlete became a staple of media coverage, while at the same time the Olympic credentials of IOC members and other Olympic officials were routinely flagged. Ironically, this information amply demonstrated that merely competing in the Olympics was not a guarantee of good character or ethical behavior. John Coates, Phil Coles, Anton Geesink,

Pirjo Haeggman, Paul Henderson, Peter Tallberg, and Paul Wallwork were all former Olympic athletes, while Agustin Arroyo, Louis N'Diaye, Lamine Keita, Un Yong Kim, and Charles Mukora had histories of coaching or sport administration. And in 1998, before the expulsions, former Olympic athletes comprised thirty-three of the one hundred and ten IOC members, a defense often used by Samaranch and Pound against the charge that it was out of touch with athletes. Given the generally unquestioned authority of Olympic athletes, the fact that they were not of one mind on the bribery controversy was not addressed. A January 1999 Associated Press story reported the views of Americans Mark Spitz and Carl Lewis that corruption in Olympic bids had been rampant for some time, largely because of a flawed bid process and the IOC's unregulated power (Business as usual, 1999). Canadians Tewksbury and Read were more idealistic, viewing IOC members' conduct as both a personal disillusionment and a betrayal of the Olympic Movement (Read, 1999; Grange, 1999). Meanwhile, Australian athletes drew up an agreement on team values for Australian athletes, including rejection of doping and cheating, and graciousness in defeat (Athletes . . . , 1999).

While rejecting the unfair and often racist stereotypes of athletes as "dumb jocks," it is important to acknowledge that Olympic athletes, like members of any occupational category, are not an undifferentiated group. As well as the obvious variables of gender, social class, race/ethnicity, sexuality, religion, and national origin among Olympic athletes, there are important differences in their political perspectives, educational backgrounds, and analytical skills and insights. In short, the experience of being an Olympic athlete does not transcend all other categories of social analysis, nor does it transform every Olympic participant into an expert Olympic analyst. Moreover, those who have developed analyses of Olympic sport will be positioned along a political continuum, from radical to conservative, and, in the face of Olympic industry hegemony, those with a radical analysis are least likely to be given voice.

This was a clear pattern in the selective media coverage of Olympic athletes' views: those who most closely resembled the "pure athlete" gained the lion's share of media attention. Canadian (former) Olympic athlete Ben Johnson, one of the minority of Olympic athletes ever actually caught and punished for taking steroids, was critical of the IOC double standard that exonerated dishonest members while punishing dishonest athletes. While Johnson, a Black man, received some local coverage (Starkman, 1999g), Tewksbury and OATH commanded international media attention in January and February 1999. Most, although not all, of the founding members of OATH were young and White; they were liberal and idealist rather than radical and jaded, and their reform agenda was palatable to generations of consumers raised on Olympic rhetoric. Richard Pound, in fact, was one of the few critics of an initiative that most observers applauded. The fact that the OATH platform called for new wine in old bottles was rarely identified as a limitation.

CONCLUSION

It is clear from the preceding discussion that democracy often fell victim to the pressures of a hallmark event. Unlike other urban renewal projects, a world fair or an Olympic Games had an unforgiving deadline for the construction of venues and the completion of infrastructure supports. Local politicians and boosters often used the excuse of hallmark construction to bypass the usual stages in urban development applications, including social and environmental impact assessment, public hearings, etc. (Hall, 1989; Thorne & Munro-Clark, 1989).

Despite rhetoric to the contrary, a "private" Olympic project is a contradiction in terms. Not only does the IOC demand financial guarantees to cover Olympic debts, which in the majority of cases are underwritten by city, state, or national levels of government, but all recent Olympic Games have required major infrastructure projects—highway, airport, transit improvements—subsidized by state and national funds. As a result, certain negative patterns emerged in Olympic host cities: when infrastructure projects were speeded up, other public works were delayed or displaced. The channeling of a large proportion of state funds into one metropolitan area during Olympic construction resulted in fewer infrastructure projects in other regions, and in suburban areas remote from Olympic venues (Rutheiser, 1996).

Furthermore, when state and federal governments contributed to what was purportedly a private urban megaproject, significant numbers of citizens were not only disenfranchised but also unfairly taxed to pay off one city's debt. The promised employment opportunities associated with Olympic construction, retail trade, and the tourist industry were often short-lived. And although there have been examples of Olympic villages later converted to affordable housing, they are more often rented or sold at market value, on the grounds that a commercially profitable development would leave the taxpayers with a lower debt, and the government with more funds for post-Olympics social programs. The next chapters will demonstrate these outcomes in a number of Olympic host cities.

6

Up Against the Olympic Industry
international resistance

T HE IOC, ALONG WITH local Olympic organizers and public relations experts, have largely succeeded in maintaining the illusion that, while international tensions may manifest themselves in boycotts or violence, host cities and countries are unequivocally supportive of the Olympic enterprise. Since the 1960s, suppression of local dissent has included such actions as the 1968 massacre of student protesters in Mexico City, the arrests of dissidents in Moscow in 1986 and Barcelona in 1992, and the criminalization of poverty in Atlanta prior to the 1996 Olympics. Equally effective strategies for suppressing public debate have been the successful campaigns to contain local media coverage of Olympic bids and preparations in Berlin, Toronto, Atlanta, Sydney, and elsewhere (see chapter 9).

Unlike those who reap the benefits and privileges of the Olympic industry, anti-Olympic and watchdog groups usually operate with minimal funding and volunteer labor. Moreover, with the terms of Olympic debate firmly established by those in power, grassroots critics are often placed in a reactive rather than proactive position. Even under these conditions, groups such as BNC succeeded in redirecting public discourse toward economic and social impact issues, while the Berlin anti-Olympic group and Sydney's Bondi Olympic Watch delayed or even stopped the progress of the Olympic machine. As well as this collective resistance to hosting the Olympics, many individuals successfully used the event itself as a vehicle for political protest.

This chapter will document political repression associated with the staging of the Olympics, and the resistance work of the major anti-Olympic and Olympic watchdog groups concerned with social, economic, and political impact. The next chapter will focus specifically on the Atlanta and Sydney situations. Two Australian environmental groups—Greenpeace Australia and Green Games Watch 2000 (GGW 2000)— will be discussed in chapter 8.

THE THREAT TO HUMAN RIGHTS

Since at least 1968, there has been extensive repression of "undesirables" and dissidents before and during the staging of the Olympic Games. While political repression has been well documented, the equally harsh treatment of poor and homeless people has only recently received attention.

Rule 61 of the IOC Charter (1997) requires the host city to guarantee that there will be no demonstrations or "political, religious or racial propaganda" in or near Olympic venues. The IOC rule, however, is more concerned with maintaining law and order than with combating racism. Australian Aborigines, for example, can expect to be arrested if they assemble near Olympic sites in September 2000 to protest White Australia's racism. In fact, with the long-standing historical association between the Olympics and the repression of students, the Left, workers, and other social change movements, it is likely that the Sydney Olympics will be used as a pretext for further Aboriginal repression (Russell, 1994).

The suppression of political protest required by the IOC Charter constituted a clear infringement on citizens' right to free assembly in a democratic society. Many anti-Olympic groups, however, were successful in mounting public protests in the period before the Games—for example, during IOC sessions and IOC members' visits to bid cities. Mass protests, such as those organized by Berlin's Olympic opponents, sent a clear message to the IOC that community dissent would damage the Olympic image for tourists, television viewers, and, most importantly, sponsors.

Although the IOC rule demanded a protest-free zone, it did not specifically require the street sweeps that by the 1980s had become a standard feature of most hallmark events. On these occasions, homeless people, sex trade workers, and beggars were harassed by police, evicted from downtown neighborhoods, and often arrested. Such street sweeps have been documented during all Summer Olympics since 1984—Los Angeles, Seoul, Barcelona, and

Atlanta (Cox, 1998; Beaty, 1999)—and there are already warning signs in Sydney, as the discussion in the next chapter will demonstrate.

IOC evaluations of candidate cities throughout the 1980s and 1990s routinely included comments on the domestic political climate: the degree of financial and political support offered by various levels of government, and the extent of organized community opposition, if any, to a bid. There were, of course, no references to poverty or prostitution; these urban "problems" were either removed, avoided, or ignored during official IOC visits.

OLYMPIC PROTEST, 1968–1992

Mexico City, Mexico

The Mexican student protest was one component of the reformist movement working toward democratization and an end to three decades of one-party government under the Institutional Revolutionary Party. Students' demands included freeing of political prisoners, and freedom of speech and association. On October 2, 1968, shortly before the Olympics began, thousands of Mexican students gathered in Tlatelolco Plaza to protest the government's lavish Olympic spending: $200 million was transferred from the social services budget to city improvement projects in an elaborate urban and national "re-imaging" campaign.

The student protest, like many other popular movements of the preceding decade, was quickly quashed by the Mexican army and paramilitary squads, with more than three hundred students massacred, more than two hundred student leaders jailed and tortured, and thousands more arrested and beaten (Paz, 1972). These events were of sufficient concern to the IOC to call an emergency meeting, but the motion to cancel the Games lost by one vote. The remainder of the Student Strike Committee called a truce during the Olympics, but at the medal ceremony, African American athletes Tommie Smith and John Carlos protested with the raised fists of the Black Power salute. In response to IOC pressure, USOC expelled Smith and Carlos from the American team and the Olympic village. However, when another medal winner, George Foreman, waved an American flag after his victory, this was not censored as a "political" demonstration.

Unlike Tiananmen Square, the Tlatelolco Plaza massacre did not command world attention at the time, largely because of media silence and the U.S. backing of the Mexican government. Almost thirty years later, however, two survivors of the student movement became elected representatives in the new democratic government, a "truth commission" was established, and the legitimacy of the 1968 student movement was finally recognized (Orozco, 1998).

Differences in outside reporting of the Mexico City massacre are both illuminating and disturbing. The *Guardian*'s (UK) figure of 325 student deaths is generally cited in progressive accounts, including those of Hispanic radio news director Samuel Orozco and Mexican poet and former ambassador Octavio Paz, who claimed that no Mexican newspaper in 1968 dared to print the real figure (Paz, 1972). The blatantly pro-American Grolier publication *Pursuit of Excellence: The Olympic Story* (Associated Press & Grolier, 1979) made an attempt to situate the massacre in the context of worldwide student protest, with Mexico City itself characterized in the racist metaphor of "a mariachi band in discord." The account went on to trivialize the preceding three decades of repression as follows: "There are any number of versions of what started the trouble. They range from a fight between two students over a girl [*sic*] to long-term distress over the plight of Mexico's poor. . . . More than 30 [*sic*] students were killed in riots. More than 100 were injured and more than 300 were jailed" (Associated Press & Grolier, 1979, p. 279).

Munich, West Germany

The deaths of five members of the Palestinian Black September group, eleven Israelis, and a German police officer during the Munich Olympics commanded international attention in 1972, as did the IOC decision to continue the Games rather than to be seen as yielding to criminals. The Munich events were largely responsible for the subsequent preoccupation with Olympic security and the threat of Olympic "terrorism" directed at athletes and Olympic family members, although, as the bombing in Atlanta later demonstrated, somewhat less attention was paid to security outside Olympic villages and venues.

In a less-publicized political protest in Munich, African American medallists Vince Matthews and Wayne Collett refused to stand to attention during the anthem, and were subsequently banned from further competition. Such behavior was seen as fundamentally contrary to the "Olympic spirit" and required "immediate and harsh repression" (Russell, 1994). These actions were not without precedent. In 1964, when Australian swimmer Dawn Fraser "souvenired" a flag from the imperial palace in Tokyo, the Australia Olympic Committee initially banned her from swimming for ten years, then reinstated her as an amateur after four years, with the result that she missed the next Olympics. In Fraser's case, this was not even a political protest, but simply a victory prank.

Montreal, Quebec

The 1976 Olympics are remembered primarily for the $1 billion debt that Montreal taxpayers were still paying off into the late 1990s. This aspect, which has been widely documented (e.g., Auf der Maur, 1976; Ludwig, 1976; Wright, 1978) can largely be explained as a product of undemocratic local government decision making under the leadership of Mayor Jean Drapeau. In terms of its other legacy—sporting facilities—these included a stadium for Montreal's professional baseball team, the Expos, and a velodrome that was subsequently closed down.

Prompted by events in Munich, Montreal Olympic organizers deployed at least 16,000 soldiers as well as security officers and provincial and city police to protect athletes and Olympic family members, at a cost of more than $100 million (Wright, 1978). The campaign of political repression that started the year before the Games is more difficult to rationalize. Stuart Russell documented his own experiences and those of other members of left-wing organizations who were employed as office workers by the Montreal organizing committee. By July 1976, about twenty political activists had been fired without reason; it was subsequently revealed that the personnel director labelled them "security risks" following Royal Canadian Mounted Police (RCMP) security checks. Other activists were simply warned by the RCMP to leave town during the Games.

Some of those fired subsequently lodged complaints of political discrimination under the Quebec Charter of Human Rights and Freedoms, but the RCMP refused to provide information or documents as evidence, invoking Crown privilege based on "national security" (Russell, 1994). All of Russell's later applications to gain access to his security files were dismissed. In short, the RCMP's refusal to release documents sealed the fate of the human rights complaints and protected the organizing committee's reputation.

Denver, Colorado

Denver has the distinction of being the only city to reject the IOC's offer to host the Olympic Games, and serves as an example of successful community organizing against the Olympic machine. The IOC awarded the 1976 Winter Olympics to Denver in 1970, but concerns over finances and environmental impact subsequently resulted in a "no" vote in state and city referenda held in November 1972.

The Denver bid and organizing committees were controlled by business leaders whose goal of uncontrolled economic development fitted well with Olympic industry values. Environmentalists and other protesters formed a group called Citizens for Colorado's Future, and succeeded in politicizing financial and environmental issues through a proposal to cut off state funding for the Games. Concerns included negative environmental impact and uncontrolled urban and regional growth as a result of hosting the Games (Katz, 1974). International sport federations' demands for costly changes and improvements to facilities and venues also fuelled Colorado residents' concerns about the potential long-term tax burden. While the overwhelming vote against the Games represented a victory for community activists, few county or state environmental controls were put in place at the time, and the next twenty-five years were marked by rapid regional and urban growth.

Los Angeles, California

The USSR's boycott of the 1984 Olympics was the most salient political aspect of these Games. In their rationale for the boycott, Soviets cited concerns about athletes' security: fears of harassment, kidnapping, and defections. An American group, the Ban the Soviets Coalition, was named as a threat by the Soviets, but dismissed by USOC officials as insignificant (Shaikin, 1988). Constitutional guarantees of freedom of speech and peaceful assembly extended to all such groups as long as they did not demonstrate in Olympic villages or venues. However, there were documented reports that public demonstrations were banned and homeless people detained without charge (Levinson, 1993, cited in Cox, 1998). And, as Borowy (1999) pointed out, the spectacle of low-income Black women selling oranges outside the village raised serious questions about access to resources in a city focused on the Olympics. The organizing committee's priorities were clearly illustrated in the distribution of the $222 million surplus: 6,500 paid employees, comprising less than 10% of the Games work force, were given bonuses, while 50,000 volunteers received nothing (Shaikin, 1988).

Seoul, Korea

Like many hallmark events, the 1988 Olympics provided the impetus for major urban redevelopment in Seoul. Traditional communities of wooden and tile-roofed houses were replaced with middle-class high-rise residential areas. The trend, common in Third World cities, began in the 1960s with Korea's transformation from an agrarian to an industrial economy. The Asian Coalition for Housing Rights (1989) documented multiple forced evictions numbering in the millions, and claimed that these were among the most extensive of any city in the world during the 1970s and 1980s.

The neighborhood of Sang Kye Dong, for example, was home to people who had been evicted from other areas in the 1960s to make way for redevelopment. In 1986, with this area slated for Olympic redevelopment, residents organized resistance to the Olympic project and the threatened evictions. Riot police and men hired by private construction companies attacked protesters, young and old, burned down tents used as community centers, and cut off the water and electricity supply.

A few months later, the remaining 380 residents and their belongings were removed by a force of more than three thousand men. Subsequently, as urban squatters, these people's new "homes" on a plot of land in central Seoul were torn down because they were within sight of the Olympic torch route, and they were forced to live in holes in the ground or plastic shelters. As part of the same Olympic "beautification" program, the government demolished any "slum" housing that was visible from main roads, Olympic facilities, or hotels, and evicted whole communities that might be visible to the media covering the torch runs (Asian Coalition, 1989). Between 1984 and 1988, more than one million people were "relocated" in this brutal manner (Mulling, 1990). On the matter of street sweeps, it is important to note that, in the case of Seoul, some officials appeared to view prostitution as an asset rather than a liability. The government engaged in "shameless" selling of sex tourism in their marketing of Korea to the outside world and dissidents were justly critical of the exploitation of women in the sex industry (Mulling, 1990).

As was the case in Mexico, the Korean dissident movement mobilized in the period leading up to the Olympics. Mulling (1990) described how the democratization movement of students, workers, farmers, and radical church groups had been politically active since the 1970s on behalf of the common people. In 1987, faced with government calls to maintain political and social stability and postpone reform until after the Games, the dissident movement engaged in demonstrations across the country. Like other organizers of hallmark events—but in this case aided by a repressive, authoritarian regime—the government used the "ticking clock" argument of inflexible Olympic deadlines to justify its repressive actions. Labor disputes and student demonstrations were terminated with tear gas, and dissidents were detained and jailed. Some short-term gains were made, prompted largely by the government's fear that domestic unrest would cause it to lose the Games, and, more importantly, the opportunity to enhance Seoul's image in the world business and diplomatic communities. Indeed, many Korean critics drew comparisons between these Games and the 1936 propaganda event of Hitler's Nazi regime.

Dissidents in Seoul, like Olympic critics in many other countries, were also concerned about costs; the initial estimates of $2.3 billion in 1981 were surpassed in the final official figure of $3.1 billion. They also suspected (correctly) that indirect costs were excluded, a finding that Seoul organizers justified to critics as a "special security matter" (Mulling, 1990, p. 404). (Lest this appear a uniquely Korean situation, it should be noted that Sydney's bid and organizing committees, as well as Toronto's two bid committees, managed, at least for a time, to avoid public accountability because of their exemption from Australian and Canadian Freedom of Information laws.)

Some commentaries have credited president Samaranch with a significant victory in international diplomacy because of his concerted efforts to promote dialogue between North and South Korea on the potential co-hosting of the Games, which in the end failed to materialize. According to Richard Pound's account of "secret negotiations" behind the Seoul Olympics, the IOC, led by "a president of remarkable ability," kept both parties at the table through "the right blend of idealism and cynicism" (Pound, 1992, p. xi). Korean IOC member Un Yong Kim claimed that the Seoul Olympics served to bring (South) Korea "into the ranks of the world's advanced nations" (Kim quoted in Hill, 1992, p. 213). Finally, critical Olympic scholar Christopher Hill (1992) claimed that the Games played a part in pushing North Korea toward reunification through emphasizing its isolation by comparison with the South's new international status as an Olympic host country.

Barcelona, Spain

Police crackdowns on petty crime, street sweeps targeting prostitutes, transvestites, and homeless people, and arrests of dissidents before and during the 1992 Games have been well documented. A social impact study conducted after the event estimated that about four hundred homeless people were subjected to "control and supervision" during the Games (Barreiro et al., 1993, cited in Cox et al., 1994).

On the security issue, there had been violent attacks on human targets (as opposed to acts of sabotage) in Spain in the five years leading up to the Games, and at least two such groups had declared their opposition to the Olympics. These groups were alleged to have sabotaged a gas line and an electricity pylon, the latter part of a plan to disrupt the Olympic opening ceremonies. Authorities considered that Olympic security and Spain's antiterrorism strategies minimized violent attacks during the Games (Thompson, 1996), but it is difficult to ascertain the extent to which these preventive strategies interfered with civil rights.

A group called NOOOOO a la Barcelona Olimpica (the five O's representing the Olympic rings) was active in the 1980s on a number of Olympic issues. Terming the bid "the biggest propaganda campaign ever seen here" (with a budget of more than 1.2 million pesetas), this group sought to promote public debate through establishing the Commission

Against the Barcelona Games composed of more than twenty tenants' rights, ecology, and other social justice groups. Its major concerns included undemocratic decision making, threats to the environment posed by Olympic construction, potential suppression of Catalan language and culture, and the diversion of public funds into elite projects and away from much-needed housing and recreational facilities in working-class neighborhoods. On the topic of urbanization and the plan for the "Great Barcelona" unification, the group pointed out that such a plan fifteen years earlier had produced the biggest-ever tenant protest and had been shelved; among its negative impacts was the planned takeover of twenty-seven independent districts near the city into one megacity (NOOOOO a la Barcelona Olimpica, n.d.). Protests against various aspects of Olympic construction were commonplace from 1987 on.

The major urban renewal projects prompted or accelerated by the Olympics—roads and transportation, sewage, green space and beaches, housing, hotels, commercial space, and sports facilities—were generally heralded as a huge success, as was the project of urban image making—the "redefinition" of Barcelona as an economically thriving city of international status and an attractive tourist destination (Brunet, 1995; Sudjic, 1992). The mayor of Barcelona at the time of the bid later became Spain's deputy prime minister, and thus was able to direct national government funds into Olympic-related projects that transformed and modernized the city, according to most reports, after decades of poverty and neglect.

Barcelona City Council's 1988 Economic and Social Strategic Plan focused on consultation with the corporate sector and put business promotion before social objectives. A 1992 economic impact study conducted by the City identified infrastructure investment (more than 80% of the budget), the generation of 128,000 jobs in the previous five years, and an influx of 250,000 tourists in 1992.

Not surprisingly, the Olympics were experienced quite differently by people "at the bottom of the food chain." Spanish journalist and novelist Manuel Vazquez Montalban, one of the early critics, identified some of the contradictions: the city's 1986 promise to include subsidized housing in the post-Games Olympic village, and the fact that by 1992 most of the six thousand units had been sold on the open market for 240,000 pounds sterling; the construction of a "spectacular upper-middle-class residential city" on former factory and warehouse sites, adjacent to "fragile working class communities . . . or the huge islands of deprivations like la Mina, a highrise gypsy estate"; and the "relentless destruction and construction" of entire city blocks with little or no concern for conservation or history (Montalban, 1992, p. 6). As one

Barcelona resident told Jan Borowy, it would take her three lifetimes to be able to afford to live in the new housing (Borowy, 1999).

The Barreiro et al. study of social, economic, and urban impact conducted after the Games (cited in Cox et al., 1994) confirmed a profoundly negative impact on disadvantaged populations. In the period 1986–1992, new house prices rose by 250%, with an accompanying increase in the numbers of renters and widespread rent increases. There was also a significant decline in new subsidized housing developed under a government funding scheme involving community organizations as well as provincial and local government bodies. As the demands of Olympic construction took priority over subsidized housing, the pattern of outmigration of disadvantaged groups from the city was exacerbated, with a more than 50% increase in the number leaving in 1992 compared to 1986. Other post-Games social and economic concerns included sustaining long-term employment growth, a slump in the housing market, and public debt as a result of Olympic-related infrastructure costs (Cox et al., 1994, pp. 37–39).

Amsterdam, Netherlands

This city was an unsuccessful bidder for the 1992 Olympics, which were awarded to Barcelona. The well-organized coalition of opposition groups, called No Olympics Amsterdam, produced a detailed report on the potential problems in *The People's Bidbook*, which was formally presented to Samaranch in February 1986. Environmental, financial, and social concerns were paramount, including the proposed Olympic village location in a market gardening region, the threat to green areas and established vegetation, and lack of consideration for the historic structure of the city.

Like many protest groups, they called on politicians to give top priority to solving urgent social problems such as housing shortages and lack of funding for local recreational programs and facilities. Furthermore, they stated that there had been insufficient public consultation. Almost all of the locations had been selected without the participation of those affected, and protesters had been "dispersed violently" by the police. Citing earlier riots prompted by evictions of squatters, No Olympics Amsterdam warned that the authorities could expect violent resistance if they proceeded with the bid. They also pointed out that the Netherlands' business links with South Africa (at this time still under apartheid) could well result in boycotts if the Games were held in Amsterdam, with serious implications for Games budget projections and possible debt for the local government. In 1985, a protest group called Autonomen, adopting the slogan "No bread, no Games," destroyed flowerbeds that promoted Olympic bid "propaganda"; in a creative fund raising endeavor, they then sold photographs of their actions.

Calgary, Alberta

As was the case in other recent Olympics, the budget for Calgary's 1988 Winter Olympics could be read as either a profit or a loss, depending on the inclusion or exclusion of government money in the calculations. Like the 1998 audit of Sydney 2000's budget, a 1993 audit of Calgary's books showed an operating profit of $38 million (CAN) or an operating deficit of $14 million. Federal, provincial, and local governments spent about $461 million on the construction of the village and most of the facilities (Walkom, 1999).

As a result of Olympic construction, the university gained $103 million worth of facilities, including a new speed-skating rink, new student housing, and the expansion of the Physical Education building and the Saddledome Stadium—later home to professional sports teams. The lion's share of this construction budget was provided by the provincial and federal governments. A group of citizens called HALT (Human Action to Limit Taxes) protested this use of public money for largely professional sports facilities (Reasons, 1984). Similarly, in terms of post-Games legacy, bobsled, luge, and ski-jumping activities were not widely practised by local recreational users, many of whom were not able to afford the high admission prices to these facilities. The university's speed-skating rink, however, was opened to the general public.

One of the most widely known protests associated with the Calgary Games was mounted by First Nations people and their allies. The Lubicon band had a longstanding land claim involving resources and lands exploited by Petro Canada, a crown corporation that was one of the sponsors of the Olympic Torch relay. The protesters chanted "Shame the flame" as the relay passed by. When they tried to set up an information table on Lubicon land rights, they were picked up by the RCMP; one of the leaders reported that she left town during the Games rather than suffer continued RCMP harassment. Many protesters had been banned from the University of Calgary campus earlier when they had tried to engage in similar protests and educational actions during Olympic test events.

The problems of displacement and forced evictions of tenants in Calgary prior to the Games have been extensively documented (Olds, 1998). The existing Landlord and Tenant Act did nothing to prevent eviction without cause (given ninety days' notice) or rent increase of any size. Occupants of student residences, residential hotels, and rooming houses had no protection from eviction or rent increases. More than two thousand people were temporarily or permanently evicted to provide accommodation for Olympic visitors; financial incentives were offered to some tenants, but not to the one thousand university students.

The proposed siting of the Olympic Stadium in a low-income inner-city community adjacent to the site of the famous Calgary Stampede rodeo resulted in a controversy involving citizens' groups, professional sport representatives, and the organizing committee. As was the pattern in hallmark construction, the development application was accelerated through the usual approval process by a provincial government order-in-council, thus putting a speedy end to community consultation and the democratic process (Olds, 1998; Macintosh & Whitson, 1992). At the same time, some houses in this neighborhood, called "the near slum district" by one Olympic booster, were painted in order to enhance the tourist image.

In summary, as Olds convincingly argued, "The goals of a relatively powerless, low-income residential community next to one of the perceived 'engines' of economic and cultural significance in Calgary [the Calgary Stampede], in conjunction with a spectacle of international scale [the Olympics], had little hope of being achieved . . ." (Olds, 1998, p. 27).

Melbourne, Australia

This city was one of the unsuccessful candidates for the 1996 Olympics. During the 1989–1990 bid process, Toronto's BNC developed links with a Melbourne coalition of community groups with the same name. In May 1990, Melbourne BNC distributed an Alternative Bid Book similar to Toronto's People's Bid Book. With the motto "No Justice, no Games," Melbourne BNC called for a range of government initiatives related to employment, environment, health, housing, transport, and social services. The Alternative Bid Book identified the interests of the Melbourne bid committee: almost half were corporate representatives, and only one was a woman. Fifty percent of the $20 million (AUS) bid budget was provided by state government and city council funds, making the bid clearly a public concern, not simply a private business deal. The Bid Book also documented links between eleven corporate donors and/or companies represented on the bid committee, and their financial dealings with South Africa (still under apartheid in 1990) as well as the poor environmental records of twenty of these companies (Melbourne Bread Not Circuses, 1990).

The state government of Victoria promised $212 million in cash and land for the Olympics, while private business interests anticipated the usual profits, or, as the Melbourne critics explained it, the redistribution of wealth from the public to the private sector. Even though the government set up an Olympics Social Impact Assessment Panel during the bid process (in contrast to Sydney's neglect of social impact issues until after the Games were won), housing advocates were cynical in the absence of government commitment to act on the panel's findings. In a similar situation in 1998, the Toronto 2008 bid committee and Toronto Council failed to incorporate the

Olympic principles developed during community consultation into the bid (see chapter 4).

The Melbourne bid committee commissioned a social impact study in 1989, a year before the bid was submitted. On the question of potential negative impacts, it identified diversion of public funds from essential services, increases in housing costs and homelessness, a post-Games decline in employment, and environmental degradation. A 1990 Community Services Department report also predicted an increase in homelessness as a result of loss of single-room accommodation in the inner city. It recommended prioritizing of public housing construction and funding for community support services. In contrast, when Sydney faced the same problems in 1993, a government spokesperson claimed that it would be "a waste of taxpayers' money to do a major social impact assessment ahead of knowing whether we've got the bid or not" (Cronau, 1990).

A Melbourne housing worker, Greg Neville, identified the potential housing problems associated with Melbourne's plans. With 71,000 people on the public housing waiting list, he asked how the athletes' village—four thousand new units costing more than $350,000 each—would alleviate the housing crisis. He noted the need for rent control, especially for low-income tenants, and the problem that current infrastructure needs—transport, sewage, and water supply—were likely to be pushed down the list of priorities to pay for the Olympics (Neville, 1990). BNC's Alternative Bid Book also revealed that both the athletes' and media village sites had been earmarked for housing development well before the bid. Summing up this particular Olympic myth, it stated: "It's not new land. . . . It's not new housing. . . . It's not affordable housing" (Melbourne Bread Not Circuses, 1990).

Nagano, Japan

The Japanese group called the Anti-Olympic People's Network has been active since the late 1980s, initially in opposition to Nagano's successful bid for the 1998 Winter Games. One of their recent actions, a letter to Samaranch dated March 12, 1999, provides a concise summation of most anti-Olympic groups' concerns. Among its eleven reasons for demanding the dissolution of the IOC following the bribery scandal were the following:

- environmental destruction;
- huge and expensive facilities financed with taxpayers' money but not serving the needs of local communities;
- restrictions on citizens' freedom of movement and civil liberties during Olympics;

- Olympic venues and infrastructure given priority over more important public services;

- distortions in local economy and hindrance to sustainable economic development;

- students and children mobilized as "volunteers" and deprived of their rights under the Convention on the Rights of Children;

- corruption in the host city selection process;

- impossibility of democratizing sport under Samaranch;

- commercialism of athletes, sport, and sport venues, resulting in damage to individuals and the environment. (Anti-Olympic People's Network, 1999)

Berlin, Germany

The successful Berlin NOlympic group, organized in 1993, represented politicians, churches, labor unions, and academics who were opposed to Berlin's bid for the 2000 Olympics. Their activities ranged from lobbying and peaceful demonstration to direct action and sabotage. Like many activist groups, they drew attention to the problem of public money diverted from housing and social services to expensive Olympic projects, and the exacerbation of existing environmental problems. Their advertising efforts dwarfed the official bid campaign, as they plastered Berlin with anti-Olympic banners and slogans (Jennings, 1996, p. 188). They even spray-painted Olympic House in Lausanne, an act that no doubt soured IOC members toward Berlin's bid. Other actions included public "die-ins" on playing fields during international soccer tournaments and noisy demonstrations whenever IOC members visited the city. It is interesting to note a similar protest in Toronto when, on the eve of the IOC evaluation visit in 1990, unidentified protesters spray-painted all the bid committee's banners.

When the IOC selection committee visited Berlin, its chair agreed to the request to meet with leaders of the Berlin group to discuss their concerns. A protest demonstration of between ten and fifteen thousand people also took place during the visit. However, according to the IOC evaluation report: "The Commission feels that whilst vocal opposition to the bid does exist, this is a minority group. The majority of the population supports the bid" (IOC 2000 City Bid, 1993). While it is difficult to believe that the IOC dismissed a protest of this size so quickly, there is evidence from other cities—Toronto, for example—of the IOC's overall reluctance to validate Olympic resistance by admitting that such groups have had any influence over their decision making.

The Greens, a political party active in Europe, Australia, and elsewhere, participated in Berlin's anti-Olympic efforts, and, more recently, were reported to have disclosed details of Samaranch's and fifty-six other IOC members' visits, which cost the Berlin bid committee $1.53 million (Demands for Samaranch, 1999). In Rome, too, Green Party members in 1997 joined the alliance opposing the bid for 2004, primarily on environmental grounds, while in Sydney in 1999, a Green member introduced a bill to protect tenants from eviction and rent gouging during the 2000 Olympics.

Salt Lake City, Utah

While there is little evidence of organized anti-Olympic groups in the 1980s during Salt Lake City's various bids for Winter Olympics, the discussion in chapter 1 showed that many individuals, including SLOC board member and whistle blower Ken Bullock, had been raising ethical and financial issues for years.

Four years before the bribery scandal, the Olympic watchdog group, Utahns for Responsible Public Spending (URPS), led by Steve Pace, had tried to get an Olympic-related question on the state ballot. In December 1998, Pace was quick to criticize the bid committee's "scholarship" program in an often repeated quote: "This looks like, walks like and quacks like a bribe" (Pace quoted in Gorrell, 1998b). The group delivered a cake with a protruding metal file to SLOC's December 19 meeting, with Pace "half-joking" to journalists that someone would need the file after the U.S. Justice Department review.

A coalition of minority, antipoverty, women's, and disability rights groups—Salt Lake Impact 2002 and Beyond—was formed in 1995 to address issues such as post-Games affordable housing, diversification of SLOC, conflict of interest on the board, and protection of civil liberties of street people during the Games. The group called for SLOC resignations in December 1998 and again in January 1999, as well as proposing a more open and public process with relation to SLOC documents and board meetings. In a letter to Governor Mike Leavitt, the group demanded the resignations of two board trustees whose business enterprises—a construction company and a ski resort—benefited from the Olympics (Heilprin, 1999).

In February, the more radical URPS responded to the SLBE report in a detailed press release that described it as "a total coverup of SLOC trustee responsibility" (Pace, 1999b). URPS subsequently received approval from the Utah governor to distribute a citizen initiative petition in order to put the following measure on the 2000 ballot: "The state of Utah shall not indemnify, guarantee, or reimburse the debt or obligations incurred by any organization, public or private, to host, solicit, organize, schedule, conduct, book, or operate the Olympic Winter Games in the State of Utah" (Pace, 1999a).

Such a measure, if successful, would challenge the 1991 contract between the state and the IOC concerning its responsibility for Olympic shortfalls. By April 1999, the group had gathered three thousand of the required 35,000 signatures. Some Olympic boosters, however, strongly objected to this democratic project. In a February 22 news release, Pace documented statements made on air by KALL 910 radio host Tom Barberi, who routinely conducted personal attacks on Pace. Barberi had urged listeners to sign URPS petitions using false or forged names, to "drive the Lt. Governor's office crazy" and to sabotage the petition drive. Pace requested the lieutenant governor to investigate this subversion of Utah electoral law (Pace, 1999c). For his part, Barberi cited his First Amendment rights and claimed that Pace's action was a publicity stunt (Gorrell, 1999c).

A group called Utah Citizens for True Repentance (CTR) was established by Mike Ridgway, a Mormon, in early 1999. Although not endorsed by the Mormon church, Ridgway used its "Choose the Right" directive to support his position that Salt Lake City should give back the Games so that church members would not be forever branded as cheats (Fantin, 1999b). The official position, however, was that the Mormon Church was supportive of the Olympics and satisfied with the proposed SLOC reforms.

Salt Lake City's Mormon religion and heritage produced an unexpected threat to Olympic boosters in 1998 with the formation of an advocacy group called Tapestry of Polygamy to address the physical and sexual abuse of girls and women in some Mormon communities. In 1999, state senator Scott Howell introduced a bill to target polygamy; arguing that this was a civil rights issue for the girls and women and involved, Howell warned: "We've got all the world coming to town for the Olympics. Do we really want to be known as the place where we let old men marry little girls?" For their part, some of the Tapestry women said they intended to use the opportunity provided by the 2002 Olympics to tell their stories to the international media (Egan, 1999).

The International Network Against Olympic Games

In 1998, four European groups organized the International Network Against Olympic Games and Commercial Sports, primarily to oppose their countries' bids for the 2006 Winter Games, in Turin and Trieste, Italy, Helsinki, Finland, and Poprad-Tatry, Slovakia. Their opposition was based, for the most part, on environmental concerns—not surprisingly in view of the generally negative impact of Winter Olympics on alpine villages and venues, as seen, for example, in Nagano. Toronto BNC was invited to join the Network in December 1998, and did so under the category of an Olympic critic rather than a member group, since at that early stage, BNC had not declared a position for or against the Toronto 2008 bid (although it clearly qualified as an anti-Olympic group in 1989–1990).

The larger aim of the International Network was to address problems caused by Olympics and commercial sports, and to bring about radical change to end the Olympics as presently constituted. Electronic communication, specifically e-mail correspondence and web sites, facilitated cheap and speedy international networking between groups in Nagano, Sydney, Toronto, Salt Lake City, and elsewhere.

In this venture, the International Network carried on the work begun by groups in Melbourne, Atlanta, Toronto, and elsewhere ten years earlier, when international connections and information sharing had been developed without the benefits of electronic networks. At that time, BNC stressed that their opposition to Toronto's 1996 bid was in no way NIMBYism (Not In My Back Yard); rather, BNC challenged the imposing of the Olympics, as presently constituted, on *any* city's residents. BNC's political project was global as well as local: to forge links between Olympic watchdog groups around the world, to exchange information, resources, strategies, and personnel—in short, to develop an anti-Olympic solidarity movement. For example, it was at this time that BNC and the Atlanta Task Force for the Homeless began a collaborative relationship that continued into the late 1990s with BNC's critique of the 2008 Toronto bid (Borowy, 1999).

Other examples of international networking include Anita Beaty's 1998 visit to Sydney where she made a number of presentations to community groups, politicians, and participants at a national housing conference. One outcome of her visit was a memorial service, similar to one held in Atlanta, for more than two hundred homeless people who had died in Sydney in the preceding three years. Beaty and the legal director of Georgia's American Civil Liberties Union (ACLU) also visited Salt Lake City in 1999 to speak at a public forum organized by Salt Lake Impact 2002 and Beyond, Utah Housing Coalition, and Utah ACLU. During my Sydney visit in April 1999, I brought news of BNC activities to Shelter New South Wales, Rentwatchers, the Nongovernmental Task Force on Homelessness, Greenpeace, and GGW 2000, and in return took their news, information, and reports back to Toronto. In short, in the face of rhetoric that claimed Olympic monopoly over "international understanding," these groups embarked on their own international exchange projects (Borowy, 1999).

The International Network's statement specified that those with nationalist or extreme right-wing arguments were not welcome. Similarly, the Turin group noted that it was nonviolent, and while the Helsinki group made reference to "direct action," this was obviously in the Greenpeace tradition of nonviolence and civil disobedience. In the case of Toronto BNC, the only instances of violence involved BNC members as the recipients, not the perpetrators: harassing phone calls, death threats, and libellous media attacks on individual members by rabid Olympic boosters were routine in 1989–1990 and again in the late 1990s (Borowy, 1999; Shapcott, 1999).

The Helsinki group was organized in 1997 to spark public debate about the IOC, the threat to the environment, and the use of public money. Their position statement included a critique of Helsinki's marketing slogan of "equality and sustainability" as a public relations gag. Noting that cities with "strong opposition" are seldom selected, they cited opinion polls from 1997–1998 reporting that 30% of Finns were already opposed to the Helsinki bid; the IOC, on the other hand, noted the *support* of approximately 70% of the population in its evaluation report for Helsinki (IOC City Bid, 1998).

Like the Japanese group, the Anti-Olympic Committee of Finland wrote to Samaranch to express their critique and concerns. Their notably less restrained letter dated November 14, 1998, ten days before the Salt Lake City disclosures, made reference to all the issues of IOC hierarchy, elitism, corruption, conflict of interest, commercialism, etc. that a few weeks later were the focus of international attention. It concluded with an unequivocal message:

> Radical direct action is growing in Finland. Campaigns including direct
> actions are raised more and more against massive projects damaging the
> environment and violating the principles of democracy. IOC can't expect
> to be able to carry through the Olympic Games in Finland without
> resistance. The Anti Olympic Committee wants the IOC to retire and
> give up irritating decent people with its corrupt games. (Anti-Olympic
> Committee of Finland, 1998)

Given the fact that Sion was the favorite largely because of its location in Switzerland, home to the IOC, the announcement of Turin's win was a surprise to many observers, who then attributed the decision to IOC members' anti-Swiss (more specifically, anti-Hodler) sentiments. Moreover, Turin's success was a bitter disappointment to its Nolimpiadi Committee, which had been campaigning against the bid because of the threat to the environment posed by the construction of ski courses, roads, hotels, and housing.

THE UNIVERSITY CONNECTION

There are two key dimensions to the relationship between universities and the Olympic industry: firstly, university administrations' complicity in the Olympic industry, and secondly, resistance to that complicity, and to the Olympic industry in general, organized by students, staff, and faculty. The central role of students in the Mexico City protest has already been discussed. While it may be accurate to view the 1960s as the peak of student protest in North America, Europe, and elsewhere, it is important to recognize the continuous history of university-based political radicalism, prompted by both external and internal injustices.

From the perspective of the Olympic industry, the creeping corporatization of North American universities made them fertile grounds for Olympic "partnerships." Whereas university buildings and facilities used to be named after dead White men, they now increasingly bear the names of multinational corporations or living (White) millionaires. Canadian critics have noted the recent change from the university as a public institution promoting academic freedom and public debate to a private, profit-making organization controlled by corporate elites. At the University of Toronto (U of T) and elsewhere, when these corporate leaders are also university governors, they are in clear conflict-of-interest situations as they make decisions about tuition fees and university spending priorities (Schmidt, 1998; The corporate shuffle, 1999). And when overlapping corporate elites control bid committees and universities, there are equally serious consequences. It is not coincidental that free university tuition for family members was one of the favors sought by IOC members and/or offered by bid committees; university administrators and governors who also served on bid committees were well placed to facilitate such arrangements.

An ongoing conflict-of-interest debate at the U of T has direct implications for the university/Olympic industry connection. President Robert Prichard had been under attack since 1993 by medical faculty, students, nonsmokers' rights groups, and others, because of his directorship in Imasco Ltd., owner of Imperial Tobacco, which controls about 60% of Canada's tobacco industry. A U of T research team's report on youth smoking addiction specifically identified Pritchard as an example of the tobacco industry's strategic board appointments and the universities' "institutional addiction" to tobacco money, despite the fact that a university with a medical school has a clear mandate to improve community health. The report recommended that universities and hospitals sever all links with tobacco companies in light of evidence of the industry's unethical behavior (Papp, 1999). There are clear parallels with the Olympic example: a university with a mandate to promote ethical business practices should not form partnerships with the unethical Olympic industry. However, there is little indication that universities will respond to either of these moral imperatives.

Bid committees have often chosen universities as sites for Olympic activities and accommodations in the hope of a mutually beneficial arrangement: enhanced sport facilities and student housing for the university, and a more generous injection of state and federal money into the Olympic budget. These outcomes have benefited the small and mostly privileged sector of the population who were university students, staff, and faculty, at a significant cost to the public purse. A minority of North American and Australian universities have allowed local residents some access to their recreation facilities, while the majority have either excluded nonuniversity members or charged an entry fee. Hence, to call university sport facilities an Olympic legacy for the community is somewhat misleading.

As already noted, the 1988 Calgary Winter Olympics provided a university "legacy" of facilities largely funded by public money and subsequently used, with a few notable exceptions, by professional teams and university and national level athletes. In Atlanta, the Atlanta University Center benefited from new and renovated athletic facilities, while at Georgia Tech, the Olympic Aquatic Center, minus its water polo pool and much of the spectator seating, was used for student recreation and swimming competition after the Games. Georgia Tech and Georgia State Universities both gained dormitory facilities for more than two thousand students. Only 17% of the cost was provided by the Atlanta Committee for the Olympic Games, with the remainder financed by the University System of Georgia (French & Disher, 1997). Not all the legacy was positive: three of the dormitory buildings proved to have defective foundations, and the University System of Georgia (and taxpayers) were subsequently liable for dealing with these problems (Rutheiser, 1996).

When the BNC coalition began organizing in Toronto in 1989, a number of university-based groups, including the U of T Women's Center and a branch of the Canadian Union of Educational Workers, joined the group of endorsers. U of T's Graduate Student Union and the York University branch of the Ontario Public Interest Research Group (OPIRG) also joined in 1998, and many students, staff, and faculty were associated with the coalition throughout its existence.

OPIRG's activities included public meetings, Internet exchanges, and distribution of a brochure titled "Why does Toronto need an Olympics?" in November 1998. At that time, TOBid was still considering using York campus for Olympic housing and sports venues. The key questions raised in this publication are relevant to any university associated with a bid:

- Will students be denied residency or removed from residency?
- Will students pay an Olympic levy on tuition?

- Who is paying for any cost overruns?
- What access will students have during the Olympics and preparations?
- Will York attempt to win favor by granting honorary degrees?

On this last point, it noted that IOC president Samaranch had received honorary degrees during past bid processes—in 1990, for example, from a Tokyo university. However, any illusion that Toronto university administrations would heed campus protest on this issue had been shattered in November 1997 at U of T, when widespread opposition to former U.S. president George Bush's honorary degree was ignored. More than a thousand protesters, surrounded by mounted police and security, assembled outside the hall where the Bush convocation was held. Over thirty professors in academic gowns, led by peace activist Dr. Ursula Franklin, walked out in the middle of the ceremony in a planned protest. Two months before the convocation, information was leaked to student newspapers that Bush was a member of the international advisory committee for Barrick Gold, one of two companies that were donating $6.4 million (CAN) to the university. This connection, as well as Bush's relationship to various human rights atrocities, prompted the mass protest.

The OPIRG brochure identified York's president, two sport administrators, and one governor who were members of the TOBid Committee. Corresponding overlaps for the U of T included the president, the chancellor, one administrator, three governors, and a fundraising committee member. In total, twenty-three of the 103-member bid committee had overlapping university involvement. Among those with university affiliations and powerful positions on the bid committee was Steve Hudson, chair of TOBid executive; in his other role, he was president of Newcourt Credit, North America's second largest non-bank lending institution, a job that paid $4.2 million in salary and bonus in 1995 (Ferguson, 1999). Richard Pound, a member of TOBid until the end of 1998, was named the next chancellor of McGill University in Montreal, where he had served on the board of governors since 1986. The university's press release noted that Pound had "excellent international and Canadian stature" (IOC's Pound, 1999)—the former probably carrying more weight in the age of the corporate university.

Prior to the January 23 release of the IOC Commission of Inquiry's first report, U of T compiled a list of eight faculty members for media contact. While admittedly not a complete list, it fell short of the UNSW Center for Olympic Studies' 1997 directory of sixty-five—evidence that hosting the Olympics helped to generate academic interest in Olympic-related issues. Two faculty from U of T's Rotman School of Business, whose names were on the list, had a special interest in promoting a positive image of the IOC: Leonard Brooks had completed a consulting contract, including work on a code of conduct, with the COA and Richard Leblanc was working with Olympic Advocates Together Honorably (OATH), a group of Olympic athletes seeking IOC reform.

Star ombudsperson Don Sellar subsequently documented discussions between *Star* sports writer Randy Starkman and Brooks about ethical issues involving the public relations firm Hill and Knowlton working for both the IOC and TOBid. Brooks had explained that it was essential to have a "firewall" to prevent exchanges of inside information (Starkman, 1999f). When Starkman asked Brooks about Carol Anne Letheren's consultancy with the 1996 Toronto bid committee, he stated that he didn't have enough information to make a judgment. Starkman later discovered from old COA documents that Brooks had a 1997 contract with COA, under Letheren's leadership, to write a code of conduct; Brooks claimed to have told Starkman, who did not recall or have written notes on the issue. Sellar concluded that, regardless of Brooks's and Starkman's conflicting recollections of these events, it was important for readers to know that such a contract existed (Sellar, 1999).

In Barcelona, the university connection was firmly established in 1995, when the IOC and the Autonomous University of Barcelona signed an agreement that created the International Chair in Olympic Studies. Two IOC and two university representatives served on the Chair's Coordination Commission, and it was administered by the Center for Olympic and Sport Studies, a consortium formed by the University, Barcelona Provincial Council, Barcelona City Council, and the Spanish Olympic Committee. The purpose of the chair was to promote "research into, training in and dissemination of the ideal of the Olympic Movement at the university level, as well as cooperation between the Olympic movement and universities (International Chair, 1997). With these structural arrangements, there was clearly not an arm's length relationship between the IOC and the center.

In 1995, the chair collaborated with the University System of Georgia (United States) and the Georgia Public Telecommunication Commission to produce a distance learning course titled "The Impact of the Olympic Movement." In 1998, it organized the World Congress for Sport for All in Barcelona, as well as other symposia, in collaboration with the IOC Museum, which focused on Olympic ceremonies, Olympic villages, television, and the Internet. In 1995, the chair began offering a credit course on Olympism, sport, and society, and subsequently developed a second course on Olympics in the information age. A Sport Marketing and Sponsorship course has been offered to sport professionals since 1995, and a diploma in sports communication and marketing since 1998. It was a copublisher of *The Keys to Success* (Moragas & Botella, 1995) as well as several other books.

With Sydney as the site of the 2000 Olympics, university interest is high. All universities and postsecondary institutions in the Sydney area have some involvement, including the following functions: accommodating athletes and officials, leasing pre-training facilities to teams, training volunteer interpreters, housing noncredentialled media, and leasing student housing, meeting rooms, and conference facilities to visitors (A degree, 1999). General volunteers will be trained by the Department of Technical and Further Education, and volunteer recruitment drives were conducted in all universities in 1998–1999. Sydney University and SOCOG began negotiations in April 1999 to secure new university student housing—an expensive high-rise development within easy access of the Homebush Olympic site—as accommodation for 1,300 technical officials during the Games (Moore, 1999d). All universities are to be closed during the Olympics to allow students to volunteer—but they will be open during the Paralympics.

The Center for Olympic Studies at UNSW with its sixty-five faculty affiliates has the most Olympic involvement of all Sydney area universities. Established in 1996, the Center was funded largely by the university, as well as by donations and publication sales revenue. The center has sponsored conferences and symposia including the Green Games, The Olympic Athlete, the Olympics in the Next Millennium, the Cultural Olympiad, and Aborigines and the Games. Two courses developed and taught by center head Richard Cashman and executive director Tony Hughes—The Olympics: The Event and its Impact, and The Modern Olympics—usually attracted large numbers of students, some of whom went on to internships with the Olympic Coordination Authority (OCA). Future links between the center and the AOC and the IOC were explored in the late 1990s, the latter initially for the purpose of producing a Directory of Australian Olympic Research. However, in light of the Autonomous University of Barcelona example, such arrangements might impose limitations on the center's potential role as Olympic critic.

A more disturbing example of university Olympic involvement was disclosed in May 1999, when a document obtained by a Sydney daily newspaper showed that the UNSW vice-chancellor, John Niland, on behalf of the university, had applied to purchase a twenty-seat corporate box at a cost of $245,000 (not including the required catering package) for the duration of the 2000 Olympics and Paralympics. Part of Niland's stated rationale was to use the occasion to host an educational round-table for leaders of sixteen top universities, including Oxford, Cambridge, Harvard, Stanford, Toronto, Edinburgh, Glasgow, and Hong Kong. These (mostly) men were invited to attend Olympic events as well as the conference largely at UNSW expense (Porter, 1999). An equally important rationale for the box was to promote fund raising by rewarding past donors and encouraging others to support the university using the lure of prime seats at Olympic events (A degree of help, 1999). Without an invitation to a corporate suite, a person seeking the best seats for the opening ceremonies would expect to pay $1,382 per ticket.

Niland asked SOCOG for support for the application because of UNSW's contribution to SOCOG and the Olympic movement—presumably through the Center for Olympic Studies, the OCA internships, etc. He also drew attention to university administrators' general interest in promoting Australia as the "clever country" during the Olympics by using the opportunity to recruit international students (Uni's suite deal, 1999; A degree of help, 1999). UNSW was, however, the only university to purchase a corporate suite.

Not surprisingly, protest was quick to follow. As the newspaper article pointed out, three university departments, including the widely recognized Faculty of Mathematics, had been under threat of closure a month earlier because of student levels and funding. The future of student associations was also in jeopardy at the time because of federal government plans to introduce voluntary rather than mandatory student union fees. In this generally bleak climate, an arbitrary expenditure of this amount of money on a largely public relations gesture generated extensive student and faculty criticism, notwithstanding UNSW administrators' argument that the benefits would far exceed the expense and Niland's press release, "UNSW's Olympic suite an investment" (1999), which made the same argument.

A group of students organized a mock Olympics satirizing the vice-chancellor, and academic staff subsequently suggested events such as "The 70 Hour Work Week Marathon—winner gets to do it again next week, so do the losers" and "Swallow the Managerialist Hype Iron Person Race." On a more serious note, at the May 18 and May 26 general meetings of the UNSW branch of the National Tertiary Education Union, academic staff unanimously passed the following two resolutions:

- This meeting condemns UNSW management for paying exorbitant sums for a Stadium Australia suite for the Olympic Games 2000. This decision is particularly insulting given the failure by management to allocate adequate funding for salaries.

- That this meeting resolves to hold a stop work meeting of all members on Tuesday 1 June 1999 . . . for a protest at the Vice-Chancellor's forum over (a) the lack of an improved salary offer and failure to reach agreement in the current round of enterprise bargaining, despite seven months of bargaining, and (b) the low priority given to staff salaries in the University's spending as indicated by the recent purchase of an Olympic Suite. (UNSW Branch, 1999)

On the general question of Olympic benefits, Tony Hughes's more realistic assessment, cited in a May 1999 *Herald* article, was that universities would only make "miniscule" financial gains compared to the resources—the student and staff volunteers—that they were putting into the Games (A degree of help, 1999).

CONCLUSION

The successes of some anti-Olympic and Olympic watchdog organizations, while limited, provide hope for future interventions aimed at stopping the seemingly inexorable progress of the Olympic machine. However, with the huge public relations budgets at the disposal of Olympic boosters, the challenge to grassroots protesters is formidable.

The task facing Olympic resisters goes beyond ensuring community involvement in publicly subsidized hallmark events. If it were simply a matter of demanding democratic decision making, it is unlikely that Olympic watchdog groups would be the targets of ongoing harassment, innuendo, and vilification. Rather, this has become an ideological battle. The pseudo-religious rhetoric of the Olympic industry, while obscuring the negative social, political, and environmental impact that has been the fallout of most recent Olympic Games, delivers a clear "Olympic spirit" message: to criticize or oppose Olympic bids and preparations is to be unpatriotic, to lack civic pride, and, most seriously, to betray the young athletes who are the "heart and soul" of the Olympics. Finally, university collusion in the Olympic industry—one more feature of the creeping corporatization of universities—has a chilling effect on critical research, open debate, and campus activism. In short, all these factors disempower citizens, while providing fertile ground for extravagant Olympic promises to evolve into long-lasting financial burdens.

7

Resistance in
Atlanta and Sydney
bread, not circuses

L IKE TORONTO, ATLANTA WAS A CITY favored to win the 1996 Summer
Olympics. The organized opposition to the Toronto bid has been discussed in detail in chapter 4. Unfortunately, in the case of Atlanta, community groups such as the Metro Atlanta Task Force for the Homeless did not
mobilize until after the city was awarded the Olympics in 1990, and as task
force co-director Anita Beaty often pointed out, this was a serious mistake.
As early as 1990, Atlanta's working poor and homeless people began to experience the negative impact of Olympic preparations, and their suffering continued until at least the end of the decade. In fact, it could be argued that
Atlanta surpassed most other recent host cities in the degree of direct damage inflicted on disadvantaged populations.

The usual rhetoric about "Olympics as opportunity" was present in
politicians' and organizers' public statements during the Atlanta bid process.
From city council members to former president Jimmy Carter, Georgia residents heard promises of solving a range of social problems—homelessness,
crime, poverty, drug abuse, and teen pregnancy—as a result of the Olympic
project. The occasional references to improving the "image" of Atlanta, however, implied quite a different political agenda—one borne out by subsequent events.

In one of the most comprehensive critiques of Atlanta politics during this period, urban anthropologist Charles Rutheiser used the term *imagineering* to describe the process by which the Atlanta Committee for the Olympic Games (ACOG) and other private business elites engineered an image of Atlanta as a world-class city, "the human rights capital of the world," and a city "too busy to hate" (Rutheiser, 1996, pp. 227–231). Undivided community support and corporate backing for the bid were central components of this image. Critics were dismissed as "having the wrong attitude" and "lacking cooperative spirit" (Sheehan & Buggs, 1995, p. 4; Rutheiser, 1996, p. 241). Mayor Bill Campbell, for example, resorted to the usual defense by urging critics to remember, "You are filling a glass that was completely empty and complaining that it is not to the brim" (quoted in Sheehan & Buggs, 1995, p. 4). And, in his own imagineering in 1995, the only Black member of the ACOG executive, former Atlanta mayor Andrew Young claimed: "These will be the affirmative action Olympics. Atlanta can become the center for the export of Southern idealism" (Young quoted in Longman, 1995). However, as Rutheiser and others have convincingly demonstrated, the Olympics in fact served to exacerbate social problems and deepen existing divides among residents: Black and White, rich and poor, inner city and suburban, immigrant and nonimmigrant.

SOCIAL PROBLEMS

When Olympic preparations began in the early 1990s, housing and related economic issues were central concerns for both organizers and critics. In September 1992, when the Olympic flag arrived, five thousand protesters assembled to draw public attention to the costs of hosting the Games and the limited benefits to Atlantans. The organized labor movement also marched in protest at ACOG's failure to make a commitment to use union labor for construction of venues. Their fears were well justified: ACOG used extensive day laborers, recruited at homeless shelters, as well as illegal immigrants (Rutheiser, 1996). In 1992–1993, the task force and other advocacy groups succeeded in getting city and state legislation regulating labor pools in order to address the pressing problems of very low wages and hazardous working conditions. However, as of 1999, the legislation had not been enforced and the only cases litigated were brought by public sector attorneys (Beaty, 1999b).

In December 1992, about a hundred members of the Atlanta Olympic Conscience Coalition—whose members included neighborhood groups, labor, students, Black clergy, and homeless advocates—held a protest inside

the ACOG offices, and left with promises of regular community consultations, which ultimately proved to be "empty rhetorical exercises" (Beaty,
1999b). This coalition, together with Atlanta Neighborhoods United for
Fairness and the Metropolitan Atlanta Task Force for the Homeless, were the
most active protest groups from 1992 on.

The huge number of homeless people on Atlanta streets and in shelters,
along with the poor state of existing low income housing, made this a central concern for advocacy groups. At the time of the bid, 30% of the population lived below the poverty line and estimates of the number of homeless
people ranged from 22,000 to 28,000 (Beaty, 1999a). For its part, the city,
under Mayor Maynard Jackson's leadership, established the Corporation for
Olympic Development in Atlanta (CODA) in 1992; this was a nonprofit,
quasi-public organization with the mandate to organize, fund, and imple-
ment the masterplan to revitalize neighborhoods near Olympic venues.

As Rutheiser explained, Jackson was promoting "the by no means novel,
but certainly dated, notion that the elected government officials should have
a major say in shaping major redevelopment projects within city boundaries"
(Rutheiser, 1996, p. 245). In very similar scenarios in Sydney and Salt Lake
City, elected representatives who also served on Olympic organizing committees—in the case of SOCOG, as its president—experienced conflicting pressures to represent taxpayers' interests, on the one hand, and to maximize
Olympic profits, on the other. Moreover, given the axiom in planning circles
that the Olympics are first and foremost an urban development project
(Sudjic, 1992), it follows that elected representatives should have a central role
in the decision-making process in order to protect the public good.

CODA's efforts at community revitalization, like many other Olympic-
related initiatives in Atlanta, produced mixed results. In its 1995 report, the
Task Force for the Homeless listed numerous broken promises, including
neighborhood involvement in decision making, no displacement of low-
income people, and rehabilitation of public housing. The report even used
Olympic boosters' own language in an attempt to make corporate and political leaders recognize the homelessness emergency, by calling on them to take
the opportunity to prove that Atlanta cared about disadvantaged people. As
Anita Beaty reflected in 1998, task force members had naively believed that
it was reasonable to ask the city to develop a humane housing plan in order
"to present the city's best face" to Olympic visitors and the world. In 1989
during the bid process, when there was already serious unmet need (30% too
few beds for homeless people), the task force developed three "bottom lines":
no loss of current shelter or accommodation beds, no cutbacks to emergency
services, and no erosion of human and civil rights.

The task force proposed that all homeless people should be provided with safe accommodation: emergency shelter during the Olympics and permanent low-income housing created out of the athletes' and media villages afterward (Beaty, 1999a). Atlanta Olympic organizers ignored all of these "bottom lines." Four shelters were lost, and church basements formerly used by the homeless were converted into backpacker accommodations during the Games. Human services organizations were offered financial incentives to convert their services for two weeks to accommodate tourists rather than low-income people, and some agencies accepted offers of free Olympic tickets and other benefits (Beaty, 1998b).

Atlanta serves as an illuminating case study of negative social impact, as Olympic construction and preparations took a heavy toll on already disadvantaged populations. About fifteen thousand residents were evicted from two of the oldest public housing projects in the United States when five thousand units were demolished to make way for Olympic accommodation. Only 30% of about two hundred new houses and townhouses were affordable, in an area where the average annual income was only $7,800. The task force estimated that a total of 9,500 units of affordable housing were lost between 1990 and 1995, and $350 million in public funds was diverted from much-needed low-income housing, social services, and other support services for homeless and poor people to Olympic preparations during the same period (Beaty, 1999a). One year before the Games, apartment rents rose by 20–25% and many tenants were told that their leases would expire before the Games, as landlords planned to reap high profits from the influx of tourists. Atlanta lacked rent controls and in fact allowed landlords to evict tenants with only seven days' notice.

One of the few successful protest initiatives was prompted by the organizing committee's proposal to locate Olympic volleyball in Cobb County, a region with openly homophobic policies. Opposition organized by the Olympics out of Cobb Coalition in November 1995 resulted in the relocation of the volleyball competition. While not detracting from this victory for lesbians, gays, bisexuals, and their allies, it is important to recognize that groups advocating for this particular form of social justice had more success in stopping the Olympic machine than organizations working on behalf of low-income and homeless African Americans. In the latter case, protesters achieved a small victory by standing in front of bulldozers in order to save a neighborhood day care center, which is now located in the middle of acres of parking lot (Beaty, 1999b).

THE STADIUM CONTROVERSY

From the outset, controversy surrounded the $209 million Olympic Stadium to be built in the suburb of Summerhill, one of the oldest Black neighborhoods in Atlanta. Following the 1960s construction of the highway, the Atlanta-Fulton Stadium and parking lots, and the displacement of 10,000 residents, little remained of this formerly thriving Black community. Summerhill neighborhood groups, some of the earliest organized Olympic critics, mobilized as soon as the venue was announced in 1990, and their actions included a candlelit vigil outside Billy Payne's home in the exclusive Atlanta suburb of Dunwoody.

However, by 1992, Summerhill Neighborhood Inc. and the Neighborhood Planning Unit, rather than opposing the stadium, developed a plan to use its construction to revitalize the neighborhood. Their proposals included a limit on parking spaces, a share in parking revenues, and the construction of a retail complex for the community. Secret negotiations resulted in a plan released in February 1993 that failed to incorporate any of neighborhood groups' proposals; in fact, it gave the Atlanta Braves, the future stadium owners, total control and almost all the parking revenues, as well as 3,500 more parking spaces than originally planned. These events amply demonstrated the contempt of a predominantly White and wealthy executive committee toward a low-income Black neighborhood group.

An alliance of Black Democrats and antitax Republicans, led by Martin Luther King III, a Fulton County commissioner, mounted a campaign against the plan and its unfair impact on county taxpayers. King also critiqued ACOG's "greed, exclusivity and elitism" as well as its exploitation of the symbol of his father to sell Atlanta. For their part, as Rutheiser explained, ACOG members viewed the "free" stadium as "an act of civic philanthropy not appreciated by their critics" (p. 252)—a classic response from the privileged White majority. Not surprisingly, in the subsequent negotiations, ACOG made fewer concessions than the stadium opponents, who eventually agreed to a revised agreement that limited taxpayer liability, reduced parking spaces and provided 8.5% of parking revenues for community development. In fact, in Beaty's assessment, King compromised in exchange for mere "crumbs," which the neighborhood did not even receive (Beaty, 1999b). ACOG agreed to hire more Black administrators and contractors, but, shortly after this agreement was reached, it hired the Black woman who was serving as president of CODA to fill the new position of senior policy advisor, thus clearly demonstrating cooptation at work.

THE CRIMINALIZATION OF POVERTY

A trend that Task Force for the Homeless leaders termed "the criminalization of poverty" showed clear signs of escalating shortly after Atlanta won the bid. Atlantans already had experience with "street sweeps" during hallmark events; the task force documented the jailing of homeless people for three to six days during the Super Bowl, the Democratic National Convention, and even the Lutheran Young People's Conference (Beaty, 1999a). City ordinances adopted in 1991 criminalized a wide range of common survival strategies of people living in poverty: "aggressive" panhandling, loitering, "camping" in public, "remaining" in a parking lot without having a car parked there, being in an abandoned building, washing a car windshield, urinating in public, and generally acting "in a manner not worthy of a law-abiding citizen." A bylaw prohibiting lying down on a park bench was repealed in 1993 as a result of the efforts of the task force, the American Civil Liberties Union (ACLU), and other advocacy groups. Park benches were then renovated so that an arm every three feet prevented people from lying down. Spikes placed around trees stopped public urination, and there were no public toilets.

In 1993, there was an unsuccessful attempt to criminalize poverty at the state level: the "Trash Bill" would have made it unlawful to remove any item from a county-provided trash container, with a fine of up to $100. Some Atlanta restauranteurs tried to drive away homeless people by pouring chlorine bleach over the leftover food in the dumpsters (SpoilSport, 1996).

A 1994 measure passed by Georgia's general assembly empowered police to enforce the county loitering ordinance by arresting violators on site; formerly, police had simply cited violators, who were arrested only if the court found them guilty. The arrests of more than nine thousand homeless African American men—who not coincidentally made up about 90% of homeless people in Atlanta—under these ordinances were recorded by the task force. In light of these statistics, Beaty's term—"ethnic cleansing"—to describe the gentrification of downtown areas and the increased policing of urban space is chillingly accurate (Beaty, 1998b). This is not to suggest that city or state officials actually targeted African Americans; their targets were homeless people. However, regardless of intent, in a social context where racism and classism constitute powerful interlocking systems of oppression, the outcome is the same.

A flyer circulating among Atlanta's homeless people in 1996 explained their rights: It was "legal" to be homeless, and "police can't arrest you in a public place if you: sleep, smell bad, talk to yourself, eat garbage." However, you could be arrested if you "beg, cause a disturbance, obstruct a sidewalk, spit on a sidewalk, urinate" (Blount, 1996). While on the one hand Olympic organizers boasted that Atlanta was among the top American cities for business, the National Law Center on Homelessness and Poverty included Atlanta in the five American cities with the "meanest streets" (Hulchanski, 1998). Clearly, the criteria used to evaluate Olympic impact need to include the view from "the bottom of the food chain."

The task force report pointed out the cost to the taxpayer—$57 per day—of using the city jail as a shelter for homeless people arrested under these draconian measures. Significantly, a new jail was one of the first Olympic construction projects to be completed. However, it appeared that police and city officials used the ordinances to legitimize harassment and exploitation of homeless people rather than to provide them with the benefits of "free" shelter in jail. A system of "community courts" was established to process ordinance offenders who, rather than being imprisoned, were sentenced to perform free community service such as cleaning the streets.

In 1995, the ACLU represented Phillip Williams, a homeless man, in challenging the constitutionality of Atlanta's ordinance prohibiting "remaining in a parking lot." It was claimed that the law violated Williams's constitutional right to travel and free association. Evidence was presented to show that 43% of 115 people arrested during a four-month period were marginally homeless. Williams had been threatened twice, and arrested and jailed overnight for past violations, and claimed in his appeal that his status as a shelter resident and therefore technically a homeless person made him susceptible to future arrests (*Williams v. City of Atlanta*, 1995).

In another official "cleanup" initiative in 1995 and 1996, Atlanta police implemented the city's goal of driving homeless people out of town. Hundreds were taken by truck to the outskirts of the city and threatened with six months' jail if they returned. In a sinister cooptation of community groups, Project Homeward Bound provided between $500,000 and $750,000 to nonprofit organizations to bus homeless people out of town if they certified that they would not return. As Beaty explained, the official "euphemistic" rationale was "to return homeless people to their original support systems" (Beaty, 1999a, p. 50; Beaty, 1999b).

A key instrument in the cleanup campaign was the business community's private security force. Downtown businesses had taxed themselves in order to hire a special so-called "hospitality force" of private security guards officially called the Ambassador Force—but termed the Pith Police by the Atlanta Olympic Conscience Coalition because of their pith helmets. Visitors who felt uncomfortable in the presence of homeless people were advised to call an Ambassador, who would then contact the police to remove the "offender." Thus, as Beaty convincingly argued, privatizing the policing of downtown urban space also constituted a form of class control (Beaty, 1998b). By 1998, the National Law Center on Homelessness and Poverty had documented laws and policies in more than fifty American cities directed at homeless people, many of which were discriminatory and/or unconstitutional: public place restrictions, sweeps, panhandling laws, discrimination, and limits on service providers (National Law Center, 1998).

In a 1996 federal lawsuit, five homeless men sued the City of Atlanta police force for wrongful arrest. Their case included documentation of arrests and harassment of homeless people, loss of shelters, affordable housing, and public housing as a result of Olympic preparations. The federal judge issued a temporary restraining order and preliminary injunction two days before the Olympic opening ceremonies—thus causing considerable embarrassment for the city. The subsequent settlement in mid-1998 included $3,000 compensation for each person, mandatory training of police on dealing with the homeless, and forced the city to acknowledge the task force as the official monitor of police activity and allegations of police abuse toward homeless people (Beaty, 1998a).

The actions of the task force, ACLU, and other advocacy groups were not limited to lobbying and legal interventions. They organized numerous protests in response to the various city ordinances that targeted homeless people and, during the Olympics, were permitted by ACOG to demonstrate in fourteen areas near Olympic venues—in other words, they were granted their Constitutional right to assembly. However, regarding a related right—freedom of speech—Georgia State University professor Charles Rutheiser, author of the critical work *Imagineering Atlanta* (cited above), was denied tenure in 1999—in Anita Beaty's view, on account of this critique (Beaty, 1999b).

SYDNEY'S OLYMPIC CORRIDOR

Sydney, Australia, showed signs of following Atlanta's example of gentrifying neighborhoods in the Olympic corridor and sweeping the streets of beggars and homeless people in the years leading up to the 2000 Olympics. As was the case in Atlanta, the dual problems of homelessness and the shortage of affordable housing and shelter beds were exacerbated by Olympic preparations.

Olympic corridor refers to a twelve-kilometer spine going west from the city center along the harbor and the Parramatta River to the Homebush Bay site of the main Olympic villages and venues. Many of the suburbs in this corridor were formerly occupied by low-income tenants, and in some western Sydney suburbs, particularly those with high proportions of unskilled workers, Aborigines, and single parents, unemployment was as high as 38% (Horin, 1999). Sydney house prices rose by 7% above inflation in 1998, compared to the usual 2% (Real Estate Institute, 1999); in the Olympic corridor, according to real estate figures provided in a Homebush housing developers' brochure, these increases ranged from 13 to 23% in 1997–1998. While developers presented this (artificial) rise in real estate prices as a lure for speculators, housing and homelessness advocates cited the figure as clear evidence of an impending crisis, with the trickle-down effect placing home ownership, rented flats, and even boarding house accommodation out of the range of low-income residents.

In the municipality of Auburn, where Homebush is located, a 1998 council study investigated the longterm financial implications of the $2 billion (AUS) Olympic construction project on local rate payers. Among the factors contributing to the rate revenue problem, at least until 2007 when the Olympic Village housing developments would be fully occupied and rate paying, was the loss of $3.7 million in rates from the former state abattoir site when the government changed its rating status to accommodate Olympic construction (Moore, 1998a).

On the topic of post-Olympic housing, it is important to note that all the new housing at Homebush Bay was (or will be) sold or rented at market value. The first phase of the three major developments on the site, Newington, was completed and up for sale by 1999, with houses ranging from $380,000 to $540,000 and apartments $295,000 to $525,000. At that stage, future residents of the two thousand homes and apartments had only promises of the schools, day care centers, and other community facilities that would be built after 2000.

In March 1999, before the state elections, both the *Rentwatchers Report* and *Tenant News* (Tenants' Union of NSW newsletter) published the major parties' positions on housing policy, particularly in relation to the Olympic impact. The Greens' policies were the most comprehensive and socially just, while the Labor government position was, for the most part, inadequate. It had rejected the Tenants Union's proposals for legislative protection against eviction and rent increase for the 1.5 million tenants in NSW. The minimal action that the government had taken focused primarily on monitoring the rental market and educating tenants about their rights. Landlords, however, were not ignored by the government, which enacted the new Residential Tribunal Act in 1998 to allow landlords to be awarded costs at the tenant's expense. And in 1999, it passed the Residential Tenancies Amendment, which made it easier to evict "problem tenants" from public and community housing; the Opposition even tried to extend the Act to cover the private rental market, where tenants' rights were already limited. In June 1999, the Green Party member of the NSW Legislative Council proposed an amendment to the Residential Tenancies Act to protect tenants against rent increases and unfair evictions, but the bill was defeated in October.

ABORIGINAL HOUSING: THE BLOCK

Another important Olympic housing issue involved the proposed redevelopment of an area known as the Block in the inner-city suburb of Redfern, an area that had been home to urban Aborigines since at least the 1940s. In 1973, with a number of Aboriginal squatters occupying derelict houses in Redfern, the Federal (Labor) Government provided a $500,000 grant for them to purchase and renovate forty-one houses. As a result, the Aboriginal Housing Company (AHC) was formed, and these events marked the first time that land had been returned to Aboriginal control and a major step toward self-determination. Many Aborigines continue to view the Block as the birthplace of Black activism in Australia (Laanela, 1999).

In 1997, with increasing problems of petty crime and drug trade/use involving White as well as Black youth, the AHC began demolishing some of the housing. By 1999, only one legal tenant and ten terrace houses remained. As part of the gentrification process in the adjacent suburbs, new residents set up "law and order" committees and even hired private security guards; according to popular wisdom, it wasn't safe for the (White) police to enter the neighborhood. Not surprisingly, there was a range of views within Aboriginal communities regarding the future of the Block—a fact that some racist commentators exploited to justify its redevelopment. Some Aborigines supported the fight against crime and drugs but wanted to keep the long-standing Aboriginal community alive; they believed that the perception of a "standoff" between the community and "law and order" was being exploited to suit redevelopers' purposes (Hughes, 1998). Moreover, the forced dispersion, the rupture of community networks, and the relocation and attempted assimilation of Aborigines into predominantly White neighborhoods was as inhumane as the displacement of poor people in Seoul and Atlanta.

Others, like the AHC, believed that the Block could not survive without government subsidies and that demolition and redevelopment were the only solutions. Both sides recognized that Redfern's location on the Olympic corridor and the thriving real estate market in adjacent areas obviously made its redevelopment an Olympic issue, regardless of some White "experts'" assertions to the contrary. By 1999, the Aboriginal and Torres Strait Islander Commission (ATSIC) had cut funding to programs in the Block, a move that some saw as ATSIC's capitulation to government pressure, so that AHC in turn would evict residents and redevelop before the Olympics (Laanela, 1999). Aboriginal activist and former chair of the Aboriginal Legal Service, Lyall Munro, captured the key problems of the Block in the following statement: "There is a human rights issue here, not just a beat up crime rate. This place is an indictment of everything the Australian Government has done to Aborigines. This place has got to be seen as the eyesore that it is, by the eyes of the world during the Olympics. ATSIC has a lot to answer for" (Munro quoted in Laanela, 1999, p. 14).

SOCIAL IMPACT ASSESSMENTS

In 1993, during the late stages of the bid preparation, the NSW Government Office on Social Policy prepared its first social impact assessment (SIA), but it was not released to the public until after the IOC decision in September. Housing and tenant advocates, citing evidence of the negative social impact of hallmark events on Australian cities in the past, were justly critical of the Sydney bid committee's secrecy and lack of preparedness. The NSW Council of Social Service (NCOSS) had been asking for government funds to conduct its own SIA since 1991.

Shelter NSW, a peak housing group established in 1977 to advocate for low-income and disadvantaged consumers of housing, began extensive research and lobbying on Olympic social equity issues in 1994. A study it commissioned at that time, titled *The Olympics and Housing*, provided a thorough analysis of the impact of six international events on local communities—Fremantle's America's Cup, Brisbane Expo, Sydney Bicentennial, Barcelona Olympics, Atlanta Olympics, and Melbourne's bid for the 1996 Olympics—and the potential impact of Sydney 2000. This report provided irrefutable evidence that, in the absence of appropriate policy measures, hallmark events had a negative impact on housing, particularly on low-income private renters, who were least able to afford adequate housing. The necessary policy measures identified in the study were: monitoring the housing market; strengthening existing planning controls; stronger residential tenancy legislation; control of private rentals; and an increased supply of low-cost accommodation (Cox, Darcy, & Bounds, 1994).

In 1995, the NSW government commissioned a preliminary SIA (Keys Young, 1995), a report that some housing advocates viewed primarily as a blueprint for future SIAs. Shelter NSW submitted its Housing and Olympics study and a supplementary report, but none of their policy recommendations was included in the Keys Young report. Among its thirty-seven proposals were: a consumer protection strategy; community consultation; and a working group to report on housing and accommodation issues. One of its more creative recommendations—and one that failed to attract any government followup—called for an Olympic Social Development Fund to distribute the economic benefits of the Games widely in the community.

The report also warned that people "will want to 'tag' issues . . . on to the Olympics and Paralympics, even if there is little objective connection" (Keys Young, 1995, p. i)—in other words, they will unfairly blame the Olympics for negative social impacts. Olympic minister Michael Knight repeated this warning at the 1997 housing conference organized by NCOSS and Shelter NSW. Like other Olympic boosters who resented the implication that they bore any responsibility for urban social problems, Knight stated: "The Olympic Games should not be held hostage to those pushing a wider social agenda" (Moore, 1997). Charges of being unpatriotic or, worse, unAustralian, struck a chord with many otherwise critical people, and statements such as Knight's would have had a chilling effect on many Olympic critics. For example, several housing advocates with whom I had discussions in April 1999 did not support the idea of organizing a protest during the Games, because they did not want to be seen as detracting from the event or using it opportunistically.

In 1995, the change in NSW government to Labor was accompanied by the passing of the OCA Act to consolidate the government's role. Despite attempts by the Green Party—and the fact that this would have been a good opportunity for the new government to demonstrate its more progressive politics—the OCA bill failed to include social and environmental impacts. Over the next few years, NCOSS, Shelter NSW, and the Uniting Church Board for Social Responsibility made repeated attempts to press for government action on the SIA, but by 1999, the vast majority of the Keys Young recommendations were still being ignored (Herbert, 1999; Plant & Roden, 1999). In fact, by late 1998, the government's major single contribution to the Olympic housing problem was to provide $300,000 for a Homeless Action Team in the Department of Housing to help secure public housing for current shelter users and to provide temporary accommodation for homeless people during the Olympics.

In another government initiative on these issues, a Social Impact Advisory Committee (SIAC) was established in 1996 to provide advice on social impacts through the OCA to the Olympic minister who in turn reported to the premier every six months. Its chair, the Reverend Harry

Herbert, as well as committee member and NCOSS director Gary Moore, reported frustration at OCA's repeated failure to consult with them or even to share basic information. For example, SIAC did not receive a copy of the Department of Fair Trading report on residential tenancy until after the government had announced its response, which was in fact to reject about half of the recommendations (Herbert, 1999). By mid-1999, the issue of exorbitant ticket prices for Olympic events became an additional concern for SIAC, but on this matter, too, its efforts were largely ignored.

COMMUNITY ORGANIZATIONS AND RESISTANCE

A coalition of community groups—Redfern Legal Center (serving an inner-city neighborhood), the NSW Tenants' Union, Tenant Advice Services, and Shelter NSW—formed in 1997 under the name Rentwatchers. The coalition structure was a strategic move to protect individual member groups so that they could criticize the government without fear of defunding. With this protection, the coalition generally engaged in more critical analysis and more radical tactics than many other homeless advocacy groups. One of Redfern Legal Center's initiatives to address the gentrification trend in the Olympic corridor was to produce and distribute "Going Thru the Roof," a tenant's guide to fighting rent increases in the Residential Tenancies Tribunal. Rentwatchers kept a database of these cases as a resource for other tenants, as well as documenting rent increases in the Olympic corridor. As one inner-city tenant, Janine Toms, observed about her modest housing on Parramatta Road, "[I]f it's on the way to Homebush [Olympic site] the streets are paved with gold in the eyes of your landlord." In a classic example of "the view from the top," the president of the Real Estate Institute told Toms: "Rent control has been described as the quickest way to clear a city of investment property . . ." (Toms, 1997, p. 17). Without rent control, however, the 31% of Sydney residents who were tenants faced the threat of unchecked rent increases before and during the Olympics.

Rent increases, in turn, produced an increase in the number of homeless people. A shortage of shelter beds in Sydney in 1997 prompted a supplementary system called brokerage to be put in place, where community organizations provided emergency shelter of up to two weeks in private accommodation beds purchased by Sydney City Council and the NSW Department of Housing. The council's Homeless Persons' Information Center coordinated the service, which placed about 4,500 people a year (Brokerage for the homeless, 1998; Horin, 1998). The center reported in 1997 that inquiries had almost doubled since 1992, with nearly half of those assisted being single parents with children. Other center statistics for 1997 confirmed the new profile of shelter users: 60–70% had never used shelter accommodation before; there was an increase in those with psychiatric disabilities; and more than half came from outside the city, including the western suburbs of Parramatta and Blacktown, close to the Homebush Olympic site (Rentwatchers Report, 1998).

In 1998, three Parramatta residents began organizing a twice-weekly barbecue in a local park to feed up to sixty homeless people living in shelters, or in fields and caves on the river bank and, in December 1998, a western suburbs branch of Rentwatchers was launched in response to the growing problem of rent increases in the Olympic corridor. A Rentwatchers analysis of Department of Fair Trading figures for January–March 1997 and 1998 provided clear evidence of rent increases ranging from 15 to 40% in these suburbs (Rentwatchers Report, 1998).

In November 1997, NCOSS sponsored the *Living in the Olympic State Conference* (Roden & Plant, 1998). Participants included housing advocates, university housing specialists, SOCOG members, and community workers. Key recommendations were: legislative protection of private renters, boarders, and lodgers during the Olympic period; provision of adequate emergency accommodations; protection of low-income housing stock; and the establishment of a social development fund from Olympic revenues to subsidize low-income housing construction after 2000.

As a result of Rentwatchers' noisy demonstrations outside the NCOSS conference, a meeting was organized with Olympic Minister Michael Knight, the minister for fair trading, and the minister for housing in November 1997. Although it was a breakthrough to have these three ministers come together to discuss social impact, the promised followup meetings were postponed to June 1998, and the necessary structural changes never came about. Shelter NSW representatives reported that Knight would not direct these ministers to include Olympic social impact in their portfolios. Knight claimed that his own job was only to put on the Games, not to deal with health and housing, while premier Bob Carr refused to consider that the housing market was affected by any factors other than market pressures (Plant & Roden, 1999).

Rentwatchers used the occasion of an OCA meeting on housing in June 1998 to perform a Housing Medals Ceremony in the center of Sydney's business district. The bronze medal was awarded to landlords for "opportunism and self-gain," the silver to real estate agents for "ingenuity and greed," and the gold to developers for "world record profits in these hard times." Tenants received the Wooden Spoon award for coming last, and the

Zero Tolerance award went to "The Capsicum (pepper) Spray for the Homeless." This street theatre event attracted media and public attention (Olympics: developers win gold, 1998). A similar mock event is planned by Townsville (Queensland) activists for 2000; called "Not the Olympics," it will feature races such as "Beach Strolling."

The Department of Fair Trading Ministerial Task Force on Affordable Housing finally released its report later in 1998; it showed, amongst its other findings, that 94% of very low-income renters spent more than 30% of their income on rent. A June 1998 report from the Smith Family, a charitable agency, found that figure to be 40% (Rentwatchers Report, 1998). The Inner Sydney Boarding House Report predicted that, at the current rate of loss, most Sydney boarding houses would be lost within a decade. The vast majority of boarding house residents were elderly, or had physical or mental disabilities, and were living on social security incomes. In the inner-city area of South Sydney, 76% of boarding houses had been converted over a ten-year period. Most former residents had been paying between $70 and $100 per week, well below the median rent even for the cheapest one-bedroom apartment. Rentwatchers viewed these findings as evidence of the government's and local councils' failure to protect low-cost housing (Boarding houses, 1998). But, as University of Western Sydney housing specialist Michael Darcy pointed out, the report "was at pains to avoid linking rising rents to the Olympics" and the government ignored the recommendations for increasing protection of low-income tenants and boarders on the grounds that there was "insufficient evidence" that any problems would arise during the Olympics (Darcy, 1998). This call for "hard evidence" was a standard response on the part of Olympic and government officials in the face of social and environmental problems created or exacerbated by Olympic preparations.

Sydney's experiences of unexpected tourist demand during Bicentennial events and the resulting temporary conversion of many boarding houses into backpacker accommodations suggested that a similar crisis was likely in 2000. As Rob Plant explained, there is a "downmarketing" process when tourists experience problems with their initial accommodation plans and settle for the next level: for example, from one-star hotel down to backpacker hostel. He also predicted that landlords would not even need to "gentrify" accommodations after evicting low-income tenants; they would simply throw a few mattresses on the floor and charge whatever they could to desperate tourists. One budget hotel manager confirmed housing activists' worst fears: when asked by *Herald* reporters if he would cooperate with the Department of Housing plan to prebook rooms for the homeless (as part of the brokerage program) during the Olympics, he replied, "I'm going to stand out the front and auction my rooms to the highest bidder" (Horin, 1998).

The Olympic Homestay Homehost programs, managed by Ray White Real Estate, were designed to provide either vacant furnished rental accommodations or bed and breakfast for visitors. By the end of 1997, they had produced three thousand homes for short-term rent, the majority offered by homeowners rather than landlords. Toward the end of 1998, in an effort to promote more participation, Ray White embarked on a direct-marketing-style campaign, with letters promising homeowners: "You will be rewarded for your involvement, firstly by sharing the Olympic spirit and playing host to international and national visitors, and secondly, financially" (Renters beware, 1998). In light of the other evidence, it could be argued that the appeal to Olympic Spirit was gratuitous. Indeed, by mid-1999, Ray White had rented four hundred properties, including harborside accommodation at $18,000 per week. At least three houses listed in the program cost more than $20,000 per week, while, at the low end, the cheapest nightly rate was $90 per bedroom for "standard" accommodation in the less desirable or more remote areas (Moore, 1999e; Ray White, 1999).

MORE CRIMINALIZATION OF POVERTY

By 1998, there were signs of the beginnings of a criminalization of poverty campaign. At least four local councils, including Sydney City, Liverpool, and Waverley sought wider powers to deal with beggars and loiterers in their local government areas. In the public outcry that followed, each council claimed that it was targeting "aggressive" street vendors, not homeless people; on talkback radio, on the other hand, the idea of "getting rid of homeless people" met with general approval. Not coincidentally, Bondi Beach, the proposed site for Olympic beach volleyball, was in the Waverley area (see chapter 8).

NSW premier Carr subsequently assured the public that there would be no campaigns to harass homeless people during the Olympics: "Any idea that we behave like Hitler in 1936 by getting unfortunate people off the streets to present a false image to the world should not be embraced. It's not going to be done as a special artificial, cosmetic measure for the Olympics" (Carr quoted in McEnearney, 1999). Another politician evoked the "swagman" (a rural transient) of "Waltzing Matilda" fame to assure citizens that, in a country that had a homeless person as a national icon, homeless people would not be harassed. Some of the housing advocates whom I interviewed in 1999 expressed caution in making connections between the Olympics and increased policing of homeless people, because they wanted to avoid unfairly criticizing those who had good records on this issue. For example, they stated that rangers in the Domain, a parkland area adjacent to the Sydney business district, were generally humane in their treatment of the seventy homeless people who lived there (Plant & Roden, 1999).

In other criminalization of poverty initiatives, new laws allowed police to search people "suspected" of carrying a knife, and to "move on" groups of young people; pepper spray was introduced to NSW police; surveillance cameras were set up in "crime hot spots"; and local business owners in the inner-city area of Darlinghurst/Surrey Hills were reported to have asked police to move vagrants off the streets (A tale of two cities, 1998). All these moves resembled Atlanta's pre-Olympic police and legislative initiatives.

In 1999, there was additional evidence of this trend. Residents of newly gentrified streets in Chippendale adjacent to Aboriginal neighborhoods hired private security guards to deal with the "Aboriginal problem"; two Sydney councils—Hurstville and Sutherland—employed their own special constables, and three others, including the Olympic corridor suburb of Auburn, were reported to be considering this move (Clennell, 1999). Homeless people in the Paddington and Darlinghurst area were "moved on" in order to make way for the 1999 Gay and Lesbian Mardi Gras celebrations, and this large influx of visitors clearly demonstrated that accommodations traditionally available for brokerage within a radius of 25–30 km from Sydney disappeared during a hallmark event (Plant & Roden, 1999).

In 1999, following the Atlanta example, Sydney's "Street Furniture Program"—a deceptively appealing name for a social control initiative—provided park benches of a design that prevented lying down. Some benches in inner-city bus shelters that had served as beds for homeless people were simply removed; in one well-known case a few years earlier, people brought bedding and lawn furniture for an old woman who had lived on a Surrey Hills bus shelter bench.

ABORIGINAL ACTIVISM

As noted in chapter 4, the Sydney Olympic organizers capitalized on "Aboriginality" from the outset, by ensuring that prominent Aboriginal leaders had some role, however small and tokenistic, in the process, as well as capitalizing on Aboriginal culture to sell the bid and the Games to the rest of the world. The political climate in Australia during the 1990s was increasingly hostile to Aboriginal issues; progress on land rights was slow, with some earlier gains lost, while the political success of the openly racist One Nation party in Queensland and elsewhere tapped the extremes of White racism.

The problem of cultural appropriation of Aboriginal images and designs by White Australians has a long history, and very little progress has been made in efforts to safeguard authenticity and reward artists fairly. As Aboriginal activist Darren Godwell explained:

> The selection and display of images of Australia's indigenous peoples is consistent with fundamental assumptions and stereotypes of race relations in Australia. Indigenous cultures are distilled into a narrow definition of "real Aboriginal culture." These Aboriginal stereotypes are permitted because . . . they do not challenge the fundamental power relations between peoples of privilege and peoples of disadvantage. (Godwell, 1999b)

Examples abound in relation to the Olympic industry in Australia, where a little bit of "Aboriginality," to use Rod McGeoch's term (McGeoch & Korporaal, 1994, p. 68)—a boomerang, or some dots to signify a Central Desert Aboriginal style of dot painting—became essential features of Olympic representation. This "Olympic branding of Aborigines," as Godwell explains, entrenches historic conceptions of Australian race relations that "have sought to disempower and dehumanize Aboriginal and Torres Strait Islanders" by focusing almost exclusively on their abilities as artists, dancers, and performers. In material as well as symbolic terms, these practices were offensive; not only did such images denote a narrow, primitive stereotype but the work of the artists involved was consistently underestimated and undervalued (Godwell, 1999a; 1999b).

Lobbying the IOC during the bid stage invariably included Aboriginal music and dancing; a dance troupe was commissioned to accompany the Sydney bid committee to Monte Carlo for the 1993 IOC session. SOBC was not the first to commit this kind of exploitation: the Calgary bid committee brought two Blood Indians to the IOC session in Baden Baden as example of "down-home culture" (Reasons, 1984, p. 123). Similarly, when the Melbourne bid committee discovered that the IOC "loved the Aboriginal angle," it located an Aboriginal didgeridoo player who appeared at every official function. Samaranch even requested a dot-style painting that incorporated the Olympic rings, and the Melbourne bid committee found an artist to produce it (Godwell, 1999a).

In 1992, the NSW Aboriginal Land Council gave its support for the bid, while the Aboriginal Legal Service announced a campaign to oppose the bid as a protest against the treatment of NSW Aborigines, and called on the IOC to disqualify Australia (Hewett, 1992). Shortly after, another prominent activist, Burnham Burnham, spoke out in favor of the bid and volunteered to promote it around the world (North, 1992).

Following discussions of Native Title legislation at a 1993 meeting of seven hundred Aboriginal and Islander leaders in Canberra, it was reported that there was support for demonstrations and boycotts. Aboriginal activist Charles Perkins, who had been involved in the bid process, called for an alternative Aboriginal Olympics in 2000 because of SOCOG's failure to include any Aborigine on its board. SOCOG appointed its first Manager of Aboriginal Affairs, Steve Comeagain, in 1994, but as Godwell (1999b) pointed out, he had little experience in sport management, arts administration, or community relations. One of his roles was as an Aboriginal "talking head" for SOCOG and OCA video infomercials.

It was not until late 1997, in the face of continued threats of boycotts, that SOCOG announced the establishment of a National Indigenous Advisory Committee (NIAC) under the leadership of former ATSIC leader Dr. Lowitja O'Donoghue. NIAC met with Olympic organizers four times per year to "advise" on Aboriginal and Islander issues and involvement and cultural appropriateness.

There was extensive discussion of planned protests and boycotts throughout the 1990s, including proposals by Lyall Munro and the coordinator of the Carpentaria Land Council to lobby South Africa and other countries with indigenous-controlled governments to boycott the 2000 Olympics in solidarity. During the bid process, representatives from the NSW Land Council had met with African IOC members but, as Godwell (1999a) explained, there were profound differences between the two groups, and "not some implied brotherhood because they're Black."

When IOC president Samaranch visited Sydney in 1996, he issued warnings about Aboriginal "highjacking" of the Games. Perkins subsequently accused SOCOG of orchestrating these remarks and failing to consult with Aboriginal people; since Michael Knight had issued a similar warning only a week before, the complaint seemed justified. Moreover, as political analyst Stuart Russell argued, the real hijacking was the IOC's "transforming a threat of peaceful protest into a criminal act of terrorism" while failing to meet with Aboriginal people during the visit (Russell, 1996). The next year, Mick Dodson, the federal Aboriginal Social Justice Commissioner, stated that Aborigines would use the Olympics to draw attention to the continued problem of Black deaths in custody: "If our people continue to die as the year 2000 approaches, we'll make damn sure the whole world knows about it" (Dodson quoted in Mitchell, 1997).

Faced with the possibility of well-known indigenous athletes such as Cathy Freeman and Nova Peris-Kneebone boycotting the Games, SOCOG appointed several prominent athletes, including Kneebone, tennis star Evonne Goolagong Cawley, and Charles Perkins, a former soccer player, to NIAC. Cawley, who had been part of the bid presentation team in Monte Carlo, was openly critical of the calls for boycotts (Indigenous leaders, 1998). By late 1998, however, NIAC was threatening a mass resignation. A vacancy on SOCOG's board following Rod McGeoch's resignation was filled, not by an Aborigine, but by another White Australian, former sprinter Marjorie Jackson-Nelson, who also happened to come from the marginal Labor seat of Lithgow. O'Donoghue accused Knight of making a political appointment while Perkins labelled the action "a slap in the face" and a racist act. Both Perkins and O'Donoghue accused SOCOG of tokenism in creating NIAC and failing to take Black issues, including boycott threats, seriously (Evans, 1998a; 1998b). The Carpentaria Land Council again called for a boycott and warned of protests in Sydney streets, while others planned mass demonstrations on the airport runways when the Games began. In his 1999 presentation to the United Nations Working Group on Indigenous Peoples, Aboriginal leader Les Malezer called on other governments to reconsider their support for Sydney 2000 unless Native Title laws were changed (Jopson and Martin, 1999) while ATSIC chair Gatjil Djerrkura was unequivocal in his call for UN support for Aboriginal self-determination (Djerrkura, 1999).

CONCLUSION

Atlanta and Sydney were hosts to the last two Summer Olympics of the twentieth century. These cities also represented disturbing examples of negative social impact, largely as a result of Olympic bids and preparations that were undertaken with little or no community consultation. The problems of disadvantaged populations, particularly in relation to housing and homelessness, were exacerbated by the Olympics, police powers were enhanced in an attempt to render urban problems invisible to the outside world, and many citizens were disenfranchised in the face of a public spending spree presented as a private enterprise. That these events took place in two democratic societies attests to the power of the Olympic industry, which succeeded in shaping urban development at both the material and ideological levels. Huge Olympic construction and infrastructure projects served as visible symbols of a new era in city building, while Olympic spirit and world-class city rhetoric was used to conceal the true impact of the Olympic industry on poverty, homelessness, systemic racism, and other pressing social problems.

The vicious aftermath of events in Atlanta continues to be experienced by members of the Task Force on the Homeless; harassment ranges from constant audits, funding cuts, vilification on the front pages of the *Atlanta Journal Constitution*, even death threats. As Anita Beaty summarized, the organization "will never be 'forgiven' for embarrassing Atlanta" and its leaders in the national and international media on the eve of the Games (Beaty, 1999b). In 1996, when these events took place, the Olympic rings were relatively untarnished. By mid-1999, with the IOC scandal still a top international news story, Sydney's preparations faced more public and media scrutiny that Atlanta's. Despite Sydney's more critical climate, however, racism and classism remained powerful forces in determining which aspects of Olympic resistance would succeed and which would fail.

8

Corporate Environmentalism

olympic shades of green

S USTAINABLE SPORT IS a relatively new concept in both sport and environmental circles. There is little research on the complex relationship between sport and the environment—specifically, the detrimental impact of sporting activities on the environment, and the negative effects of a degraded environment on sport participants. With the exception of golf and downhill skiing, which have regularly come under criticism for the obvious damage they inflict on the natural environment (e.g., Weiss et al., 1998), most sporting activities and venues escaped the attention of environmental activists and researchers until the 1980s.

This is a particularly serious omission in the case of international multisport events such as the Summer and Winter Olympic Games, which result in an influx of thousands of participants and spectators to one urban or mountain area. Like all hallmark events, the Olympics pose many environmental problems, including waste management, energy consumption, transportation, materials recycling, and negative impact on the natural environ-

This is a revised version of an article published in the *International Review for the Sociology of Sport* 33:4, 1998, pp. 341–354, titled "Sport and Corporate Environmentalism: The Case of the Sydney 2000 Olympics."

ment. Furthermore, mounting an Olympic Games invariably demands extensive new construction that may impact negatively on the environment, and many sport-specific venues, media facilities, and television hookups are subsequently demolished because of their limited usefulness to the local community. Temporary structures in Atlanta, including the velodrome, water polo pool, rowing venue, and archery facilities, as well as extensive bleacher seating, fencing, and tent space, were dismantled after what some critics termed "the Disposable Games" (Rutheiser, 1996). Such practices clearly failed to qualify as ecologically sustainable development.

Canadian David Chernushenko was one of the first environmentalists to develop a detailed application of ecologically sustainable development (ESD) principles to sport and recreation management. The objective of his 1994 book *Greening our Games: Running Sports Events and Facilities That Won't Cost the Earth*, as stated in the promotional brochure, was "to identify opportunities for [sport/recreation] decision-makers to reduce the impact of their activities while *capitalizing* on the savings that often accompany better environmental practices" (emphasis added). Although the book represented an important first step, Chernushenko's appeal to sport managers' financial self-interest was problematic. The fact that he became a member of the IOC's environment commission as well as TOBid's environment subcommittee suggested that his particular approach to environmentalism was palatable to these conservative, market-driven organizations.

WHAT DOES GREEN MEAN?

At this point in time, after more than thirty-five years in the evolution of environmentalism as a global social movement, "green" has become an imprecise term in environmental as well as industrial and commercial contexts. The notion of a continuum has often provided the theoretical framework for understanding social movements, with a liberal/reform position at one end and a radical/transformative approach on the other. In examining various environmentalist positions, however, I am persuaded by the argument that the differences between liberals and radicals are too profound to situate both on the same continuum. University of Wollongong (Australia) environmental engineer Sharon Beder, discussing the "light green" and "dark green" positions, argues convincingly that there is in fact a paradigm shift between the two groups, rather than a spectrum on which each can be situated. Material values, most specifically the goal of economic growth, characterize the (light green) dominant paradigm, with the environment valued as an economic resource. This position, in Beder's assessment, focuses on "putting a price on the environment" in order to protect it, "unless degrading it is more profitable" (Beder, 1994, p. 37). This has also been termed the technocratic position (O'Riordan cited in Beder, 1991). In the alternative paradigm espoused by dark green environmentalists, also known as the ecocentric position, the natural environment is seen as having intrinsic worth, and existing political and economic systems are to be challenged when they pose a threat to the environment. In the case of Sydney 2000, Beder's explanation is helpful in understanding the positions of various stakeholders, many of whom do not seem to be speaking the same language. There are numerous examples to be found in the dialogue between technocrats and ecocentrists at the 1997 Green Games Conference at the University of NSW, one of the major sources that I will use in the subsequent discussion (Cashman & Hughes, 1998).

As noted above, it was clear that Chernushenko adopted a liberal or light green position regarding sport management. Noting that green is a "loosely" used term, he explained that it could be applied "when [the] level of environmental impact is at or close to the best current level available" (Chernushenko, 1994, p. 9). (The term *best practice* is commonly used in scientific environmental circles.) Chernushenko went on to state that green is "a state to which we aspire" and a step toward the "next higher level." The notion of "the greening of our games" as a process rather than a quick fix is useful in the case of the Olympics, since one of the world's largest sporting events is unlikely to change overnight. However, in the case of Sydney 2000, Beder claimed that the remediation process at the Olympic site was simply "a cheap, dirty, quick and convenient option" (Cashman & Hughes, 1998, p. 108) rather than a model of best practice. Although available data are sometimes contradictory and confusing, it will be seen that toxic contamination in and near the Olympic site poses a serious problem.

THE IOC AND THE ENVIRONMENT

Environmental issues emerged in relation to Olympic bids as early as 1972, when Denver, Colorado, held two referenda and subsequently turned down the IOC's offer to host the 1976 Winter Games. The opposition group, Citizens for Colorado's Future, succeeded in politicizing environmental issues, most notably population growth, land use, and ecology. Although the referenda provided a clear public mandate for comprehensive environmental controls in Colorado, few were developed and the state suffered the effects of relatively uncontrolled development and growth (Katz, 1974). By 1999, Colorado had some of the fastest growing cities in the United States.

In 1989–1990, opponents of the Toronto bid for the 1996 Summer Olympic Games argued persuasively that the negative social and environmental impacts must be taken into account, and the BNC coalition that organized Toronto's opposition included a number of environmental organizations. Similarly, in the 1997 bid process for the 2004 Summer Olympics, influential environmental groups in Italy, including the Green Party, launched a campaign to undermine Rome's bid on the grounds that the ancient city could not cope with the influx of tourists and that big construction companies would be the only ones to profit from the expensive and unwanted megaprojects planned for the Games (Owen, 1997).

In 1991, the IOC amended its charter to include ensuring that Olympic Games were held under conditions that demonstrated a responsible concern for environmental issues. Among other initiatives, it introduced environmental requirements for bidding cities, developed an environmental policy, created a Commission on Sport and the Environment, and hosted a biennial international conference on sport and the environment. Olav Myrholt, then head of the Lillehammer umbrella organization of environmental groups, Project Environment Friendly Olympics (PEFO), was invited to draft the first environmental policy and action plan, and subsequently became a member of the IOC commission.

Bid city requirements included carrying out environmental impact assessments of all sites and facilities, with special attention to the surrounding community, cultural heritage, protected areas and species, wetlands, mountains, and other vulnerable areas. The IOC's *Manual on Sport and the Environment* (1997) as well as the *Environmental Requirements for Candidate Cities* on the IOC website (1999) emphasized the need to minimize or, where possible, to eliminate harm to the environment, as well as to restore damaged areas such as former industrial sites (brownlands). The IOC environmental policy initially drew upon existing standards such as those set by the International Chamber of Commerce Business Charter for Sustainable Development, the Coalition for Environmentally Responsible Economies, and the Japanese Federation of Economic Organizations. "Business" and "economy" were key aspects of these organizations, while standards developed by international environmentalist groups were notably absent from the list. This market-driven approach marked the IOC's light green or corporate environmentalist position. In contrast, the most recent IOC guidelines noted the need for a "proactive" and "dynamic" approach in keeping with emerging environmental standards and knowledge—in other words, best practice.

Describing the IOC position on the environment, Richard Pound expressed great faith in the IOC's power, "just by raising the environmental issue" in its consideration of bids, to "create an increased level of awareness throughout the world" (Pound, 1997, p. 19)—a sentiment that reflected Olympic industry rhetoric rather than a realistic prediction of universal environmental education based on Summer and Winter Olympic host cities addressing environmental issues every two years.

The IOC used the World Commission on Environment and Development definition of ESD as meeting "the needs of the present without compromising the ability of future generations to meet their own needs" (Pound, 1997, p. 20). It is interesting to note, in relation to Sydney 2000, that the NSW Contaminated Land Management Act of 1997 provides a more comprehensive definition that explains "intergenerational equity" as the responsibility of the present generation "to ensure that the health, diversity and productivity of the environment are maintained or enhanced for the benefit of future generations." Other relevant ESD requirements of this Act include:

- effective integration of economic and environmental considerations;
- the polluter pays the cost of containment, avoidance, or abatement of pollution or waste;
- implementation of "the precautionary principle," that is, lack of full scientific certainty is not grounds for postponing preventive measures to avoid environmental damage.

THE BEGINNING: LILLEHAMMER WINTER OLYMPICS, 1994

At the time of the bidding for the 2000 Olympics, the first to occur after the IOC's new environmental policies were introduced, Lillehammer was probably the best existing model of a large international multisport event organized on sound environmental principles. As a Winter Olympics, however, its provisions did not cover all the issues and challenges that arise in preparing for and hosting the Summer Games, which attract up to four times as many visitors and participants. Moreover, Summer Olympic sport programs are far more extensive than Winter, and make significantly different and higher demands on the natural environment. The Sydney organizers acknowledged the leadership Lillehammer provided in its waste management practices, use of biodegradable plates and utensils, energy-saving techniques, environmental specifications for suppliers of goods and services, and the environmental legacy to the local community (Otteson, 1997). Notably absent was any acknowledgment that Lillehammer organizers eventually developed an effective model of community consultation. However, in view of the minimal public consultation surrounding Sydney 2000 at any stage, this omission is hardly surprising.

Greenpeace Australia sent Andrew Myer on a study visit to Lillehammer in February 1994, where he met with environmentalists and Olympic organizers. His report noted that after the IOC decision in 1988, it took two years of struggle before the Lillehammer Olympic Organizing Committee (LOOC) set up an environmental framework. Each section of LOOC had one person in a leadership role whose job included environmental issues, and ESD principles were promoted through educational seminars for LOOC staff and volunteers. An external committee as well as an external "expert panel" provided additional input, with mixed results. One problem that community groups faced was LOOC's exemption from Norway's freedom of information legislation because it was a private company; as noted earlier, the same problem confronted activists and journalists in Toronto and Sydney. On the positive side, LOOC's actions included relocating some Olympic facilities and resisting television stations' demands to cut down trees as a cost-saving step—they argued that the entire bobsled run could be covered by one camera if trees were removed.

Other successful aspects of LOOC's ESD approach included energy-saving measures, "green office" strategies, some recycling and the use of compostable materials, and temporary structures assigned to appropriate future use. Private cars were banned from the town, and buses and trains transported all visitors, although sometimes with long waits; politicians rejected environmentalists' proposal to fuel buses with gas from landfill sites. Billboards were removed from along the main routes despite IOC complaints of inadequate promotion of the Games (Myer, 1992).

In another assessment of the Lillehammer Olympics, the Norwegian Society for the Conservation of Nature concluded that there had been "serious attempts . . . to increase environmental awareness" and that the resulting green profile of the Games represented an important first step in the process. It concluded, however, that there was still "a very long way to go" before the Games could be termed "environmentally friendly." The list of positive results included increased environmental awareness, public involvement in planning, cooperation between private, public, and nongovernmental sectors, environmental tendering criteria, and remedial efforts. On the negative side, the report noted the problems of extensive use of land for arenas and roads, loss of forest, wetland, green space, and recreational paths, damage to lynx habitat and threat to birdlife, commercialization of former public recreation areas, and increased traffic and private car use (Chernushenko, 1994).

An evaluation by IOC Sport and Environment Commission member Olav Myrholt (1996) concluded that the Games were "certainly not ecologically sustainable" but acknowledged the positive long-term effect of raised awareness in Lillehammer, as seen, for example, in residents' ongoing opposition to oil companies' billboards and hoardings. While noting environmental initiatives made by some international sport federations, including skiing, bobsled, and luge, Myrholt concluded that, in the face of sponsors' and media demands, sport organizations would clearly benefit from strong environmental guidelines.

"GREEN" IN AUSTRALIA

There is a longstanding tradition of conservation awareness and activism in Australia, with the 1963 founding of the Australian branch of the World Wildlife Federation marking one of the first formal steps toward Australian involvement in the international environmental movement. Living on an island with a fragile ecological balance, unique flora and fauna, and regular extremes of weather—droughts, floods, and bushfires—Australians can hardly afford to ignore the environment. In an economy historically dependent on livestock and agriculture, protection of farm animals and crops remains a key concern. Many overseas visitors, for example, are surprised by Australia's strict quarantine regulations, which until recently included the spraying with insecticide of all passengers disembarking from overseas flights.

This is not to suggest that Australians' environmental awareness necessarily leads to uniformly progressive positions on this or other political fronts. In the recent widely publicized Queensland state election, for example, about 22% of voters chose candidates from the blatantly racist One Nation (*sic*) party. Similar conservatism also operates in environmental politics, where "Greenies" face public censure for both their principles (seen as too expensive, time consuming, and unrealistic) and their tactics (too "radical" and "loony"). And given the sacred place of sport in the Australian (White, male) psyche (Summers, 1975; McKay, 1991), environmentalist critics of the forthcoming Green Games are doubly at risk of public disapproval.

As Australian environmentalists have often observed, it is easier to promote support for cuddly koalas and smiling dolphins than to focus public attention on problems of water pollution and waste management (specifically, sewage disposal). Until the 1960s, for example, swimmers at Sydney's world famous surfing beach at Bondi tended to take for granted the long brown stain that flowed out to sea from the northern headland of the beach, as well as the offensive smell coming from the tall chimney known locally as the Stink Pot. And ocean and harbor beaches have for many years been considered unsafe for swimming for at least twenty-four hours after heavy rain because of the risk of contamination by sewage overflow into stormwater pipes. The fact that, in August 2000, Olympic triathletes will be swimming in Sydney Harbor adjacent to the city center is therefore a cause for concern. However, when the triathlon course was tested in April 1998 before an IOC audience, Samaranch's obvious approval of what he called "the best Olympic stadium of all" (Evans, 1998) would suggest careful public relations management of the potential water pollution problem. On another sewage issue, even though treatment procedures are now more sophisticated, is it disturbing to note that the ocean near Bondi is again slated as the site of the sewage "outfall" from the entire Olympic site at Homebush during the 2000 Games (Kieran, 1998).

REMEDIATION AND CONSERVATION AT HOMEBUSH BAY OLYMPIC SITE

Environmental issues, most specifically remediation and conservation in the Homebush area subsequently designated as the site of the Sydney 2000 Olympics, have been the subject of extensive research and commentary since the 1980s. While scientific reports often present contradictory findings, it appears that, by 1995, Olympic organizers and environmentalists were in agreement on at least three priorities: pollution control of soil, sediment and water; conservation of resources; and protection of biodiversity (the flora and fauna, and the people and their environment) (Olympic Coordination Authority, 1995).

When and if all these concerns are fully addressed, future users of the sporting venues and housing complexes, beginning with the athletes and spectators at the 2000 Olympics, will enjoy working, playing, and living in an ecologically sustainable community. If remediation and conservation initiatives are inadequate, the 2000 Olympics risk being known as the "Green Wash Games"—a term used by environmentalists to refer to the public relations exercise in which governments and corporations engage to generate an environmentally friendly public image, while, behind the facade, conditions fail to measure up to current standards of best practice (Athanasiou, 1996).

The following discussion of environmental aspects of Sydney 2000 will focus on a number of players: SOCOG, OCA, environmental groups, and the mass media. I will examine the ways in which the various players define and operationalize the notion of green in relation to the Olympics, and the negotiation of conflict between groups occupying different political positions on environmental issues.

SYDNEY 2000: ENVIRONMENTAL PROMISES

The original 1993 environmental principles developed by the Sydney bid committee stated commitment to the following goals:

- energy conservation and use of renewable energy sources;
- water conservation;
- waste avoidance and minimization;
- protecting human health with appropriate standards of air, water, and soil quality;
- protecting significant natural and cultural environments. (Sydney Olympics 2000 Bid Committee, 1993)

It is important to note that these principles, like most definitions of ESD, encompass the human as well as the natural environment, and specifically identify the social impact and effects on human health as key considerations. Evidence to date, however, suggests that social and health impacts are a low priority for Sydney 2000 designers and organizers; in fact, the social impact studies were not completed until after the bid was submitted (Office on Social Policy, 1993).

As is the practice in light green environmental circles, protection of flora and fauna—most notably, the conservation of the "brickpit" area to protect a colony of endangered green and golden bell frogs—is more likely to be the topic of SOCOG/OCA media output than soil and water remediation at the Homebush site. By 1998, the small frog, now assured that its natural home would not be destroyed to make room for Olympic tennis courts and amphitheatre, was appearing on promotional material for the Royal Easter Show, held for the first time in its new facilities at the Homebush Olympic site. If the colony had been established any closer to the river, the frog would have met a very different fate, since dioxin contamination has caused disease and mutation in fish in Homebush Bay, and fishing bans have been in effect since the late 1980s (*Background Briefing*, 1997; Beder, 1993).

It is not surprising that, in 1994, international observers such as Canadian environmentalist David Chernushenko viewed the Sydney model as "exemplary" and "revolutionary" based on its 1993 *Environmental Guidelines*. Like all bid materials, they made no mention of the fact that the pro-

posed Olympic site at Homebush and the adjacent waterway at Homebush
Bay were heavily contaminated with toxic waste, including levels of dioxin
high enough for American scientists who tested the site in 1990 to consider
the danger equivalent to, or even higher than, the well-known American
Superfund sites, such as Love Canal (Beder, 1993, 1996; Short, 1996).
(However, as recently as July 1997, OCA's Executive Director for the
Environment, Dr. Colin Grant, erroneously claimed that no dioxin waste
had been found on the site [*Background Briefing*, 1997].)

Dating back to the early 1900s, the land had been variously used for
abattoirs, brickworks, an armaments depot, chemical plants, a chlorinated
herbicide factory, and industrial and toxic waste dumps. Union Carbide,
infamous for its environmental disaster in Bhopal, India, formerly occupied
one of the factory sites. It should be noted, however, that until the 1950s,
companies that dumped toxic waste in this area were not breaking Australian
environmental law.

After Sydney had been awarded the Games, it came to light that at least
four scientific analyses of the site, with detailed remediation plans, had been
commissioned by the NSW Government between 1990 and 1992, but that
a decision was made to take no action before the bid was submitted in 1993
in order not to "jeopardize" its success (Short, 1996). As of 1997, the "cock-
tail" of contaminants in the soil and waterways include: dioxin, asbestos,
heavy metals, and phthalates (Beder, 1996; Robinson, 1997). A NSW State
of the Environment report called the remediation "one of the biggest land
clean up projects ever conducted in Australia" and the cost has recently been
estimated at $137 million (AUS). The NSW Government has committed
$21 million toward the cost of removing 30,000 cubic meters of contami-
nated sediment from Homebush Bay, not only because of its proximity to
the Olympic site, but also because property developers are planning luxury
apartment complexes on the shores (*Background Briefing*, 1997).

Greenpeace toxics and Olympic campaigner, analytical chemist Darryl
Luscombe, as well as a German chemist with extensive experience in dioxin
testing, are among the many critics who claim that the government's standard of dioxin toxicity falls short of international standards of "best practice"
(*Background Briefing*, 1997; Beder, 1996). It is also disturbing to note that
the 1997 NSW Contaminated Land Management Act requirement that the
polluter pay for remediation will not be applied in the case of the Olympic
site. According to the NSW Minister for Ports and Public Works, speaking
on Australian Broadcasting Commission (ABC) Radio in 1997, the government's legal advice has been not to sue Union Carbide or its offshoot Lednez
Industries, in part because they have (strategically, it seems) changed their

corporate structure and are virtually unassailable in terms of retrieving assets to apply to the cost of remediation (*Background Briefing*, 1997).

In 1993, bid committee media releases cited Bruce Baird, minister responsible for the bid, as saying: "No other event at the beginning of the 21st century will have a greater impact on protecting the environment than the 2000 Olympic Games in Sydney" (Sydney 2000—the Environment Olympics, 1993), while Sydney 2000 chief executive Rod McGeoch (or possibly the same media copywriter) was quoted as claiming that "the *Environment Guidelines* would make Sydney's Olympic Plan a prime example of ecologically sustainable development in the 21st century" (Sydney's Plans for an Environment Olympics, 1993). Speaking at the Green Games Conference in 1997, SOCOG environmental manager Peter Otteson also stated that Sydney's twenty-five-page *Environmental Guidelines* "were the most comprehensive and ambitious . . . ever proposed by a bidding city, and went far beyond the standard that the IOC had set in the Bid Manual" (Otteson, 1998, p. 34). In other words, Olympic organizers have unequivocally stated their commitment to "best practice" on environmental issues.

Later in his presentation, Otteson defended "environmental excellence" in part on the grounds that, contrary to the popular perception of the extra expense involved, cost-efficient resource use and improved design and choice of materials have been shown to produce "great increases in wealth and reduced operational costs" (Otteson, 1997, p. 38)—a classic light green or technocratic position.

At least one critical voice at the conference, environmental scientist Ian Lowe, drew attention to the fact that the economy is a subset of human society, which itself is "totally embodied within the natural ecology" (Lowe, 1997). In other words, the economy is socially produced, not a fixed entity external to human activity, and therefore it is open to progressive social change. This appears to be a concept alien to corporate environmentalists.

Dr. Colin Grant, OCA Executive Director of Planning, Environment and Policy, quoted with approval a statement attributed to Maurice Strong, Chairman (*sic*) of the Earth Council: "We have to start managing our earth as much as we do a business" (Strong quoted in Grant, 1997, p. 44). The reference did not go unnoticed; in his summary, Professor Ian Lowe of Griffith University correctly noted that Strong's position did not go "far enough towards an ecocentric approach in which we recognize that we are part of nature rather than charged with managing it" (Lowe, 1997, p. 112).

Another concern was SOCOG's rather dramatic retreat from the "Green Games" label at the conference. SOCOG media relations manager Richard Palfreyman blamed the media for what he called "that dreadful term" (green). He emphasized on at least two occasions that SOCOG preferred the tag "The Athletes' Games" and had never used the term Green Games even though they had no doubt that the Games would in fact be green, with small "g" (Palfreyman, 1998, p. 97)—this despite the fact that both the bid committee and SOCOG/OCA have emphasized the positive environmental aspects from the outset.

Interestingly, some other presenters affiliated with SOCOG/OCA did not object to the Green Games label. Lorraine Cairnes, for example, made the rather rash claim that "OCA has had to educate the public on the Green Games . . . encouraging some of Australia's largest design and construction and engineering firms to raise their environmental performance . . ." (Cairnes, 1998, p. 23). Cynically, one might say that SOCOG/OCA are willing to own the green label when it enhances their image, but less willing when it implies a "best practice" standard of environmental achievement against which Sydney 2000 will be measured and, quite possibly, found lacking. In any event, there is little doubt that the technocratic or light green position dominates in SOCOG/OCA.

THE DARK GREEN CRITICS:
GREENPEACE AND GREEN GAMES WATCH 2000

Probably the most widely known international environmental group, Greenpeace, has had a mixed relationship with Sydney 2000 from the outset. In 1993, Greenpeace Australia prepared one of the five prize-winning designs for an environmentally sound Olympic Village, and then collaborated with the other firms to design the final version. Greenpeace Australia Cities and Coasts campaigner Karla Bell was subsequently cited in Sydney 2000 publications as endorsing the Olympic Village (not too surprisingly, since Greenpeace worked on its design) with its incorporation of solar power, water recycling, environmentally friendly building materials, and protection of biodiversity (Sydney's Olympic Village plan, 1993). By 1997, however, Bell, now an independent environment consultant, was one of the many experts to express concern over the organizers' coverup of the toxic contamination and the current NSW government's weakened environmental guidelines that permit a cost-cutting approach to remediation (*Background Briefing*, 1997).

In June 1997, Greenpeace activists cleaned up fifty rusting barrels of dioxin found two kilometers from the Olympic stadium, on a site adjacent to the former Union Carbide factory. In a classic Greenpeace direct action and educational campaign that attracted considerable media and public attention, activists trained in safe handling of hazardous waste repackaged and secured the barrels. However, Greenpeace reported that "the official response" from SOCOG/OCA was "to refute our research and paint us as 'unpatriotic' for criticizing the 2000 Olympics" (Lethal stockpile, 1997). In September 1997, Greenpeace campaigner Darryl Luscombe was asked by ABC Radio *Sports Factor* host Amanda Smith if Greenpeace had "snuggled up too close now [to Olympic organizers] to keep a critical watching brief" (*Sports Factor*, 1997). Luscombe cited the direct action of June 1997 as an example of Greenpeace autonomy and its radical agenda, with Olympic organizers' defensive response leaving no doubt that the "snuggling up" charge was not valid.

Ecocentric environmentalists, including many Greenpeace activists, have long argued that there is no such thing as a safe landfill, and cite "best practice" in the United States and other countries, where on-site treatment, removal, and off-site treatment, or incineration of toxic waste are the three preferred methods; the Australian and New Zealand Environment and Conservation Council and the National Health and Medical Research Council (Australia) also recommend on-site or off-site treatment. The "bank vault" system of containment and monitoring of untreated toxic waste, which allows the possibility of leachate leakages contaminating soil, groundwater, and waterways—the system now in process at Homebush—is widely considered to be the least safe method (*Background Briefing*, 1997; Beder, 1993; 1996). It was therefore somewhat surprising to read, in March 1998, that a Greenpeace spokesperson praised the government, reportedly for the first time, for its remediation program, specifically the containment of toxic waste under areas of the site slated for parkland and recreation, and not for buildings (Chandler, 1998). Presumably, if toxic leakages occur, there are still health risks for recreational athletes who use the land. However, it is perhaps understandable that Greenpeace did not want to lose its credibility with the public by appearing "unreasonable" after it became clear that their lobbying was not going to change the current remediation strategy.

Sydney 2000's other major environmental critic is GGW2000, a coalition of environmental groups established in 1995 "to work with community groups and communities to achieve genuine community consultation about the Olympic Games in Australia" (Tohver & James, 1997). GGW2000 receives $80,000 per annum from the NSW government and from Environment Australia, as well as a subsidy from OCA, and operates at arm's length from funders. While GGW2000 sees a major part of its role as shifting the OCA agenda, there are some who hold the more cynical view that GGW2000 merely makes OCA look as if it is facilitating public participation. Interaction between OCA and GGW2000 takes place through the presence of representatives from community environmental groups on the OCA Environmental

Advisory Panel. Among GGW2000 projects has been the commissioning of research reports on various environment issues, including energy, transport, waste management, air quality, and biodiversity. As part of its grant conditions, GGW conducts an annual review of OCA's progress in implementing its own *Environmental Guidelines* and its other public environmental commitments.

SYDNEY 2000 AND MEDIA ENVIRONMENT CRITICS

In the early 1990s, the *Herald*, like most of the Australian media, was a consistent booster of Sydney's bid, largely, no doubt, because of Olympic organizers' control of most media coverage. By the late 1990s, some changes were apparent in the *Herald* and elsewhere. Internal conflict within and between the various Australian Olympic bodies (SOCOG, OCA, and the AOC) grabbed media attention, as did criticism of Olympic preparations by environmental groups. Although many journalists still ridiculed Greenpeace, it appeared that the media treatment of debates and controversy in the latter half of the decade might balance the uncritical media hoopla of the bid years. The *Herald's* cast of Olympic reporters expanded to include Murray Hogarth, who began work in 1996, first as a general investigative journalist and ultimately as Environment editor, and hence, almost by definition, an Olympic critic. Among his credentials was a controversial ABC TV *Four Corners* program on environmental contamination at the Olympic site. Like Matthew Moore and other *Herald* journalists, Hogarth was critical of the secrecy created by the "impenetrable" IOC, SOCOG, OCA, the NSW state government, the cabinet ban on FOI requests for Olympic documents, and, finally, "big business, with a tangled web of confidentiality agreements" (Hogarth, 1996, quoted in Beder, 1999, p. 8).

Hogarth viewed the *Herald's* earlier boosterism of the bid and the Games preparations as atypical and their tougher approach of the last few years as indicative of "business as usual." While acknowledging that it may have been uncomfortable for managers to deal with the potential conflict between critical articles and the paper's role as an Olympic sponsor, Hogarth reported that he had experienced "no suggestion of pressure" not to run these stories (Hogarth, 1999).

In his presentation to the Green Games conference, it was clear that Hogarth took his responsibility for critical coverage of environmental issues seriously, and his *Herald* articles provided a much-needed media voice for groups such as GGW2000 and Greenpeace. Hogarth experienced what he called "extreme displeasure" from Olympic organizers after his articles on the dioxin contamination, and one former ministerial adviser threatened lawsuits and discreditation, even calling Hogarth "the last toxic site on the list to be cleaned up" (cited in Hogarth, 1998, p. 102). Hogarth pointed out, however, that his concerns were validated when the NSW Environmental Protection Authority upgraded its environmental controls in September 1997.

Beder experienced similar hostility from Olympic officials in 1993, when her article critiquing the proposed remediation methods was accepted for publication in *New Science*. Two senior government officials holding Olympic managerial positions visited her and the head of her university department, and succeeded in preventing the publication of the article, which subsequently appeared in the *Current Affairs Bulletin* in 1994 (Beder, 1994; 1999). This kind of government censorship was typical during the bid period. Ironically, the *New Science* editors told Beder that the Chinese would use a critical article of this kind as ammunition against Sydney's bid, while at the same time some members of the Sydney bid were plotting exactly the same kind of strategy against Beijing (see chapter 4).

On environmental issues, SOCOG/OCA staff were prone to criticize the media for their preoccupation with "shock-horror" stories. Admittedly, there were more negative than positive environmental news stories, but Palfreyman's complaints during the Green Games Conference exemplified the defensive SOCOG/OCA response to criticism about environmental issues. Quibbling about the difference between "Homebush" and "Homebush Bay" (the latter a site of heavy dioxin contamination), he dismissed a *Herald* story about dioxins in Homebush Bay on the grounds that there was no Olympic swimming in the actual bay, which was some distance from the main stadium and aquatic center. For the record, it should be noted that the 1993 *Environmental Guidelines* encompassed rehabilitation of wetlands and maintenance of threatened ecosystems. The waterways entrance at Haslams Creek, the focal point of the original Olympic design concept in 1993, was subsequently abandoned because ferries would disturb the Bay's highly polluted sediment (Short, 1996). Therefore, Palfreyman's distinction between the water and the land was an artificial one, and betrayed the spirit if not the letter of the law regarding SOCOG/OCA's environmental commitments.

Defensiveness also characterized many of the SOCOG/OCA responses to the environmentalists, particularly when the steady stream of research reports from groups such as GGW2000 and Greenpeace attracted considerable attention in the mass media in 1997 and 1998. As Greenpeace toxics and Olympic campaigner Dr. Darryl Luscombe pointed out, environmentalists were accused of being "unpatriotic" for keeping public attention on the contamination problem in the Homebush area. Joining in the "patriotic versus unpatriotic" debate, Luscombe claimed that Greenpeace and other groups were scrutinizing the cleanup so that the "world media spotlight" would not fall on the deficiencies of the Sydney Games, as it did in Atlanta in 1996 (Luscombe, 1998, p. 15). GGW2000 coordinator Peggy James was openly critical of Sydney 2000's public relations, which she called a "Green Wash" exercise, with "a lot of hype" about the achievements, and little about the negative environmental impact (*Sports Factor*, 1997). In fact, GGW2000 obtained a copy of the government's public relations strategy, parts of which were cited on the ABC Radio National program *Background Briefing* in 1997:

> Convey a message of cooperation and openness as a means of diffusing the environmental lobby and a potentially aggressive media . . . bald announcement of [remediation] parameters could lead to them being rejected by key environmental stakeholders, whereas an appropriate message of open cooperation could lead to the same parameters being adopted. (*Background Briefing*, 1997)

While it may be heartening to see this acknowledgment of the power and rights of environmental stakeholders, the government's cynical "manufacture of consent" is both dishonest and insulting to the citizens whom it purports to serve. Equally important, the health of athletes and spectators at the 2000 Olympics, as well as the health of future recreational users of the parkland and sport facilities and future residents, will be at risk if the remediation measures are inadequate. James was justly critical of OCA's and the government's failure to communicate the true extent of environmental problems and proposed solutions, which, she claimed, would undoubtedly "undermine the community's confidence about the Green Games and the willingness of people to modify their own behavior to protect the environment" (James, 1998, pp. 78–79).

In 1998–1999, a number of new environmental issues came to light concerning the satellite Olympic venues, including Rushcutters Bay yachting facilities, Ryde water polo pool, the Eastern Suburbs cycling course, Bankstown velodrome, and the Bondi Beach beach volleyball stadium. Local residents and environmental groups organized public meetings and protests, with varying degrees of success (Banham, 1999). Bondi Olympic Watch, a group affiliated with GGW2000, managed to slow down what its organizers termed the "Olympic juggernaut." Protesters threatened to chain themselves to fences and lie down in front of bulldozers if plans for a huge beach volleyball stadium proceeded. After several public meetings involving hundreds of supporters, Bondi Olympic Watch convinced OCA to modify the plans to reduce the height of the stadium and the time during which the beach would be closed for construction. Refusing to be duped by OCA promises of "facelifts" to the existing beach pavilions and compensation to business owners, Bondi Olympic Watch organizers at the April 18, 1999, public meeting emphasized that such changes did not constitute an Olympic legacy.

CONCLUSION

The IOC acted in an uncharacteristically progressive manner in establishing environmental guidelines for bid and host cities. In fact, except for the predictable corporate environmentalist perspective, these provisions are comprehensive and proactive, at least on paper. The Sydney case study demonstrated that financial imperatives, exacerbated by the inflexible deadlines typical of hallmark events, threatened to dilute the "best practice" standard promised in Sydney's bid. While groups as diverse as the "light green" Earth Council and the ecocentric GGW2000 and Greenpeace all gave due credit to OCA's genuine achievements, most notably in the areas of renewable energy, transport, and biodiversity, they were also in agreement on one major shortcoming: OCA's secrecy and lack of transparency in decision making (Latham, 1999). It is clear that environmental critics, like all other Olympic watchdog organizations, face formidable opposition from the Olympic industry.

'She praises them, and then turns around and bites them.

9

The Mass Media
and the Olympic Industry
manufacturing consent?

MANUFACTURING CONSENT, a term first used by Walter Lippman in 1921, is central to the analysis of the political economy of the mass media developed by Edward Herman and Noam Chomsky (1988). Their insights, together with Chomsky's 1989 collection of essays, aptly titled *Necessary Illusions* (Chomsky, 1989) provide the basis for the theoretical framework used here. Consistent with the neo-Marxist explanations of ruling, which focus on the ways in which power is exercised through ideological control rather than armies, Chomsky's propaganda model states that the media reflect the consensus of corporate elites. State managers will not be protected from criticism from the powerful corporate sector, whose members may in fact use the media as a platform for an antigovernment position.

The media's occasional self-criticism and reporting of external critiques constitute additional practices that help create what Chomsky terms "necessary illusions," in this case, the illusion of freedom of the press and a democratic society. Debate is carefully managed and contained, and the public is not provided with a full view of the complexities of social problems and the nature and extent of dissident views. Views incompatible with the interests of corporate and government elites are attributed to "special interest groups" which are, in fact, the large social groupings that comprise the majority:

women, immigrants, working-class people, etc. Herman and Chomsky (1988) further demonstrate how a supply of "experts" is "bought" in order to add legitimacy to media messages that serve elite interests, with (conservative) university professors among the most popular experts. It would be relatively easy to identify propaganda if the media only promoted a single party line or, alternatively, pushed a specific antigovernment position; it is more difficult to do so when there is the illusion of balance, debate, or dissent, as seen, for example, in letters to the editor or the publication of "pro" and "con" positions by staff journalists.

It should be noted that, in the case of the 1998–1999 Olympic scandal, journalists' enthusiasm for attacking individuals within the Olympic industry did not necessarily signify that they had abandoned the propaganda model. Journalists, like the other critics discussed in chapter 5, tended to separate the "pure" athlete/sport component from bid committees, NOCs, the IOC, and what they saw as the seamier side of the Olympic industry.

In discussing effective challenges to mass media monopoly over public opinion, Chomsky identified the potential of community and workplace organizations and nonprofit radio and television to broaden public debate and provide a forum for dissent. In a rare Australian example, an article in the May 1996 issue of *Green Left* presented "Ten reasons to oppose all Olympic Games" (Martin, 1996). As well as proposing strategies for change, including transforming the ethos of competitive sport and developing new forms of cooperative games, Martin suggested that critical people should boycott Olympic sponsors, mount political protest, and refuse to watch or show any interest in Olympic sport. Given the preeminent success of the Olympic television spectacle in delivering international audiences to Olympic sponsors, the economic impact of such a boycott would be felt globally.

JOURNALISTS: WHISTLE BLOWERS OR TEAM PLAYERS?

There are two key aspects to the uneasy relationships between journalists and the Olympic industry. On the one hand, a minority of investigative journalists justly earned their reputation as whistle blowers, and hence were not welcome members of the Olympic family. If documents were said to have been "obtained" by a newspaper or television station, it was likely that whistle blowers within Olympic organizations had passed them on to their counterparts in the media. On the other hand, many journalists were unwilling or unable to write full accounts of Olympic controversies, or even to offer any critical commentaries, because their editors were pressured by Olympic organizers to publish only positive articles. In theory, when a newspaper company or radio/television station was an Olympic sponsor or a source of in-kind donations, there was a separation between the business department of the media company, which negotiated such a contract, and its editorial department, which made final decisions about content. In practice, however, the distinction was often blurred, and when editors were pressured by Olympic organizers to suppress media whistle blowers, many succumbed.

There were, of course, considerable benefits flowing from this compliance, most notably, coveted Olympic Games assignments. The IOC *Written and Photographic Press Guide* (1997), which Sydney organizers are following, requires them to provide the five thousand credentialled journalists with a fully equipped and staffed main press center and competition venue press centers; a three- to four-star equivalent media village (although accommodation is not free); free local train travel and shuttle bus service; and, in the case of the top media organizations, guaranteed tickets to high-demand events.

Beyond the official provisions for the media, there have been allegations of reporters being paid by the IOC. Jennings (quoted in Calvert et al., 1999, p. 23) alleged that "too many sportswriters in Britain and abroad have accepted money and 'freebies' from the IOC"; in one instance, a senior British sports writer was forced to resign because of undisclosed IOC links. In North America, journalists alluded to similar fringe benefits, including invitations to lavish parties held by bid committees (Harrington, 1999). In the words of *Toronto Star* columnist Jim Coyle, "It's a lot easier, and lots more fun, to collect all the trinkets and make all the trips than to offend those who might turn off the access and the perks" (Coyle, 1999). And, as Burstyn convincingly argues, NBC's multibillion dollar investment in the Olympics between 1988 and 2000 put NBC staff in the position of covering the Olympics "not as independent journalists but as employees of the investors/owners of the Olympics" (Burstyn, 1999, p. 231).

Following the media success of the 1984 Olympics in Los Angeles, teams of "Olympic-dedicated" journalists were assigned to most major print and electronic news services. Some had backgrounds in sports journalism, while others had worked in other departments, covering, for example, city hall news or environmental issues. In terms of objective news coverage, there were potential advantages in having experienced political journalists covering the Olympic controversy. However, the major newspapers under discussion here tended to assign their regular sports or Olympic journalists to the Lausanne press conferences, including *Sydney Morning Herald* Olympic business reporter Glenda Korporaal and Olympic sportswriter Jacqueline Magnay, *Toronto Star* sport reporter Randy Starkman, and Mike Gorrell, long-time Olympic reporter for the *Salt Lake Tribune*. *Deseret News* Olympics editor Rick Hall acknowledged the power that the IOC had over editors and journalists through the credentialling process. He explained that editors "sort of show them [IOC] for many years before by covering meetings in Lausanne and those sorts of things" that they are hoping to get enough Olympic credentials for their staff, and that negative Olympic stories might jeopardize the outcome (Hall, 1999).

From the Olympic organizers' perspective, the noncredentialled press, expected to number about ten thousand in the case of the Sydney Olympics, could pose a greater challenge than those who have access to the official events and the carefully staged press conferences. These are the journalists who often look for nonsport, human interest stories—urban poverty, racism, etc.—that might embarrass the host city in the world press. Indeed, by the 1990s it became axiomatic in Olympic circles that world media coverage could make or break an Olympics. The negative press that Atlanta's transport and communication problems received was a convincing example (Gratton, 1999). It is unlikely, however, that Atlanta's street sweeps and criminalization of poverty campaign, although they attracted considerable media attention from 1996 on, went down in history as marring the Atlanta Games. It remains to be seen what will happen in Sydney when Aborigines organize an Aboriginal tent "embassy" in order to direct visiting media to communities where indigenous people live in Third World conditions.

Clearly, a docile media is essential from the earliest stages of the bid. The Berlin bid committee's successful "friendship" strategy in 1990, documented by Jennings, ensured that media coverage was seamlessly supportive (Jennings, 1996). Similar campaigns in other bid cities will be discussed later in this chapter.

JENNINGS AND SIMSON: EARLY MEDIA WHISTLE BLOWERS

Investigative journalists Andrew Jennings and Vyv Simson, based in the UK, published the first major exposé of Olympic bidding processes, *The Lords of the Rings*, in 1993, followed in 1996 by Jennings's *The New Lords of the Rings*. Although their work reflected exhaustive international research, some academics stated that the books were "undocumented" (Hoberman, 1995) and "overblown rhetoric" (Hill, 1992); Hoberman did, however, defend their right to publish these critiques. For his part, Jennings (1996, p. 295) claimed that few academics had addressed "the philosophical or moral quandaries arising from the sell-out of the Games" and that, like their journalist counterparts, many scholars had in fact benefited from IOC largesse in the form of research grants, positive reviews in IOC publications, etc. (See chapter 6 for an analysis of the link between the corporate university and the Olympic industry.) On the general question of Jennings and Simson's work, my own position in January 1997 was that, even if only 10% of their allegations of bribery and corruption surrounding Olympic bids were true, this alone was ample cause for concern (Lenskyj, 1997). Subsequent events suggested that the figure was significantly higher.

Jennings soon became *persona non grata* in Olympic circles, and in 1994 the IOC invoked an old Swiss law to sue him for "lampooning" president Samaranch, an "offense" for which he received five days' suspended sentence and a fine of $2,000 (Jennings, 1996). In the world of sports journalism, too, the books were often disparaged, but when the bribery allegations became international news in 1998–1999, Jennings was in great demand, reportedly conducting fourteen straight hours of interviews at one point. His articles and chapters from the book now appeared in the *Guardian* (UK), *Toronto Star*, *Village Voice*, and elsewhere, and within a matter of days it became acceptable, even de rigueur, for every news and sport journalist to cite *The Lords of the Rings*. In 1999, Jennings, still a credentialled journalist, attended IOC press conferences in Lausanne. On one such occasion, a *New York Times* journalist asked IOC director-general François Carrard if the IOC would apologize to Jennings now that many of his allegations had proven correct. Carrard claimed, with obvious irritation, that there were "enough other lies in the book" to justify the jail sentence (Magnay, 1999a).

Although Jennings and Simson are generally credited as the earliest and most widely read whistle blowers—the books were translated into thirteen languages—there were other documented accounts of bribery and corruption on the part of IOC and bid committee members that, for the most part, went unheeded. In the following discussion, I will examine media treatment of various Olympic political issues in Salt Lake City, Atlanta, Nagano, Toronto, and Sydney.

SALT LAKE CITY MEDIA: TELLING THE WHOLE STORY

In January 1999, as various SLOC members came under suspicion, journalists with Salt Lake City's major daily, the *Salt Lake Tribune*, and other papers searched the archives for earlier scandals in which Tom Welch and Dave Johnson had been implicated. *Tribune* reporter Judy Fahys (1999) produced a story on a 1988 state audit of three Utah sport associations, led by Welch and Johnson, that later became the Salt Lake bid committee. The auditors had identified questionable accounting, possible misuse of public funds through double-billing government agencies for expensive meals and entertainment, and conflict of interest, but no action had been taken. According to these reports, the lavish entertainment had been directed at USOC officials as part of the campaign to influence their selection of Salt Lake as the next American candidate city and next Winter Olympic host.

In 1991, the USOC had been the focus of another scandal when its president and IOC member Robert Helmick resigned from both committees. This marked the first time in its ninety-five-year history that an IOC member had resigned. An investigation found that Helmick had "repeatedly violated conflict-of-interest provisions of the USOC and created a perception that he was trafficking on his Olympic positions for the benefit of private clients" (Checking out, 1999).

On June 17, 1995, when the *Tribune* announced that Salt Lake City had been awarded the 2002 Winter Olympics, it made its usual appeal to the human interest side of the story. Bid committee president Tom Welch, holding a good luck token from his young sons, was reported to have been overcome with emotion, as was vice president Dave Johnson, who "shed tears, shook hands, embraced and received congratulations" (Keahey, 1995). Welch's family appeared in the news again in 1997, this time in a tragic account of wife assault witnessed by their sons. After his no-contest response to the domestic violence charge, Welch resigned from the president's position but maintained a consulting contract with SLOC of $10,000 a month and a $500,000 pension as part of his $1.1 million severance package (Gorrell, 1999b). While details of this generous deal were probably made public earlier, 1998–1999 *Tribune* stories served to draw extra attention to Welch at a time when his conduct involving "scholarships" for IOC family members was already under public scrutiny.

Also in 1997, the *Salt Lake Weekly*, a less restrained paper than the *Tribune*, published a number of accounts of Welch's SLOC leadership with titles such as "Capitol of Hypocrisy" (Harrington, 1997) and "Losing the Holy Mantle" (Biele, 1997). Foreshadowing the subsequent scandal, reporter John Harrington claimed that Welch's priorities fitted well with the IOC's "Olympic ideal" of money. He documented Welch's indulgence in "expense-paid, worldwide, glitzy Olympic schmooze-fests" and characterized him as "a pampered figurehead who got to know Olympic delegates at lavish parties, buying them off with first-class travel and expensive gifts, even medical treatment, paid for by others." Harrington alleged that fellow committee members Mike Korologos and Dave Johnson, as well as Utah governor Mike Leavitt, protected Welch, whose public relations tactics included trading on his identity as a former Mormon bishop.

Harrington, a KTVX television reporter from 1983 to 1990, radio talk show host, and freelance journalist, had been raising critical questions about Welch and the various bid attempts since 1988. When Salt Lake City was competing for USOC selection, Welch complained about Harrington's reporting to the station's general manager, and warned sponsors and advertisers that his stories would "kill" the bid. In February 1989, Harrington obtained the Utah state auditor's report that implicated Welch and Johnson in unethical business practices. Discovering Harrington's plans to show the report to the USOC ethics panel, his producer warned him that he would be fired if he proceeded. (As noted earlier, the *Tribune* published the complete story in 1999.) Harrington continued his whistle blowing attempts, and, in 1994, his *Salt Lake Weekly* exposé of the environmental controversy at the proposed Olympic ski jump site irreparably damaged his independent sports video business, as word spread through sport business circles that he was "a liar, a horrible person" (Harrington, 1999).

Finally, in 1993, with his own radio talk show, Harrington was able to expose the Olympic bribery scandal on the air as well as in print, but he found that nobody cared. In a state with a 70% Mormon population and very high Mormon representation among Olympic organizers, adherence to high moral standards was a given, and the lack of public outcry was difficult to understand. Nancy Williams, a Utah State University journalism professor, offered an explanation. Socialized in a culture "geared to being polite" and respectful of authority figures, journalism students, in her experience, had difficulty engaging in "aggressive journalism" that required questioning a president of an organization or a Mormon bishop. Williams claimed that the major television station KSL TV, owned by the Mormon church, did not have "a really strong, investigative, aggressive profile for covering issues like this" (Williams, 1999). On the other hand, Rick Hall, Olympics editor for *Deseret News*, also owned by the Mormons, disputed the claim that repressive church influence extended into the media (Hall, 1999).

It seems likely, however, that the pervasiveness of Mormon power in Utah made it difficult even for a journalist to recognize the extent of church influence on editorial content, at least until the 1998–1999 scandal. A *Deseret News* item in January 1999, written by former Utah attorney Brent Ward, pulled no punches. In a scathing critique of SLOC's "astounding array of rationalizations" intended to confuse Utahns about the legal, ethical, and moral implications of their acts, he called on readers to demand accountability and to reject the "moral laissez-faire" that retreats from an open debate of issues of public importance (Ward, 1999). In the next few months, this paper published a number of Olympic critiques, including a reprint of a *Wall Street Journal* article on criminal investigations on four continents (Copetas & Thurow, 1999b), and another by regular sports columnist Doug Robinson that posed the question "Is it too late to return the 2000 Olympics?" (Robinson, 1999).

Former Salt Lake City councilor Sydney Fonnesbeck was among the small group of elected representatives who tried to get media support in blowing the whistle on the bid. She explained in a Canadian television interview that she wrote to a journalist about a particular budget item that constituted a lot of money, but the journalist failed to follow it up, claiming it was "just a rumor." In another attempt, Fonnesbeck "specifically referred to all that we [SLOBC] were doing for the IOC members including the travel and the gifts and the scholarships, the press was sitting there and not one person" raised a question (Fonnesbeck, 1999). Even the famous letter delivered to KTVX in November 1998 had been "floating around" for at least two months, according to Fonnesbeck, who in 1998 was serving as a member of the state legislature's committee overseeing SLOC.

Harrington's experiences of harassment by Olympic supporters paralleled those of other Olympic whistle blowers: "They attack the people as individuals. There's something the matter with them . . . they're not Mormon, they're not a team player" (Harrington, 1999). He claimed that many of the journalists and editors who ignored SLOC controversies were "living off the unspoken Olympic-beat quid pro quo." Those who refused to join the "gravy train" and tried to cover Olympic news objectively under Welch's regime put their careers in jeopardy, according to Harrington, who also claimed that some female reporters were sexually harassed (Harrington, 1997).

SYDNEY MEDIA: OLYMPIC FAMILY FRIEND OR FOE?

In the early 1990s, when the Sydney bid committee embarked on its ambitious marketing campaign to sell the bid to Australians, the world, and, most importantly, IOC members, it was standard practice for the mass media to claim that there was "no organized opposition" to the bid. When local protests could not be ignored, they were trivialized as the actions of people who were "unpatriotic" and "un-Australian." Aborigines were specifically labelled troublemakers when they threatened boycotts and demonstrations. Indeed, in the wake of the Berlin experience, bid committees were fully aware that unfettered local protest signified the death blow to a bid. The fact that protests have rarely been reported in a comprehensive way in the mass media or mainstream Olympic histories attests to the power of Olympic bid and organizing committees and the IOC, especially in the last two decades, to control mass media and manufacture consent on all political questions underlying the Olympic industry. Some of the Sydney organizers' successful efforts have already been discussed in chapter 4; what follows are the later disclosures about the Sydney bid and the media.

From the early 1990s until about 1996, the *Herald* played a key role in generating support for the bid and the Games. Coverage of the bid process was primarily in the hands of *Herald* journalist Sam North, whose articles were so uncritical that they virtually served as unpaid (or payment in kind) advertising for the bid committee. Freelance journalists who attempted to blow the whistle on questionable budget figures could not get published in any major newspaper (Bacon, 1993a). For its part, a 1993 *Herald* editorial (The media and the Olympic bid, 1993) strenuously objected to the state government's alleged attempt to "straitjacket" the media. It subsequently came to light, however, that constraints on the media had been put in place three years earlier. Former premier Nick Greiner, reviewing Rod McGeoch's book, *The Bid* (McGeoch & Korporaal, 1994) in 1994, was critical of its failure to acknowledge his own "important" role in ensuring a successful outcome. Greiner explained how, in 1990, he had called a meeting of senior media representatives in Sydney to tell them that he was not prepared to commit taxpayers' money ($7 million) without a guarantee of media support for the bid. He was pleased to note that two major companies (including Fairfax, the *Herald*'s publisher) had provided what he considered "fair, perhaps even favorable treatment" and that the mass media had generally "joined in the sense of community purpose" (Greiner, 1994)—a clever cooptation of community organizing language to conceal the predominantly corporate interest ($25 million) in the bid and to rationalize his own role in censoring the press. In 1994, neither McGeoch's book, which included clear evidence of the bid committee's questionable strategies, nor Greiner's review, which boasted of his gagging of the media, sparked any public debate. By 1999, in a greatly altered political context, the publicizing of these issues attracted a different response.

As part of the *Herald*'s ongoing coverage of the Olympic scandal, it published a special report on how Sydney "snatched" the 2000 Games from Beijing (Ryle & Hughes, 1999). The story, "Breaking China," focused on McGeoch's plan to discredit the Beijing bid by drawing world attention to China's human rights record through a research report to be published in London and therefore not readily traced back to SOBC. Careful reading shows that much of the information came directly from McGeoh's book *The Bid*, while other items appeared in the Sheridan Report, which was made public the next week. The *Herald* story, of course, reached a wider audience than either McGeoch's book or Sheridan's report. Ryle and Hughes had access to additional documents "obtained" by the *Herald*, and they also conducted interviews with key politicians and bid members. Overall, the China story provided evidence of the same kind of conduct for which the Salt Lake bid committee had been universally criticized.

In February 1999, the former NSW Liberal government minister responsible for the Olympics, Bruce Baird, now a federal member of Parliament, used a speech to Parliament to defend the integrity of the Sydney bid and to attack current Labor Olympic minister Michael Knight's independent inquiry (the Sheridan Report). He reported that he had negotiated an agreement from three major media companies, including News Limited (*Daily Telegraph*) and Fairfax (*Herald* and the *Age*) on behalf of the bid committee: "[T]hey knew we would be going into a high level of duchessing [IOC members] and they would not run the normal stories about it" (Moore, 1999c). Duchessing was defined as "fawning or treating someone obsequiously in order to curry favor" (Media companies deny deal, 1999). Baird claimed that Paul Henderson had warned him about the threat posed by the media. Toronto's 1996 bid had allegedly been "blown out of the water" by local reporting (regarding BNC's opposition). Representatives from all three companies vehemently denied that such agreements ever existed and expressed shock that they should be considered capable of dictating policy to all the editors of all their newspapers. When the *Tribune* carried the Associated Press version of the story, it omitted any reference to the denials (Did Sydney papers, 1999).

Apart from the obvious "freedom of the press" explanation, these denials are difficult to explain. As noted earlier, a *Herald* editorial at the time referred to the bid committee's attempts to "straitjacket" the mainstream media, and there was ample evidence of the generally supportive tone of most mainstream coverage of the bid (see chapter 4). The *Herald*'s "Breaking China" story referred to briefing notes that identified the need to preempt criticism from "sections of the Australian media who say we should not have the Games" (Ryle & Hughes, 1999, Part 2). In short, it is clear that most of the media complied with the bid committee's request most of the time.

While some of the dissenting points of view eventually appeared in alternative publications, there was minimal critical debate in the pages of Australian magazines and journals at the time of the bid and for the next few years. The special Olympic issue of the Australian Society for Sport History journal *Sporting Traditions*, the special issue of the University of Technology Sydney's Center for Independent Journalism newsletter *Reportage*, and the first issue of the UNSW Center for Olympic Studies newsletter *Sporting Impact* came closest to achieving this goal, but few sustained their initial efforts. *Green Left Review* and *Alternative Law Journal* were among the progressive Australian publications that included critical analyses of the politics of Olympic bids in the 1990s (e.g., Russell, 1996), while even the conservative and misogynist magazine *Inside Sport* published one article by Jennings in 1997 (Jennings, 1997).

ATLANTA PRESS: THE OLYMPIC NEWSLETTER

When Atlanta embarked on its bid in 1989, the editor of the only daily newspaper, the *Atlanta Journal Constitution*, appointed the paper's business editor, Thomas Oliver, as well as two sports reporters and three other journalists, to report on the bid committee's activities. City desk reporter Bert Roughton covered local political aspects of the bid. Obviously an "insider" from the start, Roughton accompanied bid leader Billy Payne to Lausanne and to an IOC executive meeting in Lillehammer in 1990 (Lucas, 1992). Although Oliver stated in 1993 that the paper's role was as a "watchdog" to draw attention to questions of economic costs and benefits, and to provide a forum for the Olympic Conscience Coalition (Bacon, 1993), few Olympic critics agreed with this view.

Roughton embarked on his own brand of investigative journalism in 1990, when he visited all the other bid cities and wrote articles on their strengths and weaknesses. From Atlanta's point of view, this strategy was particularly successful in the case of Toronto, which had an organized opposition and, hence, plenty of "weaknesses" to document. Roughton conducted interviews with BNC members and published at least five articles on their concerns. Toronto bid chair Paul Henderson subsequently blamed Roughton for writing negative stories that were then spread through the wire services and damaged Toronto's chances (Buffery, 1999e). Roughton, in response, claimed that his stories were fair and objective, although BNC leaders acknowledged that the negative press in Atlanta probably did harm Toronto (Borowy, 1999). The fact that Roughton later became Vice President of Media Relations at the Atlanta Games cast some doubt on his objectivity.

From the perspective of the highly organized advocacy movement working on behalf of Atlanta's low-income and homeless people in the leadup to the 1996 Games, the *Constitution* did a poor job. Anita Beaty, head of the Atlanta Task Force for the Homeless, claimed that it simply became the "Olympic Newsletter" and published no criticism of Atlanta for five years. In a classic illustration of Chomsky's propaganda model, generally pro-

Olympic historian John Lucas classified Atlanta's critics as "a hundred Atlantan *special interest groups* . . . asking for and sometimes demanding a piece of the pie" (Lucas, 1992, p. 199; emphasis added). It was not until the world media came to the city in 1996 that some aspects of the city's criminalization of poverty campaigns were more widely exposed (Beaty, 1999a).

NAGANO MEDIA: UNTOLD STORIES

While English-language coverage of the Nagano bid committee's relationship to the media is limited, one highly publicized aspect is particularly relevant because of its parallels with the Sydney bid's media strategies. In an interview with the progressive UK newspaper the *Guardian*, Junichi Yamajuchi, a key member of the Nagano bid committee, reported on the reasons behind the destruction of ten boxes of documents in 1992. He claimed that some of the sixty-two IOC members (and spouses) who visited Japan had asked Nagano officials not to publicize their activities: the fine meals and hotel accommodation in Tokyo, Nagano, and Kyoto, the entertainment with geishas, and the helicopter transportation. He claimed that Nagano officials wanted to avoid any "unpleasantness" and hence as a "courtesy" to IOC members, destroyed the records (Jordan & Sullivan, 1999).

TORONTO MEDIA, 1998–1999: CAUTIOUS CRITICS

When the Toronto bid committee first announced its plans to make a second attempt at gaining the Summer Olympics for the city, the mass media were initially supportive, with the exception of a few voices calling for caution in spending millions of dollars on another risky enterprise. A March 1998 *Star* editorial, for example, praised TOBid for its (alleged) openness and outreach "to groups that have misgivings about the Olympic bid" (No room for politics, 1998). At that stage, the degree of outreach to community organizations such as the BNC member groups was minimal, and the bid committee had failed to hold a single public meeting. July 1998 marked the beginning of a more critical approach in the *Star*, when an editorial titled "More details needed on Olympics bid" (1998) validated independent forensic accountant Charles Smedmor's (1998) critique of TOBid's budget and noted that Mayor Mel Lastman's dismissive response (claiming that Smedmor had simply "invented numbers") was "not conducive to open debate."

The Olympic scandal, of course, dramatically changed public and media opinion, leaving TOBid in a defensive position in the face of clear evidence of corruption in Olympic circles. Initially, Toronto media appeared to accept

TOBid's disingenuous position that Toronto had a great advantage in bidding under the reformed selection processes, because a bid from "Toronto the Good" (as it is often called) would be "squeaky clean" and above reproach (e.g., Olympic watchdogs, 1999). With growing evidence of TOOC's less than squeaky clean 1996 bid, media treatment of the 2008 bid grew increasingly critical. Two *Star* editorials in January and two others in March were all highly critical of the IOC "cleanup" and Samaranch's continued leadership, as well as drawing attention to the double standard that ousted six members while allowing Un Yong Kim and Phil Coles to escape expulsion (Thorough Olympic cleanup, 1999; Samaranch must go, 1999; Olympic cleanup, 1999; IOC must get rid of the rot, 1999).

The *Star* also embarked on its own investigative journalism in an attempt to uncover conflicts of interest involving Canadian IOC member Carol Ann Letheren, who served on both the 1996 and the 2008 bid committees. In a March 6 article, *Star* journalists Jack Lakey and John Spears (1999) provided details of a consulting contract between TOOC and Letheren while she was a TOOC member, thus prompting a March 9 editorial titled "Letheren owes public a full explanation" (1999). A small news item several months later revealed that Letheren had sued the *Star* for libel, and the allegations disappeared from the public domain (Ethics report withheld, 1999).

In light of the close university/Olympic connection demonstrated in chapter 6, it is relevant to examine university media treatment of the Toronto bid. The major U of T student newspaper, the *Varsity*, had a long history of forthright coverage of political issues, particularly some that were an embarrassment to the university administration, such as divestment in South Africa and the corporatization of the campus. Hence, it is fair to view this paper as an example of the "alternative press" that Chomsky and others envisioned as an avenue for resistance. However, while the *Varsity* provided coverage of several Olympic bid issues in 1998–1999, its reporters tended to treat the topic with some caution.

The *Varsity* account of the panel discussion, Olympic Dreams or Urban Nightmares? sponsored by the International Network for Urban Research and Action included the complaint from a TOBid staff member that no bid representative had been invited to speak (Luksic, 1998). It is possible that *Varsity* reporters took this as a warning that future stories should not replicate the alleged imbalance of the panel, and should include the view from "the other side." In mainstream media circles, of course, this liberal notion of balance is largely unquestioned; if a newspaper published a view "from the bottom," one expects to see the mandatory response from the relevant government or corporate spokesperson. In the case of the *Varsity*, it was widely known that the president and other prominent administrators and governors were members of the TOBid board of directors, and that these overlapping directorships were generating at least informal discussions about "partnerships" and future developments in campus housing and sport facilities—all factors that may have dampened campus media interest in developing a critique of the bid.

BNC held several of its public meetings on the university campus, and the *Varsity* continued to cover these, but always with a countering point of view provided by representatives from TOBid and/or a mainstream organization such as the Board of Trade, who could be counted on to promote the alleged economic benefits of the Games. This practice seriously diluted BNC's message to the university community. In light of Chomsky's call for the community-based media to give voice to counterhegemonic perspectives, the *Varsity*'s approach often fell short of the mark.

For its part, TOBid had a healthy public relations budget and the guarantee of generous donations in kind—free advertising—from the *Toronto Star* and the *Toronto Sun*, so it could hardly be perceived as lacking in media outlets. With no funding, BNC, on the other hand, issued regular news releases—with mixed results. While the contents were sometimes reflected in mainstream coverage of the bid, the actual BNC name received very little mention. Even after BNC's sidewalk news conference to release its report card on TOBid, the *Star* published a photo but failed to discuss BNC in the story. A column on my own academic and activist work (Coyle, 1999) also omitted any reference to BNC. All these omissions can probably be attributed to the *Star*'s editorial control rather than to individual journalists. At the other end of the political spectrum, the right-wing *Toronto Sun* began its anti-BNC campaign in January 1999, with a scurrilous personal attack on Michael Shapcott that included libelous allegations (Bird, 1999; Shapcott, 1999).

THE MEDIA AND THE SCANDAL: A NEW ERA

To say that the media engaged in a "feeding frenzy" in the wake of the bribery allegations would be an understatement. Major newspapers around the world carried front-page stories for weeks, and many established a regular section under headings such as "Olympic Bribery Scandal" and "Olympic Controversy." Their web sites were equally informative, and many provided specific "Olympic Scandal" indexes to help the reader keep up with the volume of news, which at its peak reached more than five stories per day.

From the outset, president Samaranch was the most common target of media criticism, and the universal calls for his resignation prompted the response that he was not accountable to those outside the IOC and that the media were exaggerating the scandal (Korporaal, 1999f; 1999g). The personal attacks on Samaranch also prompted an official news release that repudiated allegations about his lavish lifestyle, etc. (Korporaal, 1999g). Again in March, the media focused on Samaranch's response to the U.S. Senate investigation. Depending on the newspaper, he either "refused," "snubbed," or "declined" the "invitation" to testify, sending Anita DeFrantz in his place (Samaranch snubs Senate, 1999; Samaranch won't testify, 1999). "Mauled by the media"—a *Herald* headline in March 1999—summed up European newspapers' responses to the second IOC Commission report. Most agreed with the London *Daily Telegraph* view that IOC reform "had not gone far enough, and the way they have gone about it has revealed an organization at times like a rabbit caught in the headlights" (Bose, 1999).

The controversy provided the impetus for investigative journalists to make FOI applications to Olympic organizing and bid committees, many of whom were notoriously secretive about their activities. Just before the bribery allegations of November 1998, Olympic reporter Matthew Moore documented the occasions when Sydney Olympic organizers had refused the *Herald*'s FOI requests, and contrasted Sydney with Salt Lake and Atlanta's organizing committees, both of which had (eventually) become more open (Moore, 1998b). Throughout 1999, major newspapers including the *Herald* and the *Tribune* played an important part in opening up the process. Through their web sites, for example, they provided direct links to the IOC, USOC, SOCOG, etc., as well as to the reports of the various investigations.

When interviewed at the time of the scandal, most IOC and NOC members reported being "shocked and appalled" at the possibility that bribery had ever marred the Olympic ideal, and within their ranks were individuals who themselves came under investigation at a later stage. A *Herald* editorial in January 1999 was forthright: "The IOC and Mr. Samaranch should give away the charade that they are 'shocked' at the revelations of improper conduct" (Reform time . . . , 1999). A few Olympic officials followed Richard Pound's defensive example by making references to unsubstantiated rumors of misconduct and the IOC's inability to follow up allegations without names.

Some of the more reflective journalists—those who had been critics rather than sycophants of the Olympic industry—noted the apparent "lack of shock and outrage" in the press and in society at large in the wake of the bribery charges (Brunt, 1998). Reporters who had rarely, if ever, published a critical word about the Olympic industry were now relatively free to join the majority, and it seemed that no one wished to appear naive in the face of evidence that their former blind support for the Olympics had been misplaced. One solution to this dilemma was to focus on individual misconduct rather than to examine the system that produced it. Given the nature of the mass media in the age of the twenty-second sound bite and audiences' alleged short attention span, it is probably unrealistic to expect more than the occasional in-depth analysis of the Olympic industry. Indeed, as shown earlier, journalists were among the worst offenders in calling for a return to a Golden Age of pure Olympic sport, and in supporting athletes who shared the same naive hope. But in a context where criticism of White male Olympic officials—president Samaranch, Richard Pound, John Coates, Phil Coles, Rod McGeoch, Tom Welch, and Dave Johnson, for example—was almost unprecedented, the treatment that these men received in the mainstream press in 1998–1999 helped to move public discourse onto new ground, while disrupting the Olympic industry's generally successful campaign to maintain control over the mass media.

Australian IOC/SOCOG member Phil Coles, for example, had been in the public eye in January 1999 when conflict of interest allegations prompted (or forced) him to resign from a consultancy with a hotel designated for Olympic family accommodation. On this occasion, public and media reaction generally reflected the SOCOG view that the decision was both appropriate and smart (Evans, 1999b; Moore, 1999a). A few weeks later, the media were unrelenting in their condemnation of Coles after allegations that he had received more than $50,000 (AUS) of hospitality, gifts, and services from the Salt Lake bid committee. *Herald* headlines, for example, included: "Coles: gold medal freeloader" (Coultan & Wilkinson, 1999) and "Coles set to continue the high life" (Magnay & Riley, 1999b). The *Herald* went to considerable lengths to compile evidence against Coles, particularly when he denied knowledge of a pair of earrings (originally designed as cufflinks and allegedly a $10,000 gift to Coles from the Athens bid committee) that his former wife had been wearing in a photo published in that paper in 1990 (Korporaal & Moore, 1999b). The *Herald* reproduced the photo several times in March 1999, shortly after Coles's denial, with the cynical caption, "Oh that jewelry" (Millett & Magnay, 1999).

As demonstrated in the earlier discussion of the myth of the pure athlete, it was common to find media accounts that juxtaposed the "bad apples"—most notably the expelled African IOC members and a few others from developing countries—against the "good" Olympic athletes—mostly young and White—who would return the Olympics to their "pure" roots. In Toronto, where the athletes' advocacy group known as OATH began organizing, newspapers tended to focus on one of OATH's founding members,

Mark Tewksbury, a former Olympic swimmer who had resigned from TOBid and the COA because of the scandal.

In terms of symbolic messages, an equally serious media distortion was the practice of publishing photos of the six expelled IOC members—that is, a row of mostly Black and brown faces—beside every IOC scandal story, to serve as a constant reminder to readers that the so-called "bad apples" were not White, but that Richard Pound, whose photo appeared just as often, was (Starkman & Van Rijn, 1999; Vincent, 1999c). The *Star* published one of the few analyses of the race issue by Black Canadian author and critic Cecil Foster, who correctly identified the scapegoating at work in the IOC's so-called reform process: "Pretending that a few symbolic changes here and there—the symbolic expulsion of a [Ben] Johnson or a Third World IOC member—will not clean up the Olympics" (Foster, 1999).

Although critiques of the Olympic industry as a complete system of power and privilege rarely appeared in the mainstream press, some investigative journalists went to considerable lengths to uncover instances of individual misconduct, which they occasionally presented as symptoms of a flawed system. One such example was the case of Charles Mukora, significantly, a Black IOC member from Kenya. International journalists, including Ed O'Loughlin of the *Herald*, attended Mukora's press conference in Nairobi in January 1999. O'Loughlin then drove three hours to the location of Mukora's planned high-altitude training center—the project funded by the Salt Lake and Sydney bid committees as part of their "humanitarian aid" program—and reported that no training had taken place there until that week (O'Loughlin, 1999). Since the IOC commission had recommended Mukora's expulsion a week earlier, these journalists' investigative efforts were somewhat redundant. The AOC's donations (through John Coates) to the Kenyan and Ugandan NOC's were a major focus of the Australian media in early 1999, and Mukora's continued membership in the International Amateur Athletic Federation and his role as technical delegate to the 2000 Olympics aroused public and media concern (Jeffery, 1999; Coorey, 1999), as well as a controversy over a missing $13,000 (AUS) donation to Kenyan athletes (O'Loughlin & Magnay, 1999). As was the case with other allegations involving White donors and Black recipients, media and public criticism of Coates's role in this affair was short-lived.

By April 1999, when SOCOG was breathing a collective sigh of relief that the scandal had abated, Ali Cromie, an investigative journalist with *Business Review Weekly*, published a three-part series titled "Is Coates fit to run the Olympics?" (Cromie, 1999a; 1999b). His overlapping directorships—SOCOG senior vice president, AOC president, deputy chair of

Kenfu Properties (owner of an Olympic family hotel), and others—raised many conflict of interest concerns. In addition to the well-known Reef Casino case, where Coates invested and lost about $5 million (AUS) of AOC funds, Cromie pursued his other "reckless" stock market investments and his extensive loans (which Coates acknowledged amounted to about $600,000) to build up the case that he had made many risky and bad judgments, involving both private and public money, in the recent past (Cromie, 1999a).

CONCLUSION

The unprecedented attack on the Olympic industry in 1998–1999 marked a new era in mass media treatment of all things Olympic. Admittedly, most critiques focused on individuals rather than extending the analysis to a flawed system, and the positions of Olympic watchdog groups continued, for the most part, to be underreported. It soon became apparent that the media's preoccupation with individual misconduct limited its effectiveness, and at times played into racist and colonialist discourses that portrayed ethnic minority IOC members as more culpable than those from the dominant White group. Widespread media calls for president Samaranch's resignation simply provoked official pronouncements from the IOC that it was not accountable to the press, a defense that any powerful transnational corporation, in the face of a similar media attack, might have echoed. Despite these limitations, it is clear from the preceding discussion that the global media did in fact play a key role in keeping Olympic controversies in the public consciousness, and disclosing information that ultimately pushed the IOC to investigate the allegations, to expel members, and to explore structural reform.

Conclusion

As with other unelected bodies which have acquired great power, the IOC's most priceless asset is its integrity. In modern times it is difficult enough for such bodies to preserve their other great asset, independence. Once corruption, or even incompetence, is suspected, hitherto quiet suggestions that they ought to be formally accountable to some broader constituency may turn from suggestion into demands and prove difficult to resist.

—C. Hill, in *The Changing Politics of Sport*

E VENTS OF 1998–1999 within the Olympic industry attest to the validity of UK Olympic scholar Christopher Hill's 1993 prediction. Calls for accountability came from all quarters following the disclosures of bribery and corruption in the bid process. For a short time, these demands did prove difficult, but, unfortunately, not impossible for the IOC to resist. Olympic boosters, particularly those likely to reap personal and business rewards, continued to indulge in Olympic industry rhetoric as they expressed their boundless faith in the proposed reforms. Incredibly, as late as August 12, 1999, after several international inquiries had exposed the extent of IOC corruption, Toronto 2008 bid committee chief John Bitove told a media briefing that the IOC, composed as it was of "dukes and princesses" and upstanding businessmen, was not corrupt.

Three key problematic features of the Olympic industry have been identified in the preceding discussion:

1. The structure and function of the IOC:

   • membership selection process;

   • elitism and sense of entitlement demonstrated by most members;

   • members' lack of accountability to those most affected by their decisions;

   • IOC exemption from OECD conventions regarding corruption and bribery;

   • and host city selection procedures, especially member visits to bid cities.

2. The Olympic industry's resistance to public oversight:

   • exemption from Freedom of Information legislation;

   • confidentiality agreements demanded by big business interests;

   • misleading budgets that render public spending on infrastructure and other areas invisible;

   • and secrecy and deceit in bid and organizing committees' communications with citizens.

3. Public relations campaigns mounted by the IOC and bid and organizing committees:

   • media complicity demanded by the Olympic industry;

   • suppression of public debate and critique;

   • information on negative social/economic/environmental impact suppressed or preempted by Olympic spirit rhetoric;

   • depoliticization of the Olympic industry through the myth of the "pure athlete" and "pure sport";

   • and assumptions that citizens are unreflective dupes whose support is easily secured through Olympic propaganda.

Evidence from three decades of Olympic industry disasters has demonstrated what is arguably the most serious and sinister implication for citizens living in Olympic cities and states: the threat of disenfranchisement. The generally negative social, economic, and environmental impacts of hallmark events, as well as the documented concerns and experiences of anti-Olympic and Olympic watchdog groups on four continents, provide irrefutable evidence that Olympic bids and preparations exacerbate the problems of already disadvantaged populations. While some of the promised economic boosts may eventuate, there is little evidence that the people "at the bottom of the food chain" will reap any benefits. A beautified, gentrified city with state-of-the art professional sport facilities has no value to men, women, and children whose basic human needs are not being met.

A democratic society is premised on citizen participation in decision making, genuine representation by elected officials, and a social safety net for those who cannot provide housing, food, health care, and education for themselves and their children. Admittedly, not all Olympic host countries are democracies, but it is important to remember that problems such as human rights abuses, criminalization of poverty campaigns, conflict of interest problems, attempted control of the mass media, and noncompliance with social and environmental impact legislation occurred in Atlanta, Sydney, and Toronto. Authoritarian regimes have no monopoly on suspending human rights and suppressing public debate in the interests of the Olympic profit-making machine.

None of the proposed IOC reforms to date addresses these kinds of problems. Image issues were seen as central from the outset. Both president Samaranch and vice president Richard Pound lamented the fact that there was such extensive misunderstanding about the structures and functions of the IOC, especially in the area of generating and dispersing of funds. One of the IOC's early responses to the scandal was the appointment of a public relations company that was infamous for its success in selling unpopular and unethical causes.

The IOC 2000 Commission, whose mandate included developing recommendations for structural reform, produced its intermediary report in June 1999. Replete with the usual rhetoric about Olympic ideals, values, uniqueness, heritage, benefits, etc., the report recommended that "every effort be made, through an evolutionary (as opposed to revolutionary) process, to democratize the movement behind [the athletes] whilst maintaining its autonomy and independence" (IOC 2000 Commission, 1999, p. 3). The notion of "evolution not revolution" resonated not only with IOC members but also with the athletes' advocacy group OATH, whose own mission, developed at its "Ignite the Democratic Flame" symposium in June of the same year, included challenging the IOC to *restore* Olympic ideals to the movement, in part through democratic governance initiatives. This implicit invoking of an earlier "Golden Age" when Olympic sport was pure and true obscured the reality that the organization of the Olympic Games has always been shaped by social, political, and economic forces operating globally.

Transparency and communication were identified in the IOC 2000 Commission report as two key reform principles, not just because of the need for accountability, but mainly to address the problem of public opinion that tended to "disassociate" the Olympic Games from the IOC and failed to recognize the IOC's contributions in developing sport "as an instrument of peace and reconciliation" (p. 4). Ironically, the goal of reconciliation has been central to Australian Aborigines' struggles with the government for decades, and it is hardly likely that they would view the Olympics as helpful in achieving this objective. Indeed, like other disadvantaged minorities, their voices have been suppressed in the interests of the Olympic industry, and they plan to draw international attention to racist injustice during the Sydney Olympics

Overall, the 2000 Commission report perpetuated the myth that the Olympics was a "movement" and not an industry. Players in this "movement" were identified as the IOC, organizing committees, international federations, NOCs, and athletes (p. 5). Proposed structural changes called for greater representation of federations, NOCs, and active athletes in the IOC and in its executive board, a proposal that would achieve the goal of involving more Olympic athletes in decisions that affect their lives. However, athletes are not the only constituency currently underrepresented in the Olympic industry, nor is their underrepresentation the most serious problem. None of the proposed IOC reforms addresses the social, economic, and environmental impact issues: for example, the fact that Olympic preparations are demonstrably responsible for exacerbating the problems of the most vulnerable populations in host cities and states. Not only is there the inevitable negative fallout of a hallmark event, but there are two other equally serious issues: attempts to silence opposition through Olympic industry rhetoric—most notably, the myths of the pure athlete and pure sport—and the disenfranchisement of citizens regarding public spending incurred during Olympic preparations that masquerade as private enterprise.

What is needed is the dismantling of the Olympic industry as presently constituted. It is naive to expect that those with the most power and privilege will voluntarily forfeit their status and fall in line with the proposed reforms. Indeed, IOC members' backlash to the interim city bid selection process and their opposition to the 2000 Commission's proposed limits on bid city visits provide ample evidence of their determination to maintain the status quo. It is equally naive to rely on some mythical notion of the redemptive power of sport and to pretend it is uncontaminated by capitalism, racism, sexism, classism, or any other form of systemic oppression. Athletes, coaches, and sport officials, while admittedly lacking the material privileges of most IOC members, are complicit in the industry when they perpetuate these dangerous myths, and when they dismiss intelligent critics as "unreasonable" or unmoved by the "magic" of Olympic sport. In the same vein, universities are complicit when they trade student democracy for new sport facilities. There is no evidence to date that any reforms originating within or outside the IOC will generate a humane, socially conscious alternative to the current Olympic industry product.

An essential first step in disabling the Olympic machine is to develop structural barriers that prevent elected representatives, university administrations, and the mass media from being coopted into the Olympic industry. This requires the complete demystification of the Olympics through grassroots community education and organizing. The goal of this enterprise would be to demonstrate that, behind all the rhetoric, the so-called Olympic movement is simply a transnational corporation that in many instances exploits young athletes' labor and aspirations for its own aggrandizement and profit. Furthermore, the educational agenda must include exposing the real nature of the Olympic legacy, which, in many recent worst case scenarios, has meant huge deficits borne by taxpayers, the suppression of public debate and dissent, and the oppression of disadvantaged urban populations. Indeed, I would argue that people who enjoy sport and value democracy would be ill-advised to support any aspect of the Olympics, and that their energies and talents would be better directed toward other regional, national, and international sporting competitions that are currently conducted in more ethical and less exploitative ways.

For their part, citizens need to demand accountability from politicians at all levels of government and from the administrations of publicly funded universities, regarding financial commitments, overlapping directorships, and other kinds of Olympic-related alliances. Finally, since freedom of the press is only maintained through vigilance, its frequent cooptation in the service of the Olympic industry should be strenuously resisted. When the global media present all Olympic news as good news, as they are often pressured to do by bid and host cities, one of the most important avenues for full disclosure and public debate is in jeopardy.

REFERENCES

Deseret News; <www.desnews.com>
Salt Lake Tribune (Tribune); <www.sltrib.com>
Sydney Morning Herald (Herald); <www.smh.com.au>
Toronto Star (Star); <www.thestar.com>

A degree of help for athletes. (1999). *Herald* (May 25).

Adler, J. (1996). It's the Olympic spirit that still moves them. *Newsweek* (July 22).

Alinsky, S. (1971). *Rules for Radicals.* New York: Vintage.

Anti-Olympic People's Network. (1999). Letter to IOC President Samaranch (March 12).

Armstrong, I. (1998). NSW Government: Motion of No Confidence. Legislative Assembly Article, Hansard (September 8).

Asian Coalition for Housing Rights. (1989). Evictions in Seoul, South Korea. *Environment and Urbanization,* 1:1, 89–94.

Askin, L. (1989). Deputation to the City of Toronto Olympic Bid Committee (November 28).

Associated Press and Grolier. (1999). *Pursuit of Excellence: The Olympic Story.* Danbury, CT: Grolier.

A tale of two cities. (1998). *Rentwatchers Report,* 1:2, 4.

Athanasiou, T. (1996). *Divided Planet: The Ecology of Rich and Poor.* Boston: Little, Brown & Co.

Athletes draw up team values. (1999). *ABC News* (February 19).

Atlanta Task Force for the Homeless. (1995). *Advocacy: The criminalization of poverty.* <www.leveller.org/tfp/MAMBO/advocacy/html>.

ATSIC. (1995). *Recognition Rights and Reform*: Sport and recreation. <www.atsic.gov.au/library/recognit/45.htm>.

Auf der Maur, N. (1976). *The Billion-Dollar Games.* Toronto: Lorimer.

Background Briefing. (1997, October 26). Bay of Secrets. ABC Radio National Transcripts.

Bacon, W. (1993a). Atlanta's watchdog. *Reportage* (September), 6.

———. (1993b). Media's role questioned. *Reportage* (September), 1–2.

Baird, J. (1998). Olympic deal not bribery, say African athletes. *Herald* (December 17).

Bale, J., and Moen, O. (1995). *The Stadium and the City.* Staffordshire: Keele University Press.

Banham, C. (1999). Stopping the Olympic juggernaut. *City Hub* (May 6), 11.

Beaty, A. (1998a). E-mail communication to Bread Not Circuses (June 4).

———. (1998b). Extracts from August 10 Speech to NSW Parliament. *Rent Report* 2 (December).

———. (1999a). The homeless Olympics? In James, C., Plant, R., South, J., Beeston, B., & Long, D., eds., *Homelessness: The Unfinished Agenda*. Sydney: University of Sydney, 46–51.

———. (1999b). Personal communication (November 12).

Beder, S. (1994). Sydney's toxic Green Olympics. *Current Affairs Bulletin*, 70:6, 12–18.

———. (1996). Sydney's Olympic landscape: A toxic coverup. *Search*, 27:7, 209–211.

———. (1999). Media self-censorship in Australia's Olympic bid. *PR Watch*, 6:2, 7–8.

Benedict, J. (1998). *Athletes and Acquaintance Rape*. Thousand Oaks, CA: Sage.

Biele, K. (1997). Losing the holy mantle. *Salt Lake City Weekly* (September 4).

Bird, H. (1999). Olympics fight turns personal. *Toronto Sun* (February 2).

Blizzard, C. (1999). Keep it clean, and drink your milk. *Toronto Sun* (February 7).

Blount, R. (1996). Outta there. *CNN Weekly News* (July 29).

Boarding houses. (1998). Rentwatchers Report #2 (December), 6–7.

Booth, D., & Tatz, C. (1994). Sydney 2000: The Games people play. *Current Affairs Bulletin*, 70:7, 4–11.

Borowy, J. (1999). Consultation re Bread Not Circuses Coalition (July 16).

Bose, M. (1999). IOC meeting: Samaranch holds on but chaos and confusion reign. *Telegraph* (UK) (March 18).

Boulton, G. (1999). IOC spouse had job help from SLOC. *Tribune* (February 6).

Bread Not Circuses. (1998). Democratic, financial and social accountability and Toronto's bid for the 2008 Olympics (June 30).

Bread Not Circuses Coalition. (1990). *The Anti-Bid Book*. Toronto: Bread Not Circuses.

Brokerage for the homeless. (1998). *Around the House*, 30 (November–January), 6–7.

Brown, M. (1998). City "cleansing" fear for Games. *Herald* (June 3).

Brubaker, B. (1999). Ex-Olympic official admits violation. *Washington Post* (February 19).

Brunet, F. (1995). An economic analysis of the Barcelona '92 Olympic Games. In Moragas, M., & Botella, M., eds., *The Keys to Success*. Barcelona: UAB, 203–237.

Brunt, S. (1998). Olympic scandal triggers yawns. *Globe and Mail* (December 15).

Buffery, S. (1999a). 96 bid victim of scams. *Toronto Sun* (January 13).

———. (1999b). IOC member's 1989 hiring questioned. *Toronto Sun* (January 15).

———. (1999c). 96 bid group on defensive. *Toronto Sun* (January 19).

———. (1999d). T.O. boss rips media. *Toronto Sun* (January 24).

———. (1999e). Atlanta smeared us: TOOC. *Toronto Sun* (March 6).

Burstyn, V. (1999). *The Rites of Men*. Toronto: University of Toronto Press.

Business as usual. (1999). *Associated Press* (January 13).

Byers, J. (1999). El Farnawani's trip to Spain shrouded in mystery. *Star* (January 29).

———. (1989). "Fair" media coverage urged for Olympic bid. *Star* (November 14).

Cairnes, L. (1998). Perspectives. In Cashman & Hughes, *Green Games*, 23–25.

Calvert, J., Connett, D., Gillard, M., & Mackay, D. (1999). Games up for sale to highest bidder. *Guardian Weekly* (UK) (January 31), 23.

Canadian Folk Arts Council. (1990). Intervenor Report (January).

Caplan, G. (1990). Olympic bid is a shameless con job. *Star* (January 28), B3.

Carr, R. (1998). Royal Easter Show: Questions without notice. Legislative Assembly Article, Hansard (April 28).

Carter, M. (1998). IOC official criticizes SLOC for scholarships. *Tribune* (December 10).

Cashman, R., & Hughes, A., eds. (1998). *The Green Games: A Golden Opportunity.* Sydney: Center for Olympic Studies, UNSW.

Cates, K. (1998). Park City leaders ask SLOC to disclose all. *Tribune* (December 12).

Chandler, M. (1998, March 25). Homebush and dry: a green seal of approval for Olympic gains. *Australian Financial Review*, 38.

Checking out past Olympic scandals. (1999). *USA Today* (January 27).

Chernushenko, D. (1994). *Greening Our Games: Running Sports Events and Facilities that Won't Cost the Earth.* Ottawa: Centurion.

Chomsky, N. (1989). *Necessary Illusions.* Toronto: CBC Massey Lectures.

Christie, J. (1990). Games' legacy: state-of-the-art venues. *Globe and Mail* (September 7).

———. (1999a). Special consideration for IOC spouse denied. *Globe and Mail* (January 15).

———. (1999b). IOC president knew about job, rent payment. *Globe and Mail* (January 19).

———. (1999c). Toronto bid leader had secret scheme to raise funds. *Globe and Mail* (January 27).

———. (1999d). Toronto told to forget audit of failed Games. *Globe and Mail* (April 13).

Clennell, A. (1999). Second council "police force" hired. *Herald* (May 20).

Cochrane, A., Peck, J., & Tickell, A. (1996). Manchester plays games: exploring the local politics of globalization. *Urban Studies*, 33:8, 1319–1336.

Cockerill, M. (1999). Olympic spirit to make a comeback. *Herald* (April 23).

Community coalition fighting for the protection of tenants. (1998). *Rent Report* (July).

Coorey, M. (1999). Kenya's touring delegate maintains innocence. *Australian* (January 21).

Copetas, R., & Thurow, R. (1999a). IOC fears Justice probe poses its "biggest problem." *Deseret News* (January 20).

———. (1999b). Do Games hide shady dealings? *Deseret News* (March 5).

Copetas, R., Thurow, R., & Fatsis, S. (1999). Tarnished rings? *Deseret News* (reprinted by permission of *Wall Street Journal*) (January 10).

Coultan, M., & Wilkinson, M. (1999). Coles: gold medal freeloader. *Herald* (February 27).

Cox, G. (1998a). Faster, higher, stronger . . . but what about our rights? *Impact Assessment and Project Appraisal*, 16:3, 175–184.

———. (1998b). *Social Issues for Olympic Cities.* Cox Consulting Pty Limited, Darlinghurst.

Cox, G., Darcy, M., & Bounds, M. (1994). *The Olympics and Housing.* Sydney: Shelter NSW (September).

Coyle, J. (1999). Olympic critic finally gets to say "I told you so." *Star* (January 30).

Cragg, A. (1998). Business, globalization, and the logic and ethics of corruption. *International Journal* (Autumn), 641–660.

Crombie, D. (1998). *CTV News* (September 17).

———. (1999). Green Olympics panel discussion, Toronto (January 23).

Cromie, A. (1999a). Mr Olympics chases his own gold. *Business Review Weekly* (April 16), 85–91.

———. (1999b). Five rings, four stars, no conflict. *Business Review Weekly* (April 23), 149–157.

Cronau, P. (1993). Social impact of the Games under wraps. *Reportage* (September), 16–19.

D'Alessandro, D. (1999). How to save the Olympics. *New York Times* (February 14).

Darcy, M. (1998). The Olympics: a smokescreen for dispossession of the poor. *Rent Report* 2 (December).

Darcy, S., & Veal, A. J. (1994). The Sydney 2000 Olympic Games: the story so far. *Australian Journal of Leisure and Recreation*, 4:1, 1–8.

Dehli, K., Restakis, J., & Sharpe, E. (1988). The rise and fall of the parent movement in Toronto. In Cunningham, F., Findlay, S., Kadar, M., Lennon, A., & Silva, E., eds., *Social Movements, Social Change*. Toronto: Between the Lines, 209–227.

Deister, G. (1999). Uncle Sam's Games. *Herald* (April 14).

Demands for Samaranch to resign continue. (1999). *Associated Press* (January 27).

DeMara, B. (1999a). Eggleton ignored '96 Games warning. *Star* (January 30).

————. (1999b). Games watchdog has yet to meet in public. *Star* (March 10).

Did Sydney papers agree to ignore IOC gifts? (1999). *Tribune* (February 19).

Djerrkura, G. (1999). Speech to UN Working Group on Indigenous Populations, Geneva (July 17). <www.atsic.gov.au//media/speeches_transcripts/display/asp?id=231>.

Donnelly, P. (1997). Young athletes need child law protection. In Donnelly, P., ed., *Taking Sport Seriously: Social Issues in Canadian Sport*. Toronto: Thompson Educational Press, 189–95.

Egan, C., Gardner, L., & Persad, J. (1988). The politics of transformation: struggles with race, class, and sexuality in the March 8th Coalition. In Cunningham et al., *Social Movements, Social Change*, 20–47.

Egan, D. (1999). Johnson's Olympic dream tumbles. *Tribune* (January 9).

Egan, T. (1999). The persistence of polygamy. *New York Times Magazine* (February 28), 51–55.

Eitzen, D. S. (1996). Classism in sport: the powerless bear the burden. *Journal of Sport and Special Issues*, 20:1, 95–105.

Environmental Protection Authority. (1996). *Case Study: Homebush Bay Olympic Site*. <www.epa.nsw.gov.au/soe/97/ch5/9_1/htm>.

Essex, S., & Chalkley, B. (1998). Olympic Games: catalyst of urban change. *Leisure Studies*, 17, 187–206.

Ethics report withheld. (1999). *Star* (June 11).

Evans, L. (1998). Team Oz in golden form on 2000 course. *Herald* (April 27).

Evans, M. (1998a). Perkins slams SOCOG "token." *Herald* (November 30).

————. (1998b). Knight snubbed by blacks. *Herald* (December 3).

————. (1999a). Winter Olympics city gave Samaranch gift of guns. *Herald* (January 7).

————. (1999b). Spirit breached, not the rules: Knight. *Herald* (January 15).

————. (1999c). Holden admits scandal has given it sponsorship jitters. *Herald* (February 12).

————. (1999d). You scratch my back, Sydney. *Herald* (March 16).

Evans, M., Moore, M., & Korporaal, G. (1999). Coates explains himself to IOC. *Herald* (January 25).

Fahys, J. (1999). Audit had questioned groups' practices. *Tribune* (January 10).

Fantin, L. (1999a). Utahns react to Olympic scandal: cynicism, anger. *Tribune* (January 9).

————. (1999b). Mormon man says Utah should give back "ill-gotten Games." *Tribune* (February 25).

————. (1999c). Congress next in line to run IOC through the ringer. *Tribune* (March 21).

Ferguson, R. (1999). Newcourt Credit sold to US firm. *Star* (March 9).

Fonnesbeck, S. (1999). Transcript, *CBC Sports Journal* (May 3).

Foster, C. (1999). Olympics are as tarnished as Ben Johnson. *Star* (February 1).

Freeman, A. (1999). IOC moves to expel six in bribery scandal. *Globe and Mail* (January 26).

Freire, Paulo. (1973). *Education for Critical Consciousness*. New York: Seabury.

French, S., & Disher, M. (1997). Atlanta and the Olympics: a one-year retrospective. *Journal of the American Planning Association*, 63:3, 379–393.

Gillis, C. (1998). Membership has its privileges. *National Post* (December 14).

Gittings, Ross. (1993). The case for an Olympic kick-start. *Herald* (September 22).

Godwell, D. (1999a). Consultation re Aboriginal issues, Sydney (April 26).

———. (1999b). Olympic branding of Aborigines: the 2000 Olympics and Australia's indigenous peoples. In Schaffer, K., & Smith, S., eds., *The Olympics at the Millenium: Power, Politics, and the Games*. New Jersey: Rutgers University Press.

Golden, A. (1999). Report of the Mayor's Homelessness Action Task Force, Toronto.

Gorrell, M. (1998a). Tuition paid for kin of IOC member. *Tribune* (November 26).

———. (1998b). Payments were aid, SLOC maintains. *Tribune* (December 6).

———. (1998c). SLOC payments to IOC relatives under suspicion. *Tribune* (December 9).

———. (1998d). IOC investigation gets under way. *Tribune* (December 12).

———. (1998e). IOC won't strip S.L. of Games. *Tribune* (December 14).

———. (1998f). Hodler says IOC needs to change its operations. *Tribune* (December 15).

———. (1998g). "Agent" who received IHC care named. *Tribune* (December 18).

———. (1998h). SLOC orders ethics panel to review bid. *Tribune* (December 19).

———. (1999a). SLOC top officials will step aside today. *Tribune* (January 8).

———. (1999b). Welch: I hid nothing, Joklik: That's baloney. *Tribune* (January 11).

———. (1999c). Olympic watchdog files complaint over radio jabs. *Tribune* (February 23).

———. (1999d). Documents support report on IOC member. *Tribune* (February 26).

———. (1999e). Olympic alumnus tells SL it can achieve dream. *Tribune* (February 26).

Gorrell, M., & Walsh, R. (1998). Welch to help in SLOC probe. *Tribune* (December 17).

Grange, M. (1999). IOC report on Games scandal not enough, Tewksbury says. *Globe and Mail* (January 26).

Grant, C. (1998). The infrastructure of the Games. In Cashman & Hughes, *Green Games*, 41–46.

Gratton, R. (1999). The media. In Cashman, R., & Hughes, A., eds., *Staging the Olympics*. Sydney: UNSW Press, 121–131.

Greiner, N. (1994). Inside running on Olympic bid. *Australian* (19 October).

Gross, G. (1999). Lausanne braces for IOC's day of reckoning. *Toronto Sun* (January 22).

Guttman, A. (1994). *The Olympics: A History of the Modern Games*. Chicago: University of Illinois Press.

Hall, C. (1989). The politics of hallmark events. In Syme, G., Shaw, B., Fenton, M., & Mueller, W., eds., *The Planning and Evaluation of Hallmark Events*. Vermont: Avebury, 219–241.

———. (1994). *Tourism and Politics*. New York: Wiley.

———. (1998). Imaging, tourism, and sports event fever. Paper presented to the Sport in the City Conference, Sheffield (July 2–4).

Hall, R. (1999). Transcript, *CBC Sports Journal* (May 12).

Halstead, J. (1998). Report to the Community Councils on 2008 Toronto Olympic bid public consultation (July 7).

Harrington, J. (1997). Capitol of hypocrisy. *Salt Lake City Weekly* (August 7).

———. (1999). Transcript, *CBC Sports Journal* (May 5).

Heilprin, J. (1999). Coalition calls for SLOC resignations. *Tribune* (January 3).

Henderson, P., Seagram, N., & Eggleton, A. (1991). *Report to the International Olympic Committee by the Toronto Ontario Olympic Council* (January 9).

Henetz, P. (1998). Olympic scandal may lead to housecleaning. *Tribune* (December 20).

Herbert, H. (1999). The homeless Olympics? In James, C., Plant, R., South, J., Beeston, B., & Long, D., eds., *Homelessness: The Unfinished Agenda*. Sydney: University of Sydney, 60–62.

Herman, D., & Chomsky, N. (1988). *Manufacturing Consent: The Political Economy of the Mass Media*. New York, Pantheon.

Hershman, M. (1998). Criminalized foreign bribery will improve trade. *National Law Journal* (April 27).

Hewett, T. (1992). Aboriginal group splits support for 2000 Olympics. *Herald* (October 24).

Hill, C. (1992). *Olympic Politics*. Manchester: Manchester University Press.

———. (1993). The politics of the Olympic movement. In Allison, L., ed., *The Changing Politics of Sport*. Manchester: Manchester University Press, 84–104.

Hoare, B. (1999). Consultation re Green Games Watch 2000 (April 29).

Hoberman, J. (1995). Toward a theory of Olympic internationalism. *Journal of Sport History*, 22:1, 1–37.

———. (1997). *Darwin's Athletes*. New York: Houghton Mifflin.

Hogarth, M. (1998). Media Panel. In Cashman & Hughes, *Green Games*, 101–102.

———. (1999). Consultation re Sydney 2000 and the environment (April 22).

Horin, A. (1998). Budget hotels baulk at rooms for homeless during Games. *Herald* (August 5).

———. (1999). State of despair haunts a score of western suburbs. *Herald* (June 8).

Horton, M., & Freire, P. (1990). *We Make the Road by Walking: Conversations on Education and Social Change*. Philadelphia: Temple University Press.

Hospitality the rule in Games bid. (1999). *Star* (February 27).

Houlihan, B. (1994). *Sport and International Politics*. New York: Harvester Wheatsheaf.

Hughes, A. (1999). Redfern Report (unpublished research paper, UNSW).

Hulchanski, D. (1998). Presentation to International Network for Urban Research and Action Conference, *Olympic Dreams, Urban Nightmares?* Toronto (September 15).

Hutton, D. (1987). *Green Politics in Australia*. Sydney: Angus & Robertson.

Indigenous leaders call for Olympic unity. (1998). *ABC News* (March 23).

Infantry, A. (1998). Olympic bid team working in Spain. *Star* (June 1).

———. (1999a). Games officials quit as cash-for-votes scandal grows. *Star* (January 9).

———. (1999b). Bid agents' gravy train about to end. *Star* (January 24).

Infantry, A., & Starkman, R. (1998). Toronto agent probed in Olympic bribe scandal. *Star* (December 18).

International Chair in Olympic Studies, Autonomous University of Barcelona. (1997). Informational brochure.

Intervenor Funding. (1989). City of Toronto Committee of Department Heads Olympic Task Force (October).

IOC. (1997). *Olympic Charter* (September 3).

———. (1997). *Manual on Sport and the Environment* (August).

IOC 1998 City Bid Vote Commission. (1998). *City details: Helsinki*.

IOC 2000 City Bid Vote Commission. (1993). *City details: Berlin*.

IOC 2000 Commission. (1999). *Intermediary Report* (June 2).

IOC ad hoc Commission. (1999a). *Report* (January 23).

———. (1999b). *Report* (March 11).

IOC bribes: Hodler mistrusts 25. (1998). *Herald* (December 18). (AP).

IOC members revolt against plans to change vote system. (1999). *Tribune* (February 4).

IOC must get rid of the rot (editorial). (1999). *Star* (March 16).

IOC Special Commission. (1999). *Report* (June 14).

IOC's Pound. (1999). Press release, McGill University, Montreal, PQ.

James, R. (1999). Toronto the good now shabby. *Star* (June 30).

Jeffery, N. (1993). Just 45 minutes to decide Olympic glory or gloom. *Australian* (June 23), 9.

———. (1998). Grandstanding: the pollies' event. *Australian* (October 26).

———. (1999). IOC bribe take wins Sydney post. *Australian* (January 28).

Jennings, A. (1996). *The New Lords of the Rings*. London: Simon & Shuster.

———. (1997). How Athens got the 2004 Games. *Inside Sport* (September).

Johnson, K. (1999). Utah officials saw "red flags" in '88. *USA Today* (January 22).

Jopson, D., & Martin, L. (1999). Blacks put Games threat to UN. *Herald* (July 30).

Jordan, M., & Sullivan, K. (1999). Olympic Games: multi-million mystery as lid blows off Nagano. *Guardian* (UK) (January 22).

Katz, L. (1974). *Power, public policy, and the environment: the defeat of the 1976 Winter Olympics in Colorado*. In *Dissertation Abstracts International*, 35:12, part 1 (June 1975).

Keahey, J. (1995). Utah to welcome the world in 2002. *Tribune* (June 17).

Kells, M. (1998). Debates of the Ontario Legislature: City of Toronto XXIX Summer Olympic Games Bid Endorsement Act, 1998. Hansard (December 3).

Keys Young. (1995). Preliminary Social Impact Assessment of the Sydney 2000 Olympics and Paralympic Games (January).

Kidd, B. (1992). The Toronto Olympic Commitment: towards a social contract for the Olympic Games. *Olympika*, 1, 154–167.

———. (1995). Toronto's SkyDome: the world's greatest entertainment center. In Bale & Moen, *The Stadium and the City*, 175–196.

———. (1997). Towards a pedagogy of the Olympic sports. In Donnelly, *Taking Sport Seriously*, 73–82.

Kieran, I. (1998). Opportunities for education and selling Australian environmental technology and practice. In Cashman & Hughes, *Green Games* 71–75.

Korporaal, G. (1998a). IOC should grab the chance to clean up its act. *Herald* (December 14).

———. (1998b). Sydney spared IOC inquiry. *Herald* (December 16).

———. (1999a). Suite charity: Olympic family's free ride. *Herald* (January 22).

———. (1999b). Ousting corrupt members bit of a marathon. *Herald* (January 22).

———. (1999c). Gosper defends Korean colleague. *Herald* (January 23).

———. (1999d). Kept in dark, now Gosper has to give answers. *Herald* (January 25).

———. (1999e). Baird letter "disappoints" inquiry. *Herald* (January 26).

———. (1999f). World press tells Samaranch to go. *Herald* (January 28).

———. (1999g). Samaranch is angry at media. *Herald* (February 2).

———. (1999h). IOC offers to import its own cars. *Herald* (February 5).

———. (1999i). "Lavish treatment" may not be such a terrible crime after all. *Herald* (February 12).

———. (1999j). US raises pressure on IOC over graft. *Herald* (February 26).

Korporaal, G., & Moore, M. (1999a). Coles jewels case to get high priority on ethics agenda. *Herald* (April 23).

———. (1999b). Shamed agent loses Sydney book contract. *Herald* (January 27).

Korporaal, G., & Riley, M. (1999). Bribes scandal may cost jobs of 16 IOC members. *Herald* (January 22).

Laanela, M. (1999). Bulldozed. *City Hub* (May 6), 12–15.

Lakey, J., & Spears, J. (1999). "Questionable contracts" linked to Olympics boss. *Star* (March 6).

Larkin, J., & Evans, M. (1999). Major Olympic sponsor may quit. *Herald* (February 15).

Latham, H. (1999). GGW2000 & Earth Council review the OCA. *Green Games Watch Newsletter*, 10, 1–2.

Lehmann, J. (1999a). Bid team fed Arab who talked Turkey. *Australian* (January 12).

———. (1999b). Samaranch backs off ditching host vote. *Australian* (February 20).

Lehmann, J., & Zubrzycki, J. (1999a). Olympic horse gift ends with takhi ring. *Australian* (January 29).

———. (1999b). IOC fury at dossier release. *Australian* (May 13).

Lenskyj, H. (1990). *Sex Equality in the Olympics:* A Report to the Toronto Olympic Task Force (April).

———. (1996). When winners are losers: Toronto and Sydney bids for the Summer Olympics. *Journal of Sport and Social Issues*, 20: 4, 392–410.

———. (1997). The case against Toronto's bid for the 2008 Olympics. *Policy Options* (May), 16–18.

Lethal stockpile near Olympic site. (1997). *Greenpeace Bulletin* (Spring), 4–5.

Letheren owes public a full explanation (editorial). (1999). *Star* (March 9).

Levy, S. (1996). Cultural unity through sports. *FAME Newsletter*, 15 (March), 1, 7.

Longman, J. (1995). Atlanta heats up with Olympic hopes. *Aspen Times* (July 29–30).

Lowe, I. (1998). Overview. In Cashman & Hughes, *Green Games*, 111–114.

Lucas, J. (1992). *Future of the Olympic Games*. Champaign, IL: Human Kinetics.

Ludwig, J. (1976). *Five Ring Circus*. Toronto: Doubleday.

Luksic, N. (1998). Activists meddle with Toronto Olympic bid. *Varsity* (September 17), 3, 6.

Luscombe, D. (1998). Promises. In Cashman & Hughes, *Green Games*, 14–16.

———. (1999). Consultation re Greenpeace Australia (April 23).

Lusetich, R. (1999). Samaranch implicated in Finn deal. *Australian* (January 21).

MacAloon, J. (1992). The ethnographic imperative in comparative Olympic research. *Sociology of Sport Journal*, 9, 104–130.

Macey, R. (1999). $58m to cater for media. *Herald* (February 13).

Magnay, J. (1999a). IOC refuses to apologise to journalist. *Herald* (February 3).

———. (1999b). Sydney saves pots as IOC bars lobsters. *Herald* (June 16).

———. (1999c). IOC perks police attack Knight. *Herald* (June 18).

Magnay, J., & Riley, M. (1999a). IOC clears Sydney's bid payments. *Herald* (February 3).

———. (1999b). Coles set to continue the high life. *Herald* (March 3).

Martin, B. (1996). Ten reasons to oppose all Olympic Games. *Green Left* (22 May), 13–14.

Masters, R. (1999). IOC's "family" values—pomp and pretence. *Herald* (January 23).

Mauled by the media. (1999). *Herald* (March 20).

McBride, G. (1998). Legislative Assembly Article: Appropriation Bill, second reading. Hansard (June 24).

McEnearney, M. (1999). Some dignity at last for the homeless. *Around the House*, 34, 6.

McKay, J. (1991). *No Pain No Gain: Sport and Australian Culture*. Sydney: Prentice-Hall.

Media companies deny deal. (1999). *ABC News* (February 19).

Melbourne Bread Not Circuses. (1990). *The Alternative Bid Book*. Carlton South, Victoria: Melbourne Bread Not Circuses.

Messner, M., & Sabo, D. (1994). *Sex, Violence, and Power in Sport: Rethinking Masculinity*. Freedom, CA: Crossing Press.

Metro Tenants' Association. (1990). Intervenor report (January).

Miguelez, F., & Carrasquer, P. (1995). The repercussion of the Olympic Games on labour. In Moragas, M., & Botella, M., eds., *The Keys to Success*. Barcelona: UAB, 149–164.

Millett, M., & Magnay, J. (1999). Found: the jewels Phil Coles says he's never seen before. *Herald* (March 19).

Mims, B. (1998). Experts say events mirror our society. *Tribune* (December 20).

Minister says he was asked to offer Olympic bribes. (1998). *ABC News* (December 12).

Mitchell, B. (1997). Jail deaths must end, warn black leaders. *The Age* (February 18).

Montalban, M. (1992). *Barcelonas* (translated by Andy Robinson). London: Verso.

Moore, M. (1997). Benighted minister faces Rentwatchers and wins embrace. *Herald* (November 15).

———. (1998a). Olympic hurdle too high: council. *Herald* (June 9).

———. (1998b). The secret Games. *Herald* (November 21).

———. (1999a). Coles smart to jump given 2000 guidelines. *Herald* (January 13).

———. (1999b). $2 million to Africans surprised us, Games bidders say. *Herald* (February 19).

———. (1999c). Media's "pact of silence." *Herald* (February 19).

———. (1999d). Games officials find a home in Sydney Uni housing deal. *Herald* (April 23).

———. (1999e). Olympic home away from home could cost $20,000. *Herald* (July 17).

Moore, M., & Korporaal, G. (1998). Olympic Games: whatever it costs. *Herald* (December 19).

Moragas, M., & Botella, M., eds. (1995). *The Keys to Success*. Barcelona: UAB.

More details needed on Olympic bid (editorial). (1998). *Star* (July 6).

Mulling, C. (1990). Dissidents' perspective of the 1988 Seoul Olympics. In Proceedings of Seoul Olympiad Anniversary Conference, Toward One World Beyond All Barriers, 394–407.

Myer, A. (1994). *Lillehammer Winter Olympics: Report of study visit for Greenpeace Australia* (unpublished).

Myrholt, O. (1996). Greening the Olympics. *Our Planet*, 8:2. <www.ourplanet.com.txtversn/82/myrholt.html>.

Nagano's gifts "normal." (1999). *Star* (January 27).

National Law Center on Homelessness and Poverty. (1998). Civil rights violations. <www.tomco.net/~nlchp/civil.htm>.

Native Title Act 1993. (1993). Canberra: Department of the Prime Minister and Cabinet.

Neville, G. (1990). Olympics and housing: who wins? *Shelter NHA*, 6:3, 25–26.

No Olympics Amsterdam. (n.d.). No Olympics in Amsterdam.

NOOOOO a la Barcelona Olimpica. (n.d.). No to the Barcelona Olympics (information flyer).

No room for politics in Toronto's Olympic bid (editorial). (1998). *Star* (March 8).

North, S. (1992). Black activist to back Olympic bid. *Herald* (October 31).

———. (1993a). Aid for African athletes may help Olympic bid. *Herald* (August 25).

———. (1993b). Olympic support hits record high. *Herald* (September 10).

———. (1993c). Silver lining to the cloud of defeat. *Herald* (September 18).

———. (1993d). Sydney's odds on, and deservedly so. *Herald* (June 23).

———. (1993e). Perkins abandons Olympic niceties. *Herald* (June 23).

Nunes, J. (1990). Observers question networks' support for Toronto's Olympic Games bid. *Globe and Mail* (February 2), C5.

OATH. (1999). Background: What is OATH? <www.theoath.com>.

OECD. (1998). Implementation of the Convention on Combating Bribery of Foreign Public Officials (December 12). <www.oecd.org/daf/cmis/bribery/bribimpe/htm>.

Office on Social Policy. (1993). *Sydney 2000: Approaches and Issues for the Management of Social Impact*. Sydney: Social Policy Directorate.

Olds, K. (1998). Urban mega-events, evictions, and housing rights: the Canadian case. Unpublished paper, Department of Geography, University of Singapore.

O'Loughlin, E. (1999). High and getting higher. *Herald* (January 30).

O'Loughlin, E., & Korporaal, G. (1999). IOC man speaks out: no money went to me. *Herald* (January 28).

O'Loughlin, E., & Magnay, J. (1999). The missing Olympic $13,000. *Herald* (February 2).

Olympic cleanup falls short of the mark (editorial). (1999). Star (March 20).

Olympic Coordination Authority. (September 1995). *Homebush Bay Development Guidelines*, Volume I: Environmental Strategy.

Olympics: developers win gold. (1998). *Guardian* (Sydney) (June 24).

Olympic watchdogs send right signal (editorial). (1999). *Star* (February 10).

Ontario government job went to husband of IOC member. (1999). *Canadian Press* (January 14).

Ormsby, M. (1998). Games vital to kids' hopes. *Star* (April 18).

———. (1999). Ethics issue forces TO-Bid to drop PR firm. *Star* (April 13).

Orozco, S. (1998). The massacre of 1968 and Mexico's movement toward democracy. *Colorlines* (Summer), 24–26.

Otteson, P. (1998). The Olympic Vision. In Cashman & Hughes, *Green Games*, 32–39.

Our Games (editorial). (1999). *Herald* (June 18).

Owen, R. (1997, August 1). Green alliance fights to kill off Roman Games. *Times*, 12.

Pace, S. (1999a). URPS submits petition for vote on Olympics debt (press release, January 18).

———. (1999b). Response to board of ethics (press release, February 9).

———. (1999c). URPS requests investigation into call for Olympics petition forgery (press release, February 22).

Packer, L. (1997). A federal case? *City Weekly* (October 27).

Palfreyman, R. (1998) Media Panel. In Cashman & Hughes, *Green Games*, 97–100.

Papp, L. (1999). U of T link to tobacco under fire. *Star* (May 24).

Paz, O. (1972). *The Other Mexico: Critique of the pyramid*. New York: Grove.

Peat Marwick. (1989). *Toronto 1996 Olympic Bid: Economic Impact Study*.

———. (1993). *Sydney Olympics 2000: Economic Impact Study*.

Performance Audit Review. (1999). The Sydney 2000 Olympics and Paralympic Games. <www.audit.nsw.gov.au/olympics99/>.

Perlman, D. (1989). Deputation to Public Meeting (November 28).

Pierson, R., Cohen, M., Bourne, P., & Masters, P. (1993). *Canadian Women's Issues*. Volume 1. Toronto: James Lorimer & Company.

Plant, R., & Roden, W. (1999). Consultation re Shelter NSW (April 22).

Porter, M. (1999). Playing Games at our cost. *Daily Telegraph* (May 12).

Pound, R. (1993). The IOC and the environment. *Olympic Message*, 35, 14–20.

———. (1994). *Five Rings Over Korea: The Secret Negotiations Behind the 1988 Olympic Games in Seoul*. Boston: Little, Brown & Co.

———. (1999a). Keynote address to the 1999 Sport Summit, New York (January 21).

———. (1999b). Remarks at IOC press conference (January 24).

———. (1999b). Speech to the Canadian Club (February 23).

Preuss, H. (1998). Problematizing arguments of the opponents of Olympic Games. In Barney, R., Wamsley, K., Martyn, S., & MacDonald, G., eds., *Global and Cultural Critique: Problematizing the Olympic Games*. London: University of Western Ontario, 197–218.

Price, J. (1993). Fahey, the premier spoiler of victory. *Herald* (October 20).

Ramsay, D. (1999). Government rushes tenancy laws. *Tenant News*, 64 (March), 3.

Ray White Real Estate. (1999). Ray White Residential Accommodation Program—Home owners. <www.raywhite.com.au/olympics/owners/>.

Read, K. (1999). Special to the *Calgary Herald* (January 26).

Real Estate Institute of NSW. (1999). Residential prices are likely to keep rising. *Herald* (January 9).

Reasons, C. (1984). *Stampede City*. Toronto: Between the Lines.

Reform time for the IOC (editorial). (1999). *Herald* (January 21).

Reilley, R., & Logan, D. (1999). Time for us to check out of the Olympics. *Sports Illustrated* (February 23).

Renters beware. (1998). Rentwatchers. <www.peg.apc.org/~greensnsw/archives.htm>.

Rentwatchers Report 1. (1998).

Robinson, A. (1997). Full clean-up of Bay required. *Green Games Watch Newsletter*, 6, 5, 11.

Robinson, D. (1999). Excuse me, but is it too late to return the 2002 Olympics? *Deseret News* (April 16).

Roche, L. (1999a). Tarnish of bribery scandal starts to rub off on Olympic finances. *Deseret News* (January 12).

———. (1999b). PR firm hired to fix IOC's image. *Deseret News* (January 21).

Roden, W., & Plant, R. (1998). *The Homeless Olympics?* Sydney: Shelter NSW (June).

Russell, S. (1994). The Sydney 2000 Olympics and the game of political repression: an insider's account. *Canadian Law and Society Association Bulletin*, 18 (Fall), 9–12.

———. (1996). IOC creates spectre of "terrorism" at Olympics. *Green Left* (October 30), 14.

Rutheiser, D. (1996). *Imagineering Atlanta*. New York: Verso.

Ryle, G. (1999). VIPs get all the comforts of home city contract. *Herald* (February 12).

Ryle, G., & Hughes, G. (1999). Breaking China: How Sydney stole the Games. *Herald* (March 6).

Salvado, J. (1999). Do the Done thing—lose the Games, says Coates. *Age* (January 24).

Samaranch, J. A. (1999a). Statement from the IOC regarding gifts presented to the IOC president (January 19).

———. (1999b). Transcript of Speech to open 108th Session (March 17).

Samaranch must go to clean up Olympics (editorial). (1999). *Star* (January 26).

Samaranch snubs senate. (1999). *Star* (March 31).

Samaranch won' t testify at IOC corruption hearing. (1999). *ABC News* (March 31).

Saunders, J., & Partridge, J. (1999). Toronto bid may profit from Olympic Games scandal. *Globe and Mail* (January 25).

Sawer, M. (1990). *Sisters in Suits: Women and Public Policy in Australia*. Sydney: Allen & Unwin.

Schmidt, S. (1998). U of You Name It. *This Magazine* (September/October), 23–27.

Sellar, D. (1999). An Olympic contract divulged at last. *Star* (April 24).

Selsky, A. (1999). Africans say they were IOC target. *Tribune* (January 27).

Sewell, J. (1998). Playing games with the Olympics. *Now* (February 19–25).

Shaikin, B. (1988). *Sport and Politics: the Olympics and the Los Angeles Games* (New York: Praeger).

Shapcott, M. (1991). Effective social change through coalition: the case of Toronto's Bread Not Circuses Coalition. Paper presented to Society for Socialist Studies Conference, Kingston, Ontario (June 2).

———. (1999). Consultation re Bread Not Circuses Coalition (March 2).

Share the Spirit. Sydney 2000. (June 1993).

Sheehan, R., & Buggs, S. (1995). Atlanta dreams of gold. *News and Observer* (July 23).

Sheridan, T. (1999). *Report of Independent Examiner for SOCOG* (March 12).

Short, K. (1996). *Management of Contaminated Sites for the Sydney Olympics 2000.* Prepared for Green Games Watch 2000, 1996.

Simson, V., & Jennings, A. (1992). *The Lords of the Rings.* Toronto: Stoddart.

SLBE. (1999). *Report of the Salt Lake Olympic Committee Board of Ethics inquiry* (February 9).

SLOC. (1999). Games Budget. <www.slc2002.org/info/html/budget/html>.

Smedmor, C. (1998). We risk $1 billion debt to get Olympics. *Star* (June 26).

———. (1999a). Olympic perks more imagined than real. *Star* (February 22).

———. (1999b). Olympic legacy costs money. *Star* (February 23).

Smith, C. (1999). Will our Olympics ever be the same? *Tribune* (February 28).

SpoilSport. (1996). *SpoilSport's Guidebook to Atlanta.*

Sponsors "playing games" over Olympics. (1999). *ABC News* (February 18).

Starkman, R. (1999a). No recourse to expelled IOC officials, Pound says. *Star* (January 21).

———. (1999b). Pound dines with IOC target. *Star* (March 2).

———. (1999c). Weeding out IOC's woes. *Star* (February 6).

———. (1999d). Crichlow speech shows true Olympic spirit. *Star* (February 7).

———. (1999e). Could the IOC be that dumb? *Star* (February 25).

———. (1999f). Johnson calls for ban. *Star* (March 9).

Starkman, R., & Infantry, A. (1998). Games bribery scandal grows. *Star* (December 19).

Starkman, R., Infantry, A., & Vincent, D. (1999). Olympic boss: I was offered $1m. *Star* (January 20).

Starkman, R., & van Rijn, N. (1999). Six IOC members told to go as crisis deepens. *Star* (January 25).

Sudjic, D. (1992). *The 100 Mile City.* London: Deutsch.

Summers, A. (1975). *Damned Whores and God's Police.* Ringwood: Penguin.

Sydney 2000—the Environmental Olympics. (1993). Media release, Sydney 2000 Olympic Bid Ltd.

Sydney 2000 Fact Sheets. Sydney 2000. (June 1993).

Sydney Olympic Bid Committee Ltd. (1993). *Environmental Principles.*

Sydney runs a bus past Games chief. (1999). *Herald* (February 2).

Sydney's Olympic Village Plan. (1993). Promotional material, Sydney 2000 Olympic Bid Ltd.

Sydney's Plan for an Environmental Olympics. (1993). Media release, Sydney 2000 Olympic Bid Ltd.

The corporate shuffle. (1999). *Varsity* (August), 4.

The importance of Olympics (editorial). (1996). *Globe and Mail* (July 29).

The Sports Factor. (1997). *Sydney's Green Olympics.* ABC Radio National Transcripts (September 12).

Thompson, A. (1999). Dirty deals could spark cleanup. *Star* (January 31).

Thompson, Alan, ed. (1996). *Terrorism and the 2000 Olympics.* Canberra: Australian Defence Studies Center.

Thorne, R., & Munro-Clark, M. (1989). Hallmark events as an excuse for autocracy in urban planning: a case study. In Syme et al., *The Planning and Evaluation of Hallmark Events*, 154–171.

Thorough Olympic clean-up needed (editorial). (1999). *Star* (January 23).

TOBid. (1998). Toronto Olympic Bid Corporation Corporate Bylaw (August 26).

———. (1999). Toronto Olympic Bid Corporation Source and Use of Funds from October 1, 1996 to December 31, 1998.

Tohver, L., & James, P. (1997). *Sydney Olympics 2000 Community Consultation and Participation Report 1996*. Prepared for Green Games Watch 2000 Inc.

Tomlinson, A., & Whannel, G., eds. (1984). *Five Ring Circus*. London: Pluto.

Toms, J. (1997). Rent hiking in the Olympic city. *Bridge* (August), 16–17.

Top Salt Lake Olympic officials resign, IOC reports. (1999). *Star* (January 8) (AP).

Toronto Olympic Commitment. (1989). Toronto City Council.

Toronto Ontario Olympic Committee. (1990). Proposal for the 1996 Summer Olympics Cultural Festival (January).

Uni's suite deal. (1999). *Daily Telegraph* (Sydney) (May 12).

UNSW Branch, National Tertiary Education Union. (1999). Minutes of meetings (May 18 and May 26). <www.nteu.org.au/unsw/index.html>.

UNSW's Olympic suite an investment. (1999). Media release, University of New South Wales (May 12).

US chiefs seek power control on Samaranch. (1999). *Herald* (March 5). (*Washington Post*).

USOC. (1999). Report of the Special Bid Oversight Commission (March 1).

US Olympic official out due to Salt Lake business tie. (1999). *Reuters* (January 14).

Valpy, M. (1990). Beyond hucksterism of Olympic council. *Globe and Mail* (January 29), A8.

Verma, S. (1999). Police double crime "hotspot" target. *Star* (July 23).

Vincent, D. (1999a). '96 bid chair under fire. *Star* (January 21).

———. (1999b). No place for any favours: Crombie. *Star* (January 26).

———. (1999c). IOC fingers point to colour. *Star* (February 4).

———. (1999d). Official ousted in Salt Lake Olympic scandal. *Star* (March 13).

———. (1999e). Samaranch to face vote of confidence. *Star* (March 14).

Vincent, D., & Ruimy, J. (1999). Province considering probe. *Star* (January 23).

Walker, W. (1999). Games row: when did Eggleton know? *Star* (January 31).

Walkom, T. (1999a). IOC's capo taking good care of Family. *Star* (January 26).

———. (1999b). The Olympic myth of Calgary. *Star* (February 8).

Walsh, M. (1992). Risible arithmetic on Olympic bid. *Herald* (December 23).

———. (1993a). OIympic backers fail to count the cost. *Herald* (April 9), 25.

———. (1993b). Olympic figures just do not add up. *Herald* (June 25), 21.

———. (1993c). First gold goes to cost concealment. *Herald* (September 28), 29, 32.

Wamsley, K., & Heine, M. (1996). Tradition, modernity, and the construction of civic identity: the Calgary Olympics. *Olympika*, 5, 81–91.

Warchol, G. (1999). Olympic family expects to be treated lavishly. *Tribune* (January 19).

Ward, B. (1999). Don't be confused about Olympic errors. *Deseret News* (January 22).

Weiss, O., Norden, G., Hilscher, P., & Vanreusel, B. (1998). Ski tourism and environmental problems: ecological awareness among different groups. *International Review for the Sociology of Sport*, 33:4, 367–380.

Williams, N. (1999). Transcript, *CBC Sports Journal* (May 3).

Williams, P. (1999). The rings of ire. *Financial Review* (March 5).

Williams, P. v. City of Atlanta, Georgia. Case no. 95-8752 (August 1995).

Wilson, H. (1996). What is an Olympic city? Visions of Sydney 2000. *Media, Culture & Society*, 18, 603–618.

Women Plan Toronto. (1990). Intervenor report (January).

Wright, G. (1978). The political economy of the Montreal Olympic Games. *Journal of Sport and Social Issues*, 2:1, 13–18.

Zubrzycki, J. (1999). Rail worker whistles corruption watchdog. *Australian* (January 26).

INDEX